Networking Programming with C++

Build Efficient Communication Systems

Robert Johnson

Published by HiTeX Press

For permissions and other inquiries, write to:
P.O. Box 3132, Framingham, MA 01701, USA

Contents

Introduction

Network programming is a vital aspect of modern computer science, underpinning the infrastructure that enables communication between systems across vast geographical distances. As the digital landscape continues to evolve, the demand for efficient and reliable communication systems has increased, placing network programming at the forefront of technological advancement.

This book, "Networking Programming with C++: Build Efficient Communication Systems," aims to provide a comprehensive guide for individuals seeking to master the art of network programming using the C++ programming language. C++ is renowned for its efficiency and performance, making it an ideal choice for developing network applications that require swift and precise data handling capabilities.

Throughout this text, readers will explore the foundational concepts of network programming, delve into the intricacies of vital networking protocols, and acquire practical skills in socket programming. The book is structured to facilitate a progressive learning experience, starting with an overview of essential networking principles before advancing to more complex topics such as asynchronous and synchronous communication, multithreading, and data stream management.

A significant focus is placed on the TCP/IP protocol suite, which serves as the backbone of internet communication. Understanding the architecture and functions of TCP/IP is crucial for any aspiring network programmer. Consequently, this book provides detailed insights into its components and their integration into network applications.

Security is another pivotal aspect of network programming. The text emphasizes techniques and best practices for securing data transmissions, authenticating network participants, and mitigating potential threats. This knowledge is crucial for developing robust applications capable of withstanding the evolving landscape of cybersecurity challenges.

Performance optimization forms another cornerstone of this book. By examining strategies for enhancing the speed and efficiency of network applications, readers will be equipped to develop systems that perform seamlessly under varying conditions. This includes exploring methods to identify performance bottlenecks, optimize resource utilization, and reduce latency.

The final chapters focus on practical application development, guiding readers through the process of conceptualizing, designing, and implementing network applications. Through hands-on examples and real-world scenarios, the book reinforces the theoretical concepts covered, solidifying the reader's understanding and preparing them for practical implementations.

By the conclusion of this book, readers will have a solid foundation in network programming with C++. They will be equipped with the knowledge and skills necessary to design and implement efficient communication systems, addressing contemporary challenges in network software development. With a blend of theoretical knowledge and practical application, this book serves as an invaluable resource for both beginners and seasoned developers aiming to advance their expertise in network programming.

Chapter 1

Introduction to Network Programming

Network programming forms the core of today's interconnected world, enabling diverse systems to communicate effectively across networks. This chapter lays the groundwork for understanding the essential concepts of computer networks, focusing on the fundamental principles that facilitate data exchange. Emphasizing the client-server model, it also introduces key networking terminology and explores the role of C++ in developing efficient network applications. By setting up a suitable development environment, readers will be primed to apply these concepts practically, providing a strong foundation for deeper exploration of network programming topics.

1.1 Overview of Computer Networks

Computer networks are at the core of modern communication and digital infrastructure, established to facilitate the sharing of resources and the exchange of data among multiple devices. A comprehensive understanding of computer networks encompasses the analysis of their fundamental components, purpose, types, and operational methodologies.

Computer networks are setups that connect multiple computing devices, known as nodes, to enable data exchange and resource sharing. These networks extend beyond personal computing devices to include more intricate configurations, such as data centers and cloud infrastructures. The primary objective of constructing a network is to leverage the interaction between these modern computing devices to improve efficiency, collaboration, and communication on both small and expansive scales.

A typical computer network comprises several components: physical media that carry data, hardware devices such as routers and switches that manage data flow, software protocols that govern data transmission and formatting, and network services that facilitate resource sharing and communication processes.

Types of Computer Networks

Computer networks can be categorized based on their scale, functionality, and topology. The most common types include:

1. **Local Area Network (LAN):** LANs are confined to a relatively small geographic area, such as a single building or campus. They are characterized by high data transfer rates and low latency. Devices within a LAN can communicate directly with each other, often using Ethernet cables or wireless technologies. A primary advantage of LANs is their ability to facilitate resource sharing, such as printers and local storage solutions, within a contained setting.

2. **Wide Area Network (WAN):** WANs cover broader geographical areas, often implementing satellites, leased telecommunication lines, or international networks. WANs enable connectivity across cities, countries, or even continents. A typical example of a WAN is the Internet itself, which connects disparate networks across the globe.

3. **Metropolitan Area Network (MAN):** MANs span a city or a large campus, often utilizing fiber optic connections to deliver high-speed Internet services within a metropolitan area. These

networks are typically larger than LANs but smaller than WANs. A prevalent use case for MANs is in providing broadband Internet services to a city where several buildings and homes are involved.

4. **Personal Area Network (PAN):** PAN networks are used for very short-range communication, such as tethering mobile devices. Typically, Bluetooth and USB connections realize these networks, facilitating seamless and rapid data exchange between personal devices like smartphones, tablets, and laptops.

5. **Wireless Networks (WLANs and WWANs):** These networks utilize wireless communication technologies such as Wi-Fi and cellular data networks. They align with various network sizes, including LANs and WANs, delivering flexibility and mobility, essential in today's mobile-first world.

Components of Computer Networks

A functioning computer network comprises several critical components, each playing a pivotal role in ensuring efficient communication and data exchange. The core components include:

- **Network Interface Cards (NICs):** These hardware components enable devices to connect to a network. The NIC interfaces a device's motherboard with the network medium, often offering both wired (Ethernet) and wireless (Wi-Fi) connection capabilities.

- **Switches and Hubs:** These devices facilitate data transfer within networks by connecting multiple devices. While hubs broadcast incoming data to all connected devices regardless of its destination, switches intelligently direct data to specific devices based on their MAC addresses.

- **Routers:** Routers connect multiple networks, guiding data packets between them while ensuring the best pathways are followed. They operate at the network layer, utilizing Internet Protocol (IP) addresses to determine data routes and manage traffic across the Internet.

- **Communication Media:** These include all forms of media through which data can be transmitted. Wired communication

11

often relies on copper cables, fiber optics, or coaxial cables. Alternatively, wireless communication employs radio frequencies, microwaves, and infrared signals.

- **Communication Protocols:** Protocols are systematic sets of rules that facilitate data exchange between network devices. Notable protocols include the Transmission Control Protocol/Internet Protocol (TCP/IP), defining how data should be packetized, addressed, transmitted, routed, and received on the Internet.

Network Topologies

Network topology denotes the layout and structure of network connections, depicting how various nodes are interconnected. The most prevalent topologies include:

- **Bus Topology:** A single central cable connects all network devices. However, this topology often results in data collisions, which can degrade performance as more devices are added.

- **Star Topology:** Each device in the network is connected directly to a central node (often a switch or hub). The failure of a single connection does not impact the rest of the network, making this a robust and scalable topology.

- **Ring Topology:** Devices are arranged in a circular configuration, with each node connected to two others, forming a closed loop. This topology can efficiently handle data collisions but struggles with failures, as the entire network can be disrupted by a single point of failure.

- **Mesh Topology:** Every network device is connected to multiple other devices. This comprehensive interconnectivity ensures high reliability and redundancy.

- **Hybrid Topology:** By combining several topologies, hybrid structures seek to leverage the benefits of different configurations, addressing specific network requirements.

Network Protocols and Communication

Protocols are crucial in computer networks to standardize communication, governing data formats, transmission processes, error detection, and correction. They operate across different layers of the OSI and TCP/IP models, ensuring that distinct applications and networks can interoperate efficiently.

The OSI model characterizes layers as:

- **Physical Layer:** Concerns with the transmission and reception of raw data streams over a physical medium.

- **Data Link Layer:** Manages node-to-node data transfer and error detection/correction from the physical layer.

- **Network Layer:** Responsible for path determination, routing, and forwarding of packets.

- **Transport Layer:** Ensures complete data transfer with proper error correction and segmentation.

- **Session Layer:** Establishes, manages, and terminates connections between applications.

- **Presentation Layer:** Translates, encrypts, and compresses data for communication.

- **Application Layer:** Interfaces with the end-user applications, providing network services directly.

The TCP/IP model is a streamlined suite offering practical implementations for digital network communications, emphasizing the Internet's functionality.

- **Link Layer:** Incorporates data link and physical aspects of the OSI model.

- **Internet Layer:** Corresponds to the OSI's network layer; manages routing and addressing.

- **Transport Layer:** Includes core transport functions akin to the OSI's transport layer.

13

- **Application Layer:** Combines the OSI's application, session, and presentation layers.

Integral to these models, protocols such as TCP, IP, HTTP, HTTPS, FTP, and DNS exemplify the diverse methods for ensuring reliable and effective communication across networks.

TCP provides a connection-oriented data transmission mechanism. Consider the following C++ example demonstrating a basic TCP client setup leveraging the socket programming interface:

```cpp
#include <iostream>
#include <sys/socket.h>
#include <arpa/inet.h>
#include <unistd.h>
#include <cstring>

int main() {
    // Create a socket
    int clientSocket = socket(AF_INET, SOCK_STREAM, 0);
    if (clientSocket < 0) {
        std::cerr << "Socket creation error" << std::endl;
        return -1;
    }

    // Define server address
    sockaddr_in serverAddress;
    serverAddress.sin_family = AF_INET;
    serverAddress.sin_port = htons(8080);

    // Convert IP address
    if (inet_pton(AF_INET, "192.168.1.1", &serverAddress.sin_addr) <= 0) {
        std::cerr << "Invalid address or Address not supported" << std::endl;
        return -1;
    }

    // Connect to server
    if (connect(clientSocket, (sockaddr*)&serverAddress, sizeof(serverAddress)) < 0) {
        std::cerr << "Connection failed" << std::endl;
        return -1;
    }

    // Send data to server
    const char *message = "Hello Server";
    send(clientSocket, message, strlen(message), 0);

    close(clientSocket);

    return 0;
}
```

This example demonstrates establishing a TCP connection, converting an IP address, and sending data to a server, highlighting the practical

14

aspects of network programming in C++.

Computer networks fundamentally enhance the capacity for data exchange and resource sharing, making them indispensable to modern enterprises and day-to-day personal activities. Whether facilitating communication through emails, enabling remote work, or providing platforms for online education, networks underpin much of the digital society's functionality, bridging diverse systems and users worldwide with unprecedented efficiency.

1.2   Basics of Network Communication

Network communication is essential in connecting diverse systems, enabling them to exchange data effectively across various types of networks. The principle of network communication involves a blend of protocols, devices, and mechanisms working in harmony to facilitate the transmission of information from one node to another. A comprehensive understanding of these fundamentals is crucial for developing efficient network applications and supporting seamless data flow across networks.

At the heart of network communication lies the process of data transmission between sender and receiver nodes. Communication models, such as the OSI and TCP/IP models, provide structured approaches to understanding and implementing network communications. These models break down network functionalities into layers, each layer responsible for specific network operations that collectively enable data transmission.

Communication Models

1. **OSI Model:** The Open Systems Interconnection model is a conceptual framework used to understand network interactions in seven layers.

   - **Physical Layer:** Handles the physical connection between devices, encompassing transmission and reception of raw binary data over a physical medium. This layer includes specifications for hardware elements such as cables, switches, and network interface cards.

15

- **Data Link Layer:** Facilitates reliable node-to-node data transfer and manages error checking and frame synchronization. Protocols like Ethernet and PPP are governed by this layer.

- **Network Layer:** Manages packet forwarding through routing, addressing, and congestion control. It includes protocols like the Internet Protocol (IP).

- **Transport Layer:** Ensures end-to-end communication reliability and data integrity with flow control, segmentation, and error correction. Protocols like TCP and UDP operate at this layer.

- **Session Layer:** Manages sessions and synchronization between end-user applications, providing controls for dialog coordination.

- **Presentation Layer:** Concerns data translation, encryption, and compression, converting data from network formats to application formats.

- **Application Layer:** Interfaces directly with application software, facilitating network services like file transfers, email, and browsing.

2. **TCP/IP Model:** The Transmission Control Protocol/Internet Protocol model is a streamlined model widely adopted for Internet-based communications. The TCP/IP model combines functionalities into four layers:

- **Link Layer:** Incorporates data link and physical layer responsibilities, managing data transfer between network interfaces.

- **Internet Layer:** Similar to the OSI's network layer, handling addressing and routing of packets across networks.

- **Transport Layer:** Provides data transport services with reliability, error control, and flow control, mirroring the OSI's transport layer.

- **Application Layer:** Encompasses all higher-level protocols supporting Internet applications, analogous to the OSI's application layer.

16

Components of Network Communication

Network communication involves several key components essential for establishing and maintaining efficient data exchanges:

- **End Systems, Hosts, and Nodes:** End systems, typically user devices such as computers and smartphones, serve as communication points in a network. Hosts can denote devices that offer services, such as servers, while nodes are generalized terms for any connected device within the network.

- **Network Switches and Routers:** Network switches operate at the data link layer, facilitating local network communication by receiving incoming data packets and directing them specifically to their destination. Routers function at the network layer, guiding packets between networks using IP addresses and implementing advanced routing protocols for efficient data traffic management.

- **Transmission Media:** Network communication is supported by transmission media, which include wired options like twisted pair cables, coaxial cables, and fiber optic cables as well as wireless media, such as radio waves and microwaves.

- **Communication Protocols:** Protocols define the rules and conventions for data exchange. TCP and UDP are landmark protocols for transport layer operations. TCP provides reliable, connection-oriented communication, ensuring data packets reach their destination error-free and in order, while UDP offers a faster, connectionless service, prioritized for applications where speed is crucial over reliability, such as live streams.

Client-Server Model

The client-server model is a foundational architecture in network communication wherein clients request resources or services, and servers fulfill these requests. This model underlies many network applications built for diverse environments like the web, email communications, and databases.

- **Client:** The client is a computing device or application that initi-

17

ates a request for network services or resources, acting as an active entity fetching data or executing instructions sent to a server.

- **Server:** Servers are robust machines or applications providing services over a network, often responding to several clients simultaneously. Servers host resources and services, thereby enabling clients to perform operations remotely or fetch data and applications.

Given that the client-server architecture defines many critical operations in today's networks, it's important to understand practical implementations like HTTP for web applications or FTP for file transfers.

Consider the following C++ code example illustrating a simple TCP server configuration using socket programming:

```cpp
#include <iostream>
#include <sys/socket.h>
#include <netinet/in.h>
#include <unistd.h>
#include <cstring>

int main() {
    int serverSocket = socket(AF_INET, SOCK_STREAM, 0);
    if (serverSocket < 0) {
        std::cerr << "Socket creation failed" << std::endl;
        return -1;
    }

    sockaddr_in serverAddress;
    serverAddress.sin_family = AF_INET;
    serverAddress.sin_addr.s_addr = INADDR_ANY;
    serverAddress.sin_port = htons(8080);

    if (bind(serverSocket, (sockaddr*)&serverAddress, sizeof(serverAddress)) < 0) {
        std::cerr << "Bind failed" << std::endl;
        return -1;
    }

    if (listen(serverSocket, 3) < 0) {
        std::cerr << "Listen failed" << std::endl;
        return -1;
    }

    std::cout << "Server is listening for connections..." << std::endl;

    int clientSocket;
    sockaddr_in clientAddress;
    socklen_t clientLength = sizeof(clientAddress);
    clientSocket = accept(serverSocket, (sockaddr*)&clientAddress, &clientLength);

    if (clientSocket < 0) {
        std::cerr << "Client accept failed" << std::endl;
```

```
    return -1;
}
char buffer[1024] = {0};
read(clientSocket, buffer, 1024);
std::cout << "Message received: " << buffer << std::endl;

const char* response = "Hello from server";
send(clientSocket, response, strlen(response), 0);

close(clientSocket);
close(serverSocket);

return 0;
}
```

This example illustrates setting up a simple TCP server, capable of accepting client connections, receiving messages, and sending responses back.

Peer-to-Peer Networks

Contrasting the client-server model, peer-to-peer (P2P) networks distribute network roles more egalitarian. Every node, or peer, in the network has equivalent capabilities and responsibilities, allowing for direct sharing of resources and information without relying on a centralized server.

This model is prominent in blockchain and file-sharing applications (e.g., BitTorrent), where data storage and distribution are decentralized. P2P networks enhance resilience and availability by diversifying roles and leveraging collective peer resources; however, they pose unique challenges in managing data integrity and security.

Challenges in Network Communication

Network communication presents several hurdles that must be addressed to maintain efficiency, reliability, and security:

- **Latency:** Refers to delays experienced in data processing or transferring. Network latency can affect application performance, leading to suboptimal user experiences, particularly in real-time applications.

- **Bandwidth:** Denotes the maximum capacity of a network connection. Limited bandwidth can result in congestion and slowed data transfer rates.

- **Reliability:** Encompasses the consistency and dependability of a network's data transfer capabilities. Ensuring reliability requires addressing packet loss, disconnections, and corruption.

- **Security:** Protecting data during its transit across networks is paramount. Network security employs encryption, authentication, and access control measures to safeguard data from interception, tampering, or unauthorized access.

The essence of network communication is in its ability to convey information swiftly and reliably across diverse entities and media. As the backbone of modern digital ecosystems, the mechanics of network communication lay down the frameworks allowing disparate systems to synchronize their operations and users to interact effortlessly over expansive distances. Understanding these fundamentals facilitates the creation of applications capable of leveraging the full spectrum of network capabilities, addressing latency, security, and bandwidth challenges that arise in an increasingly interconnected world.

1.3 Essential Networking Terminology

A firm grasp of networking terminology is essential for understanding how networked systems communicate and function cohesively. Networking terminology encapsulates the fundamental concepts, mechanisms, and components that facilitate data exchange across networks. This section delves into key networking terms and concepts, providing clarity on both basic and complex network operations.

IP Addresses

IP addresses are numerical labels assigned to each device connected to a computer network that uses the Internet Protocol for communication. They serve two main functions: identifying hosts or network interfaces, and providing the location of the host in the network. IP addresses are divided into two standards:

1. **IPv4:** The most widely implemented version, IPv4, uses a 32-bit address scheme allowing for approximately 4.3 billion unique

addresses. These addresses are typically represented in dot-decimal notation, divided into four octets, such as 192.168.1.1.

2. **IPv6:** Due to the proliferation of internet-connected devices and a looming shortage of available IPv4 addresses, IPv6 was developed. This standard employs a 128-bit address scheme, supporting an exponentially larger number of unique addresses. IPv6 addresses are presented in hexadecimal, separated by colons, for example: 2001:0db8:85a3:0000:0000:8a2e:0370:7334.

IP addresses also incorporate subnet masking, a technique used to divide the network into smaller subnetworks, increasing routing efficiency and address allocation.

Ports and Sockets

In networking, ports and sockets are pivotal elements in enabling concurrent communication sessions between different applications and devices.

- **Ports:** Ports are numerical pointers in each IP address that identify specific processes or services. They allow a single host to facilitate various services, each listening on a different port number. Standard Ports, like port 80 for HTTP or port 443 for HTTPS, ensure universal access to specific services.

- **Sockets:** A network socket acts as an endpoint for sending or receiving data across a computer network. Sockets leverage a combined IP address and port number to establish a two-way communication link. They are integral to socket programming, where they enable the definition of network controls for data actions like send, receive, and disconnect.

The following C++ snippet exemplifies a simple client socket setup using TCP:

```cpp
#include <iostream>
#include <sys/socket.h>
#include <arpa/inet.h>
#include <unistd.h>
#include <cstring>

int main() {
```

```cpp
int clientSocket = socket(AF_INET, SOCK_STREAM, 0);
if (clientSocket < 0) {
    std::cerr << "Socket creation failed" << std::endl;
    return -1;
}

sockaddr_in serverAddress;
serverAddress.sin_family = AF_INET;
serverAddress.sin_port = htons(8080);

if (inet_pton(AF_INET, "127.0.0.1", &serverAddress.sin_addr) <= 0) {
    std::cerr << "Invalid IP address" << std::endl;
    return -1;
}

if (connect(clientSocket, (struct sockaddr*)&serverAddress, sizeof(serverAddress))
        < 0) {
    std::cerr << "Connection error" << std::endl;
    return -1;
}

char buffer[1024] = {0};
const char* message = "Hello Server";
send(clientSocket, message, strlen(message), 0);
read(clientSocket, buffer, 1024);
std::cout << "Server response: " << buffer << std::endl;

close(clientSocket);

return 0;
}
```

Here, the client establishes a connection with a local server on port 8080, demonstrating the use of sockets to facilitate network communications.

Protocols

Protocols are extensive sets of rules allowing networked devices to communicate effectively. Key networking protocols include:

- **TCP/IP (Transmission Control Protocol/Internet Protocol):** This suite is foundational for Internet-based communications. TCP manages reliable data delivery in sequence, while IP handles packet routing and addressing. Together, they provide a framework for transmitting data across diverse networks.

- **UDP (User Datagram Protocol):** UDP offers a connectionless service for fast, but less reliable, communication. It is best suited for applications requiring speed over accuracy, such as streaming and voice-over-IP protocols.

- **HTTP/HTTPS (Hypertext Transfer Protocol/Secure):**
HTTP governs how information is transmitted over the web.
HTTPS extends HTTP by providing a secure layer through
encryption (via SSL/TLS) to protect data integrity and privacy
online.

- **FTP (File Transfer Protocol):** FTP facilitates the transmission, upload, and download of files over a network. It operates
using separate control and data connections between client and
server, often requiring authentication.

- **SMTP (Simple Mail Transfer Protocol):** SMTP is critical
for email transmission, navigating emails from senders to recipients' mail servers. SMTP servers can send and receive mail messages, often requiring encryption for security.

Network Interfaces and MAC Addresses

- **Network Interface:** A network interface could be a physical
device (such as a network card) or software program that serves
as the intermediary between a computer and a network. It directs data traffic entering and leaving a network node, functional
through both physical and logical addresses.

- **MAC Addresses (Media Access Control):** MAC addresses
are unique identifiers assigned to network interfaces for communications on a physical network. MAC addresses operate at the
data link layer, formatted as six groups of two hexadecimal digits, e.g., 00:1A:2B:3C:4D:5E. These addresses are the hardware
identifier for network adapters, immutable and assigned by manufacturers.

DNS (Domain Name System)

The Domain Name System is an essential protocol addressing
the issue of translating human-readable domain names (like
www.example.com) into machine-readable IP addresses. This
translation is necessary because, while users prefer easily
remembered names, the underlying network infrastructure relies on
numerical IP addresses for navigation and data routing.

- **DNS Hierarchy:** DNS has a hierarchical structure, starting with root servers, followed by top-level domains (such as .com, .org, .net), then second-level domains, culminating in the specific host domain names.

- **DNS Resolution:** The process whereby a DNS query is converted into an IP address, facilitating the direction of a web request to the appropriate server address. This resolution can involve multiple intermediaries such as recursive resolvers and authoritative name servers.

NAT (Network Address Translation)

Network Address Translation is a methodology allowing multiple devices on a local network to be mapped to a single public IP address for Internet communications. NAT conserves public IP address space and adds a level of security by masking internal IPs from external view.

A common use of NAT occurs with home routers, where the internal network consists of private IPs, translating outgoing traffic to the router's public IP. Upon receiving external data meant for a private network host, NAT redirects the packet to the appropriate internal address.

Firewalls and Network Security

Firewalls are network security systems designed to prevent unauthorized access while allowing legitimate communications to pass. These can be hardware- or software-based, filtering incoming and outgoing traffic based on predefined security rules.

Essential security protocols include:

- **SSL/TLS (Secure Sockets Layer/Transport Layer Security):** Protocols providing a secure, encrypted connection between devices in a network. Widely used in HTTPS transactions, they ensure privacy and data integrity.

- **VPN (Virtual Private Network):** A technology creating a secure, encrypted connection over a less secure network like the Internet. VPNs provide remote access to a private network, maintaining confidentiality and data protection measures.

Understanding these terms elucidates the intricacies of network architecture, providing a foundational understanding vital for grasping more advanced networking topics and addressing real-world challenges in system intcroperability and security management.

1.4 Role of C++ in Network Programming

C++ plays a significant and influential role in network programming, offering a blend of performance, versatility, and control. As a language that straddles low-level system access and high-level programming capabilities, C++ is a preferred choice for developing robust, resource-efficient network applications. Its relevance in network programming extends across various domains, from system-level applications to large-scale network services and telecommunications infrastructure.

Advantages of Using C++ for Network Programming

- **Performance and Efficiency:** C++ is known for its performance efficiency, an essential aspect in network programming where latency and throughput are critical. The compiler optimizations and low-level system access in C++ allow developers to fine-tune their applications for maximum speed and minimal resource consumption.

- **Standard Library and STL:** The C++ Standard Library and the Standard Template Library (STL) provide a rich set of tools and data structures, enabling efficient resource management and operations in network programming. Container classes, algorithms, and iterators in STL support complex data manipulation required in networking processes.

- **Object-Oriented Programming (OOP):** C++ provides robust object-oriented programming features, which bring modularity, reusability, and scalability to network programming. Encapsulation, inheritance, and polymorphism equip developers to design complex network architectures through organized classes and interfaces.

- **System-Level Access:** With C++, developers can interact directly with operating system resources through system calls, manipulating sockets, threads, and file descriptors. This feature is crucial for tasks such as socket programming, where precise handling of data packets and network sockets is required.

- **Cross-Platform Development:** C++ supports cross-platform development, an invaluable trait for building network applications meant to operate on diverse hardware and software environments. Libraries like Boost and Qt extend C++'s capabilities, ensuring code portability across platforms including Windows, Linux, and macOS.

- **Vast Array of Libraries:** C++ has a plethora of third-party libraries that facilitate network programming. These libraries provide higher levels of abstraction, security, and connectivity for rapid development of network applications. Libraries such as Boost.Asio, Poco, and cpp-netlib support asynchronous I/O operations, HTTP client/server implementations, and additional protocols.

Core Concepts in Network Programming with C++

- **Socket Programming:** The bedrock of network programming, socket programming in C++ involves creating, configuring, and managing network sockets to enable communication between endpoints. Using the Berkeley sockets API, C++ facilitates TCP and UDP communication.

```cpp
#include <iostream>
#include <sys/socket.h>
#include <netinet/in.h>
#include <unistd.h>
#include <cstring>

int createServerSocket(int port) {
    int serverSocket = socket(AF_INET, SOCK_STREAM, 0);
    if (serverSocket < 0) {
        std::cerr << "Failed to create socket" << std::endl;
        exit(EXIT_FAILURE);
    }

    sockaddr_in serverAddress;
    serverAddress.sin_family = AF_INET;
    serverAddress.sin_addr.s_addr = INADDR_ANY;
```

26

```
    serverAddress.sin_port = htons(port);

    if (bind(serverSocket, (struct sockaddr*)&serverAddress, sizeof(
        serverAddress)) < 0) {
        std::cerr << "Bind failed" << std::endl;
        close(serverSocket);
        exit(EXIT_FAILURE);
    }
    return serverSocket;
}

void startListening(int serverSocket, int maxClients) {
    if (listen(serverSocket, maxClients) < 0) {
        std::cerr << "Listen error" << std::endl;
        close(serverSocket);
        exit(EXIT_FAILURE);
    }

    std::cout << "Server is listening on port..." << std::endl;
}
```

This snippet demonstrates creating and binding a TCP server socket, ready to listen for incoming client connections.

- **Multithreading:** Using C++ multithreading constructs, such as the C++11 std::thread library, enhances network application performance by efficiently handling multiple simultaneous connections. Multithreading allows network applications to execute separate tasks concurrently, improving responsiveness and resource utilization.

```
#include <iostream>
#include <thread>

void handleClient(int clientSocket) {
    // Implement handling logic for each client connection
}

int main() {
    int serverSocket = createServerSocket(8080);
    startListening(serverSocket, 5);

    while (true) {
        int clientSocket = accept(serverSocket, nullptr, nullptr);
        if (clientSocket >= 0) {
            std::thread clientThread(handleClient, clientSocket);
            clientThread.detach(); // Allow independent execution
        } else {
            std::cerr << "Failed to accept connection" << std::endl;
        }
    }
    close(serverSocket);
    return 0;
}
```

Here, the server spawns a new thread for each incoming client connection, allowing concurrent handling of multiple clients.

- **Protocol Implementation:** C++ allows development of custom protocol handlers and services owing to its flexibility and performance potential. Protocol parsing, serialization, and error-handling mechanisms can be implemented with precise system-level control.

- **Asynchronous I/O:** Libraries such as Boost.Asio enable asynchronous input/output operations, crucial for non-blocking network communication where I/O operations do not hinder application throughput.

```cpp
#include <boost/asio.hpp>
#include <iostream>

using namespace boost::asio;

void asyncHandler() {
    io_service ioService;
    ip::tcp::acceptor acceptor(ioService, ip::tcp::endpoint(ip::tcp::v4(), 8080))
        ;

    auto handleAccept = [&](const boost::system::error_code& errorCode,
            ip::tcp::socket socket) {
        if (!errorCode) {
            std::cout << "Accepted connection from: " << socket.
                remote_endpoint().address() << std::endl;
        }
    };

    ip::tcp::socket socket(ioService);
    acceptor.async_accept(socket, handleAccept);
    ioService.run();
}

int main() {
    asyncHandler();
    return 0;
}
```

The example shows initiating an asynchronous TCP server using Boost.Asio, allowing it to asynchronously accept client connections.

Libraries and Frameworks

- **Boost.Asio:** Offers comprehensive support for asynchronous networking and concurrent threading without platform-specific

APIs, providing robust abstraction over operating system capabilities.

- **Poco:** C++ libraries supporting building network-centric and internet-based applications with networking algorithms, I/O operations, and protocol implementations.

- **cpp-netlib:** Widely used for implementing high-performance network servers and clients, providing protocol support and high-level abstractions.

- **QT Network Module:** Part of the Qt toolkit, it provides classes to handle TCP/IP, UDP, HTTP, SSL/TLS, and various other common networking tasks.

C++ has proven itself in diverse use cases such as real-time communication systems, gaming servers, IoT devices, and high-frequency trading platforms, where reliable performance is critical. Its robustness, combined with an expansive ecosystem, ensures C++ remains a cornerstone in network programming. Mastery of C++ for networking purposes offers enduring advantages, leveraging its power to build scalable, efficient, and cross-platform networking solutions.

1.5 Setting Up the Development Environment

Establishing a well-configured development environment is a fundamental step in network programming. It sets the stage for efficient coding, debugging, and deployment of network applications. A robust setup enables seamless integration of development tools, libraries, and version control systems essential for collaborative and scalable software development processes. Tailoring the environment to the specific needs of C++ network programming involves careful selection and configuration of compilers, IDEs (Integrated Development Environments), libraries, and test frameworks.

Choosing the Right Compiler

The compiler is a fundamental component of the C++ development environment, translating high-level C++ code into machine code executable by the system. Below are prominent C++ compilers widely used in industry and educational settings:

- **GCC (GNU Compiler Collection):** A versatile compiler that supports a vast range of programming languages, including C++. It is the default compiler for many Unix-like operating systems, providing strong compliance with C++ standards. Installation on systems like Ubuntu can be handled via the package manager as follows:

```
sudo apt update
sudo apt install build-essential
```

- **Clang:** Developed by the LLVM project, Clang is lauded for its fast compilation, detailed error messages, and compatibility with GCC. It's ideal for projects requiring analyzation tools or when compiling is integrated with IDEs like Xcode. To install Clang on Ubuntu:

```
sudo apt install clang
```

- **MSVC (Microsoft Visual C++):** A popular choice for Windows platforms, MSVC is deeply integrated with Visual Studio, providing extensive libraries and debugging features. Visual Studio also supports comprehensive project management and deployment capabilities.

- **Intel C++ Compiler:** Known for optimizing high-performance applications, it enhances execution speed on Intel processors through specialized optimizations.

Integrating an IDE

An IDE brings together editing, compiling, and debugging under a unified interface, enhancing productivity by automating repetitive tasks and providing insights and tools for code management.

- **Visual Studio Code:** A lightweight, cross-platform IDE with robust extensions for C++ development, such as the C++ extension by Microsoft, providing IntelliSense, debugging, and code browsing. To enhance network programming, integrate extensions like CMake and Git for version control.

- **CLion:** An IDE by JetBrains, tailored for cross-platform C++ development. CLion offers deep code insight, smart refactoring, and project-wide coding tools. It seamlessly integrates with CMake, a widely-used build system, enhancing its suitability for diverse projects and dependencies.

- **Eclipse CDT:** An extension of the Eclipse IDE for C/C++ developers, supporting editorial, debugging, and source control functionalities necessary for development efficiency.

- **Qt Creator:** Ideal for 'Qt' applications, it delivers an excellent development experience for GUI applications, network programming, and supports a wide array of QT modules and libraries.

Incorporating Networking Libraries

To expedite network application development, integrate C++ networking libraries that provide pre-built functionality for protocols, asynchronous operations, and data manipulation.

- **Boost.Asio:** Designed to write scalable network and low-level I/O applications, it supports synchronous and asynchronous communication, blending with Boost libraries for additional functionalities. Configuration involves integrating Boost with your compiler and setting up paths in your project.

```
sudo apt install libboost-all-dev
```

- **Poco C++ Libraries:** Provide a range of networking and data access capabilities. Include these libraries in your workflow for seamless integration and performance benefits, particularly in IoT and network-based applications.

- **cpp-netlib:** Delivering HTTP and other protocol implementations, cpp-netlib is effective for web-based network applications. Technologies like JSON parsing and RESTful API handling are facilitated by cpp-netlib.

31

Setting Up Version Control Systems

Version control is indispensable in network programming projects, especially when collaborating within development teams or maintaining an application over time.

- **Git:** Git is a distributed version control system, with comprehensive branching capabilities and collaboration support. Platforms like GitHub, GitLab, and Bitbucket offer cloud-based Git solutions, fostering team workflows and project management.

  Typical Git operations in a project include:

  ```
  git init
  git add .
  git commit -m "Initial commit"
  git remote add origin <repository-url>
  git push -u origin master
  ```

Configuring Build Tools

Build automation tools manage source code compilation and application assembly. They automate error-prone tasks, ensuring consistent builds and simplifying project management.

- **CMake:** Designed to handle project build processes in a compiler-independent manner, providing greater control and flexibility for C++ projects. CMake handles defining build parameters, managing dependencies, and creating build files.

  ```
  sudo apt install cmake
  ```

  CMakeLists.txt for a basic project might include:

  ```
  cmake_minimum_required(VERSION 3.10)
  project(NetworkApp)

  set(CMAKE_CXX_STANDARD 17)

  add_executable(NetworkApp main.cpp)
  ```

- **Makefiles:** Part of Unix-based environments, Makefiles dictate how to compile and link a program, standardizing build processes. Makefiles specify dependency checks, file compilation commands, and targets for applications.

Testing and Debugging

Testing within C++ network programming ensues validating application robustness, identifying bugs, and ensuring protocol and security compliance. Debugging tools and test frameworks complement development by providing real-time insights and automated evaluation.

- **GDB:** The GNU Debugger is a powerful tool for debugging C++ programs. It allows the inspection of variable values, program state, and execution flow. Command-line driven, GDB is suited to complex applications requiring in-depth debugging.

  Basic GDB workflow includes:

  ```
  g++ -g -o application main.cpp
  gdb ./application
  ```

- **Valgrind:** Implements dynamic analysis to identify memory leaks and threading issues, usually associated with network applications.

- **Google Test (GTest):** A unit testing framework for C++ applications, allowing automated test creation and execution. It supports assertions, test suites, and fixtures to check each part of your application.

  ```
  TEST(SocketTest, ConnectionSuccess) {
      ASSERT_EQ(connectToServer(), 0);
  }
  ```

Setting up an environment holistic to the needs of network programming in C++ extends beyond simple installations, necessitating tailored integrations, custom configurations, and strategic tool selections that align with application objectives, team dynamics, and target platforms. This meticulous preparation paves the way for developing network software with precision, efficiency, and adaptability in today's advancing technological ecosystem.

Chapter 2

Understanding Network Protocols

In this chapter, readers will delve into the critical role that network protocols play in enabling seamless communication between devices. By exploring the structure and function of models such as the OSI and TCP/IP, the chapter emphasizes how these protocols govern data exchange across networks. It examines commonly used internet protocols such as HTTP, FTP, and DNS, providing a comprehensive view of their purposes and applications. Additionally, the chapter addresses challenges in protocol implementation, preparing readers for potential issues they might encounter in practical scenarios.

2.1   Concept of Network Protocols

The concept of network protocols holds a foundational place in the domain of computer networking. Network protocols dictate the rules and conventions for communication between network devices, ensuring the reliable transmission and reception of data across diverse types of networks. These protocols are akin to languages spoken by computers, allowing them to establish clear and structured communication pathways.

In networking, understanding protocols requires recognizing their pivotal role in harmonizing data exchange processes. Each protocol is specifically designed to perform a distinct function within the network, addressing different aspects of communication such as synchronization, error handling, data packetization, and routing. The specifications of a protocol incorporate a comprehensive set of rules that include syntax, semantics, and timing. Syntax refers to the structure or format of the data, semantics pertains to the meaning of each section of bits, and timing coincides with the coordination of data transmission.

The diversity of network protocols opens up several layers of communication, which can be visualized through structured models such as the OSI and TCP/IP. These models compartmentalize network functions to provide a framework for protocol standardization and interoperability. Despite their layered approaches, the models share the objective of enhancing network communication efficiency and robustness.

Within the operational context, network protocols can be broadly classified into several key categories:

- **Communication Protocols:** These protocols establish the procedures for the transmission of data between network devices. Examples include Transmission Control Protocol (TCP) and User Datagram Protocol (UDP). Their main function is ensuring that data packets are sent and received reliably.

- **Routing Protocols:** These ensure the proper routing of data across networks, providing pathways for packet delivery. Protocols like Border Gateway Protocol (BGP) and Open Shortest Path First (OSPF) fall under this category.

- **Management Protocols:** Such protocols are used to manage network devices and troubleshoot network issues. Simple Network Management Protocol (SNMP) is a common example.

- **Security Protocols:** These protocols ensure the authentication and authorization of users and data encryption. Protocols like Secure Sockets Layer (SSL) and Transport Layer Security (TLS) are typical instances.

Each protocol brings its own set of capabilities that contribute to the efficient function of networks. For instance, TCP provides a reliable, connection-oriented service that sees to the successful delivery of data, with error detection and correction, as well as source and destination node acknowledgment before communication ensues. The simplicity and efficiency of UDP, allowing data to be sent without prior communications to set up special transmission channels or data paths, make it suitable for applications that require time-sensitive data such as streaming.

To further appreciate the importance of network protocols, one could consider a practical coding example illustrating a rudimentary implementation of a TCP client-server communication model. This scenario encapsulates the initiation, data exchange, and termination of a connection between a client and a server.

```python
# Python program for a simple TCP client

import socket

def tcp_client():
    host = '127.0.0.1'
    port = 65432

    # Create a TCP/IP socket
    with socket.socket(socket.AF_INET, socket.SOCK_STREAM) as s:

        # Connect to the server
        s.connect((host, port))

        # Send data
        message = "Hello, Server"
        s.sendall(message.encode())

        # Receive response
        data = s.recv(1024)

    print('Received', data.decode())

if __name__ == '__main__':
    tcp_client()
```

The client script establishes a connection to a TCP server specified by an IP address and port number. After setting up the connection, it demonstrates message delivery with 's.sendall()' and receives the server's reply using 's.recv()', thus completing the basic exchange cycle.

Protocols serve as blueprints for building interoperable networked environments. They enable hardware and software from various vendors to interact, fostering greater innovation in network technologies. The adherence to standard protocols ensures devices can communicate with minimal configuration, promoting a seamless user experience. This aspect is crucial in environments where equipment from multiple sources coexists.

Network protocols also address data congestion through mechanisms that regulate traffic flow. Flow control meticulously manages the rate of data transmission between sender and receiver, ensuring receivers are not overwhelmed by a data influx. Protocols such as TCP employ flow control through windowing techniques to manage buffer resources effectively.

Error detection and correction are integral to network protocols. They employ mechanisms like checksums, cyclic redundancy checks (CRC), and acknowledgments to maintain data integrity. These mechanisms detect corrupted packets and facilitate their retransmission, ascertaining that data arrives at its destination correctly.

Delving further into protocol analysis, it becomes apparent that network security protocols play an essential role in safeguarding communications. Consider the employment of TLS in securing web transactions:

```python
# Python code for a simple SSL-enabled server

import ssl
import socket

def ssl_server():
    context = ssl.create_default_context(ssl.Purpose.CLIENT_AUTH)
    context.load_cert_chain(certfile="server.pem", keyfile="server.key")

    bindsocket = socket.socket()
    bindsocket.bind(('127.0.0.1', 10023))
    bindsocket.listen(5)

    while True:
        newsocket, fromaddr = bindsocket.accept()
        conn = context.wrap_socket(newsocket, server_side=True)
        try:
            data = conn.recv(1024)
            if data:
                conn.sendall(b"Hello, SSL Client")
        finally:
            conn.close()

if __name__ == '__main__':
    ssl_server()
```

The server utilizes SSL to create a secure connection channel with the client, providing confidentiality and integrity to data transmitted over insecure channels. This level of protection is vital in modern-day applications where data privacy is paramount.

The continuous evolution of networking protocols reflects the adaptability of the technology to meet emerging requirements. From the simple data exchanges of the ARPANET era to today's complex, high-speed internet, protocols have evolved to manage increased traffic loads, more sophisticated attacks, and the unprecedented demand for real-time data processing. This evolution prompts continuous updates in established protocols and the introduction of new ones to address specific challenges.

In summary, the knowledge of network protocols empowers network administrators, engineers, and developers to architect reliable, secure, and efficient communication systems. These protocols encompass the entire spectrum of networking needs, from the fundamental handshakes that establish communication to the sophisticated encryptions that protect it. Understanding their mechanisms and applications allows for a deeper appreciation of the intricacies involved in the interconnectivity of modern devices and systems.

2.2 The OSI Model

The Open Systems Interconnection (OSI) model, established by the International Organization for Standardization (ISO), is a conceptual framework that standardizes the functions of a telecommunication or computing system into seven abstract layers. Each layer serves a specific role and communicates with directly adjacent layers to facilitate modular network architecture. Understanding the OSI model is essential for network designers and engineers to diagnose network issues and apply network protocols effectively. The OSI model consists of the following seven layers:

- **Physical Layer**: This layer is the first and lowest layer in the OSI model. It deals with the physical connection between devices and the transmission and reception of raw bit streams over

39

a physical medium. It defines the electrical, optical, and mechanical characteristics of the network's hardware interfaces. Examples of standards at this layer include Ethernet, USB, and RS-232.

• **Data Link Layer**: This layer provides node-to-node data transfer and error correction through mechanisms like checksums and frame synchronization. It is divided into two sublayers: the Logical Link Control (LLC) sublayer that manages Frame Synchronization, error checking, and flow control, and the Media Access Control (MAC) sublayer that determines permission to access the transmission medium. Protocols such as Ethernet for LANs and PPP for point-to-point connections operate at this level.

• **Network Layer**: The primary responsibility of this layer is routing—deciding the physical or logical paths for data transmission from source to destination across multiple networks. It handles packet forwarding, including routing through intermediary routers. The Internet Protocol (IP) is the principal protocol used at this layer, ensuring data packets are transferred across networks.

• **Transport Layer**: Providing end-to-end communication service for applications, the transport layer deals with error recovery, flow control, and ensures complete data transfer. It can provide a reliable connection-oriented service like TCP or a connectionless service like UDP. Error detection and correction, as well as data segmentation and reassembly, are key processes performed by the transport layer.

• **Session Layer**: This layer establishes, manages, and terminates sessions between two communicating hosts. It controls the dialogues (connections) between computers, managing data exchange and providing checkpoint and recovery measures whenever needed. Protocols like RPC and SQL are associated with this layer.

• **Presentation Layer**: Often called the syntax layer, it translates data between the application layer and the network format. It is responsible for data encryption, decryption, compression, and decompression, ensuring the data sent by the application layer of one system is readable by the application layer of another. Encryption protocols like SSL operate within this layer.

- **Application Layer**: The topmost layer of the OSI model deals with the interaction between software applications and lower network services. This layer supports network access, data integrity, and additional security features. Protocols like HTTP, FTP, SMTP, and DNS reside at this layer, serving end-user applications and facilitating data exchange between computers.

The OSI model facilitates an understanding of the complex interactions involved in network communication by separating them into more manageable and distinct functions. Such abstraction allows for the interchangeability and interoperability among products from different manufacturers, as each component only needs to adhere to specific standards relevant to its layer.

To illustrate the practical application of OSI layers in a network communication scenario, consider a simple implementation of a TCP communication that engages multiple layers of the OSI model. This hypothetical example emphasizes the encapsulation process as data moves downward from the application layer to the physical layer, across the network, then back up to the application layer on the receiving end.

- **Application Layer**: The user's action - requesting a web page through a browser initiates communication at this level.

- **Presentation Layer**: If data encryption is required, SSL/TLS encrypts the HTTP request.

- **Session Layer**: The application opens a session for HTTP communication, allowing multiple request/response transactions.

- **Transport Layer**: TCP segments the data and attaches header information for error detection and flow control, establishing a connection-oriented service.

- **Network Layer**: Each segment from TCP is encapsulated into packets, adding IP-specific routing and addressing information.

- **Data Link Layer**: The packets are framed with MAC addresses and prepared for transmission over the physical network.

41

- **Physical Layer**: The actual binary data is transmitted over physical media using electrical signals, cables, or wireless technologies.

For a further understanding, a Python example simulating a TCP Echo Server can demonstrate how transport-level protocols (such as those implemented through socket programming) manage data transmission reliability and connectivity in accordance with OSI model layers:

```
# Python program simulating a simple TCP Echo Server
import socket

def tcp_echo_server():
    host = '127.0.0.1'
    port = 65432

    # Create a TCP/IP socket
    with socket.socket(socket.AF_INET, socket.SOCK_STREAM) as server_socket:
        # Bind the socket to the address
        server_socket.bind((host, port))

        # Enable the server to accept connections, backlog queue size is 5
        server_socket.listen(5)
        print("Server listening on", (host, port))

        # Wait for client connection
        while True:
            client_socket, address = server_socket.accept()
            with client_socket:
                print("Connected by", address)
                while True:
                    data = client_socket.recv(1024)
                    if not data:
                        break
                    client_socket.sendall(data)

if __name__ == '__main__':
    tcp_echo_server()
```

In the example above, the server provides an endpoint for a client through the transport layer, handling the encapsulation of messages through TCP for reliable data transfer. The server indefinitely listens for incoming connections and, upon connection, echoes back any data received from the client. At each layer in the OSI model, data undergoes processing steps that wrap it with necessary control information, enabling reliable, scalable communication.

The OSI model is pivotal in modern network architecture, not only used for theoretical understanding but also as a reference during the troubleshooting of network issues. By providing specific roles for varying communication functions, the OSI model simplifies diagnosing process failures. For instance, a problem in inter-networking could be isolated to the network layer, whereas a data encryption issue could point to the presentation layer.

Understanding the OSI model extends beyond simply grasping the responsibilities of each layer. It involves an appreciation of how these layers interdependently operate to ensure the smooth transfer of data, from source to destination, across complex network infrastructures. With evolving technologies and new communication demands, the principles of the OSI model remain a foundational guide for developing effective and efficient communication systems.

2.3   TCP/IP Model and Protocols

The TCP/IP model, also known as the Internet Protocol Suite, is a set of communication protocols that dictate how data should be packaged, transmitted, routed, and received in a network environment. It forms the core architecture of the Internet and many local networks. Unlike the OSI model with its seven layers, the TCP/IP model comprises four layers, each contributing to the seamless transfer of data across heterogeneous systems and networks. These layers are the Link layer, Internet layer, Transport layer, and Application layer.

- **Link Layer:** The Link layer, equivalent to a combination of the OSI's Data Link and Physical layers, handles the intricacies of hardware addressing and the physical transmission of data within the same network. It encompasses protocols and hardware standards that facilitate communication over the network's physical media. Protocols like Ethernet, Wi-Fi (IEEE 802.11), and Point-to-Point Protocol (PPP) are integral to this layer, ensuring that data packets are properly formatted for transmission over the defined medium.

- **Internet Layer:** Operating independently of the underlying network infrastructure, the Internet layer's primary function is to control the routing of packets across different networks, essentially acting as the navigational component that interconnects

43

vast arrays of networks into a cohesive whole known as the internet. The Internet Protocol (IP) serves as a cornerstone at this layer, tasked with addressing and forwarding packets without establishing end-to-end connections. IP operates in two versions: IPv4 and IPv6. The availability of IPv6 addresses the limitations of IPv4 in terms of address scarcity and enhanced routing performance. Other protocols in this layer include the Internet Control Message Protocol (ICMP) for diagnostics and error reporting, and the Address Resolution Protocol (ARP) which facilitates IP addressing within local networks.

- **Transport Layer:** Comparable to the Transport layer in the OSI model, it ensures the reliable delivery of messages across networks. Transport layer protocols standardize communication endpoints called ports, distinguishing multiple applications hosted on a single device. Transmission Control Protocol (TCP) and User Datagram Protocol (UDP) are the primary protocols. TCP offers a reliable, connection-oriented delivery mechanism, using methods like three-way handshakes, acknowledgments, and retransmissions for dependable packet delivery. Conversely, UDP provides a connectionless service suitable for applications where speed outweighs reliability, such as video streaming.

- **Application Layer:** This topmost layer amalgamates functionalities of the OSI's Session, Presentation, and Application layers, addressing interaction with software applications involved in communication processes. Protocols operating at this layer include HTTP for web traffic, FTP for file transfers, SMTP for sending emails, and DNS for resolving domain names to IP addresses. Its vast array of protocols enables diverse applications to operate over the network seamlessly, ensuring data is presented correctly to the end-user.

Examining Key Protocols

- **Transmission Control Protocol (TCP):** TCP ensures secure connections and reliable data transfer between devices. By implementing flow control, error detection, and correction, TCP maintains data integrity and delivery accuracy.

44

```
# Simple illustration of a TCP client using Python

import socket

def tcp_client():
    server_address = ('localhost', 8080)
    client_socket = socket.socket(socket.AF_INET, socket.
        SOCK_STREAM)
    client_socket.connect(server_address)

    try:
        message = 'Hello, TCP Server!'
        client_socket.sendall(message.encode())
        response = client_socket.recv(1024)
        print('Received:', response.decode())

    finally:
        client_socket.close()

if __name__ == "__main__":
    tcp_client()
```

This Python code demonstrates a simple TCP client connecting to a server, sending and receiving data while utilizing TCP's promise of reliable communication through established connections and acknowledgments.

- **User Datagram Protocol (UDP):** UDP is optimized for lower overhead communication where speed is prioritized over reliability. It does not require establishing or maintaining a connection, suitable for real-time applications like online gaming or VoIP.

```
# Simple illustration of a UDP sender using Python

import socket

def udp_sender():
    server_address = ('localhost', 6789)
    udp_socket = socket.socket(socket.AF_INET, socket.SOCK_DGRAM)

    try:
        message = 'Hello, UDP Server!'
        udp_socket.sendto(message.encode(), server_address)
        print('Message sent to', server_address)

    finally:
        udp_socket.close()

if __name__ == "__main__":
    udp_sender()
```

This demonstrates sending a simple message to a server using

45

UDP, showcasing the speed and simplicity of connectionless communication.

- **Internet Protocol (IP):** IP provides navigational assistance across networks, managing addresses and data packet routing, essential for internet communication. Its two versions, IPv4 and IPv6, differ primarily in the address length, with IPv6 offering a larger address space necessary for modern network demands.

Contrast and Integration with the OSI Model   While the OSI model provides a comprehensive theoretical foundation for network communications, the TCP/IP model is practical and tailored to the designs and implementations used for internet technologies. The TCP/IP model's layers are less abstract, detailing specific protocol suites utilized in everyday networking tasks. Understanding the relationships between OSI and TCP/IP facilitates seamless troubleshooting and network analysis, with each offering separate insights into how data traverses networked systems.

The TCP/IP model substantially informs the design of network infrastructure, hosting modern, distributed applications by linking computing domains, enabling expansive connectivity, and supporting scalable architectures. Through its well-defined layers, network designers leverage TCP/IP for efficient and extensible systems, accommodating diverse protocols and legacy systems under a single, cohesive framework.

Implementing TCP/IP Protocols   Consider a simplified client-server interaction where both TCP and UDP are implemented to understand their contrast in operation.

- **TCP vs. UDP Server Implementation:**

```python
# Python code illustrating TCP vs. UDP server-side setup

import socket

def tcp_server():
    server_socket = socket.socket(socket.AF_INET, socket.
        SOCK_STREAM)
    server_socket.bind(('localhost', 8090))
    server_socket.listen()
```

46

```
    print('TCP server listening...')
    while True:
        conn, addr = server_socket.accept()
        with conn:
            print('Connected by', addr)
            while True:
                data = conn.recv(1024)
                if not data:
                    break
                conn.sendall(data.upper())

def udp_server():
    udp_socket = socket.socket(socket.AF_INET, socket.SOCK_DGRAM)
    udp_socket.bind(('localhost', 8091))

    print('UDP server ready...')
    while True:
        data, addr = udp_socket.recvfrom(1024)
        print('Connection from', addr)
        udp_socket.sendto(data.upper(), addr)

# Uncomment to run either server function
# if __name__ == "__main__":
# tcp_server()
# udp_server()
```

The TCP server establishes a persistent connection, ensuring comprehensive data transmission integrity. In contrast, the UDP server offers immediate data transmission without the need for a connection handshake, focusing on efficiency and low-latency feedback.

The TCP/IP suite's famed versatility and robust application engagement ensure it remains the backbone of modern networking, incorporating key protocol developments and reflecting evolving technologies that ensure prompt, reliable data exchange across the vast expanse of the internet. By grasping its operational paradigms, professionals in the field are better equipped to design and maintain robust network systems tailored for diverse and dynamic environments.

2.4   Common Internet Protocols

In the landscape of digital communication, common internet protocols facilitate the robust exchange of data among devices over the vast network infrastructure known as the internet. These protocols help estab-

lish connections, transfer information, and maintain reliability and security across diverse network environments. Among these, Hypertext
Transfer Protocol (HTTP), File Transfer Protocol (FTP), Simple Mail
Transfer Protocol (SMTP), and Domain Name System (DNS) stand out
due to their critical roles in web services, file transfers, email communication, and domain resolution, respectively.

- **Hypertext Transfer Protocol (HTTP)** HTTP is a foundational protocol in the World Wide Web, employed for transferring hypertext documents between clients and servers. Operating primarily over TCP, HTTP dictates the transmission of
  data across the web, encapsulating requests and responses into
  comprehensible formats for seamless user interaction with web
  resources. It resides at the Application layer of the TCP/IP
  model and leverages methods such as GET, POST, PUT, DELETE,
  among others, to perform various operations on web resources.

  - **HTTP Methods:**
    * GET: Used to request data from a specified resource,
      usually without causing any state change on the server.
    * POST: Submits data to be processed to a specified re-
      source, often resulting in state changes on the server.
    * PUT: Updates an existing resource or creates a new re-
      source with provided data.
    * DELETE: Removes a specified resource.

  The evolution of HTTP to HTTP/2 has introduced advancements
  such as multiplexing, header compression, and improved flow
  control, enhancing speed and efficiency. HTTP/3 is emerging
  with new transport mechanisms leveraging Quick UDP Internet
  Connections (QUIC).

  A Python example of a simple HTTP client using the http.client
  module demonstrates basic HTTP operations:

```
# Python HTTP client example using http.client

import http.client

def fetch_website():
    connection = http.client.HTTPConnection("www.example.com")
    connection.request("GET", "/")
```

48

```
response = connection.getresponse()

print("Status:", response.status)
print("Headers:", response.getheaders())
print("Content:", response.read().decode())

if __name__ == "__main__":
    fetch_website()
```

This script establishes a connection to www.example.com, sends a GET request, and prints the status, headers, and content of the response.

- **File Transfer Protocol (FTP)** FTP is designed for the seamless transfer of files over the internet, providing mechanisms for uploading and downloading files between computers. Utilizing separate data and control channels, FTP offers command execution and data exchange independently, often under the transport secured connection. FTP clients can interact with servers using user credentials, allowing authenticated and anonymous access modes.

  - **Active vs. Passive FTP:**
    * Active Mode: The client opens a random port and communicates to the server's command port (21), providing the IP and port to which the server connects back to establish the data transfer.
    * Passive Mode: The server opens a random port and communicates that port to the client, allowing the client to initiate the data connection.

  To highlight FTP operations, Python's ftplib library can demonstrate list retrieval and file download functionalities:

```
# Python FTP client example using ftplib

from ftplib import FTP

def download_file():
    ftp = FTP('ftp.example.com')
    ftp.login() # Anonymous Login
    ftp.cwd('some_directory')

    # List Files
    files = ftp.nlst()
    print("Files in directory:", files)
```

49

```
# Download File
with open('downloaded_file.txt', 'wb') as local_file:
    ftp.retrbinary('RETR example.txt', local_file.write)

ftp.quit()

if __name__ == "__main__":
    download_file()
```

This example logs into an FTP server, lists files in a directory, and downloads a specified file.

- **Simple Mail Transfer Protocol (SMTP)** SMTP is the de facto standard for email transmission across the internet, delineating the rules for sending, receiving, and routing email messages. SMTP typically operates over TCP. While SMTP is employed for sending emails, protocols like Post Office Protocol (POP3) and Internet Message Access Protocol (IMAP) are used for retrieving messages. SMTP uses commands like HELO, MAIL FROM, RCPT TO, DATA, and QUIT to coordinate message transactions between mail servers.

  With the advent of security requirements, SMTP supports extensions like STARTTLS for encrypted mail transfer:

```
# Python SMTP client example using smtplib

import smtplib

def send_mail():
    smtp_server = 'smtp.example.com'
    sender = 'example@example.com'
    recipient = 'friend@example.com'
    message = """\
Subject: Test Email

This is a test email sent from Python."""

    with smtplib.SMTP(smtp_server, 587) as server:
        server.starttls() # Secure connection
        server.login(sender, 'password')
        server.sendmail(sender, recipient, message)
        print("Email sent successfully")

if __name__ == "__main__":
    send_mail()
```

This script establishes an SMTP connection, encrypts it with TLS, and dispatches an email message.

- **Domain Name System (DNS)** DNS translates human-readable domain names (e.g., www.example.com) into machine-understandable IP addresses required for locating and identifying computer services and devices with the underlying network protocols. Functionally analogous to a massive distributed database, DNS resolves queries through a hierarchy of name servers, including root, top-level domain (TLD), and authoritative name servers.

  DNS records categorially include A, AAAA, CNAME, MX, TXT, and more, serving various resolving functions:

  - **A Record:** Maps a domain to an IPv4 address.
  - **AAAA Record:** Maps a domain to an IPv6 address.
  - **CNAME Record:** Maps an alias name to the canonical domain name.
  - **MX Record:** Directs email to mail servers for a domain.

  The Python library socket provides methods to resolve DNS queries programmatically:

```python
# Python DNS query example using the socket library

import socket

def resolve_domain(domain):
    ip_address = socket.gethostbyname(domain)
    print(f'The IP address of {domain} is {ip_address}')

if __name__ == "__main__":
    resolve_domain('www.example.com')
```

  This example resolves a domain into its associated IP address via DNS lookup.

Analyzing Protocol Security and Evolution

Network protocol security encompasses strategies to protect data integrity and privacies, such as Transport Layer Security (TLS) and Secure Socket Layer (SSL), which adjoin secure extensions to protocols like HTTP (resulting in HTTPS) and SMTP. Security measures such as encryption, authentication, integrity, and non-repudiation underpin protocols to counter threats in data communication.

With the internet's continued growth, protocols have adapted to encompass performance enhancements, accommodating the exponential
rise in network users and data consumption demands. Protocols ma-
ture with iterative refinements aimed at latency reduction, data compression, adaptive congestion control, and fortified security postures.

In the contemporary digital era, these internet protocols serve invaluable roles, seamlessly enabling communication and interaction on an
unprecedented scale. They form the backbone of e-commerce, online
services, cloud computing, and an ever-expanding array of internet-
dependent functionalities. Mastery of these protocols empowers developers, network engineers, and IT professionals to optimize and secure
the modern internet infrastructure, ensuring efficient and secure data
exchanges.

2.5   Protocol Implementation Challenges

Implementing network protocols involves an intricate balance of software engineering, network programming, and system design to ensure
efficient and performant communication across digital environments.
Protocol implementation challenges arise from the diverse considerations needed to maintain compatibility, scalability, security, and reliability. As networks expand and evolve, addressing these challenges
becomes pivotal for developers and engineers who aim to provide robust network solutions.

- **Compatibility and Interoperability**

Ensuring that new and existing protocols can coexist and communicate effectively across a broad range of systems and devices is a primary challenge. Different systems may use heterogeneous hardware,
operating environments, and software stacks, necessitating protocols
that can adapt while maintaining compatibility. This challenge is often addressed through adherence to open standards and specifications
that facilitate interoperability. Nevertheless, real-world implementations may encounter deviations in protocol interpretation and execution, leading to network incompatibilities.

To alleviate such disparities, thorough testing using diverse test suites and environments is essential to verify adherence to protocol standards. Simulators and network emulators can play critical roles in modeling network conditions and identifying interoperability issues.

- **Security Threats and Vulnerabilities**

Security remains one of the leading challenges in protocol implementation, primarily due to evolving threat landscapes and sophisticated cyberattacks targeting vulnerabilities. Implementing secure network protocols entails ensuring confidentiality, authentication, integrity, and non-repudiation.

Protocols must implement encryption mechanisms appropriately while balancing performance and security overheads. For example, introducing cryptographic handshakes, as in the Transport Layer Security (TLS), adds latency but provides significant security benefits. A practical challenge lies in designing protocols to minimize these performance impacts without compromising security features.

```python
# Example of TLS-encrypted communication in Python using ssl module

import socket
import ssl

def secure_client():
    hostname = 'www.example.com'
    context = ssl.create_default_context()

    with socket.create_connection((hostname, 443)) as sock:
        with context.wrap_socket(sock, server_hostname=hostname) as secure_sock:
            secure_sock.sendall(b"GET / HTTP/1.1\r\nHost: www.example.com\r\n\r\n")
            response = secure_sock.recv(4096)
            print(response.decode('utf-8'))

if __name__ == "__main__":
    secure_client()
```

This example illustrates secure communication over TLS, integral to maintaining confidentiality and integrity for HTTP transactions.

- **Scalability**

A protocol must handle increased loads without degradation in performance, which presents a significant implementation challenge. Scalability encompasses aspects such as breadth (handling more clients) and depth (handling complex transactions). As networks grow and extend, protocols must anticipate these changes to accommodate growth in user base, data volumes, and transaction complexities.

Implementing efficient data handling, load balancing mechanisms, and distributed systems are key strategies for scaling protocols. Network Load Balancers (NLBs) and Content Delivery Networks (CDNs) are examples of technologies that ameliorate scaling issues by distributing loads efficiently across multiple servers.

- **Latency and Throughput**

The opposing needs to minimize latency and maximize throughput present a technical conundrum. While high throughput ensures large volumes of data transfer efficiently, low latency requirements demand minimal delay in transmission and reception of information. Protocol designers must craft algorithmic optimizations and network behaviors to balance these factors effectively.

TCP's congestion control mechanisms, such as Slow Start and Fast Retransmit, exemplify protocol features aimed at maintaining high throughput with acceptable latency. These components must be meticulously implemented and tested to ensure they adapt dynamically to network conditions.

- **Packet Loss and Error Handling**

Protocols must remain resilient in the face of packet loss and transmission errors, ensuring data integrity and seamless user experiences. Implementing error detection and correction algorithms forms a cornerstone of reliable protocol design. Techniques such as checksums, cyclic redundancy checks (CRCs), and Automatic Repeat reQuest (ARQ) mechanisms are commonly employed to detect and correct errors.

UDP, despite its connectionless nature, often integrates with higher layer protocols to manage disorderly packets and data corruption, facilitating error handling without the extensive overhead of TCP.

```
# Python code using UDP with basic acknowledgement to demonstrate error handling
```

```
import socket

def udp_server_with_ack():
    host = '127.0.0.1'
    port = 65432
    udp_socket = socket.socket(socket.AF_INET, socket.SOCK_DGRAM)
    udp_socket.bind((host, port))

    while True:
        data, addr = udp_socket.recvfrom(1024)
        print(f"Received message from {addr}: {data.decode()}")

        # Send Acknowledgment
        ack = f"ACK for {data.decode()}"
        udp_socket.sendto(ack.encode(), addr)

if __name__ == "__main__":
    udp_server_with_ack()
```

This example demonstrates UDP communication with a simple acknowledgment mechanism, offering an alternative to mitigate dropped packets.

- **Resource Constraints**

Resource-limited environments, such as embedded systems and IoT devices, present another layer of difficulty in protocol implementation. These devices must communicate efficiently, often with limited memory, processing power, and energy resources. Protocols need to be optimized for low overhead while retaining core functionality, an area where lightweight protocols like MQTT and CoAP excel.

Designers must strategically trim resource-intensive features, emphasizing compressed message formats, streamlined operation sequences, and the use of lightweight encryption when necessary.

- **Network Topologies and Dynamics**

Protocols must adapt to various network topologies and dynamic conditions, such as mobility and environmental changes. Mobile ad-hoc networks (MANETs) and vehicular networks introduce further challenges, as protocols must accommodate frequent topology changes and varying signal strengths.

Routing protocols like AODV (Ad hoc On-Demand Distance Vector

55

Routing) have emerged to cater to such dynamics by providing self-starting, loop-free, and multihop routing for ad-hoc networks.

Conclusion

Protocol implementation stands at the nexus of innovation and complexity in network engineering. Addressing compatibility, security, scalability, performance, error resilience, resource constraints, and network dynamics are paramount to crafting robust and efficient communication systems. By navigating these challenges with informed design strategies and leveraging progressive technologies, today's engineers can develop protocols that not only meet immediate needs but also evolve to accommodate future demands in an ever-connected world.

Chapter 3

Socket Programming in C++

This chapter provides an in-depth exploration of socket programming with C++, a fundamental aspect of network communication development. It begins by defining the concept of sockets and their critical role in creating networked applications. Through detailed, step-by-step guidance, readers learn how to create and manage sockets, including binding, listening, and accepting connections to facilitate client-server interactions. The chapter further covers essential techniques for sending and receiving data, alongside effective error-handling practices, equipping readers with the skills to implement robust network applications using sockets.

3.1   What are Sockets

In computer science, a socket is a fundamental and binding interface for network communications that connects software applications over a network. Sockets play an essential role in enabling communication between different processes and systems, permitting them to exchange data efficiently through standardized interfaces. To understand sockets, one must grasp both their theoretical underpinning and practical applications.

The concept of a socket originated with the Berkeley Software Distribution (BSD) UNIX operating systems. A socket represents an endpoint for sending and receiving data across a computer network. In a Unix-like environment, it is treated like a file descriptor employed by programs to establish a communication channel to other processes, either locally on the same machine or on a remote system. This concept is extended in most other operating systems, making socket programming a universally applicable skill.

Sockets can be understood as an abstraction layer that separates the specifics of the physical network from the application layers, enabling developers to focus on higher-level concerns of data transmission without delving into the intricacies of the medium itself. Technically, a socket is defined by an IP address and a port number, forming a unique identifier for communications over Internet Protocol (IP)-based networks.

The types of sockets can broadly be categorized into several types, each catering to specific communication models and used semi-transparently to differentiate between various architectures:

- **Stream Sockets (SOCK_STREAM):** These provide two-way, reliable, and sequenced communication channels that operate over Transmission Control Protocol (TCP). Stream sockets ensure data integrity and order, making them suitable for applications where delivery order and data integrity are paramount, such as HTTP, FTP, and SMTP. Due to TCP's connection-oriented nature, a socket connection must be established and maintained, which involves an overhead of managing connection states and handshakes.

- **Datagram Sockets (SOCK_DGRAM):** These facilitate communication using User Datagram Protocol (UDP), enabling connectionless messaging where each message is an independent packet. Unlike stream sockets, datagram sockets do not guarantee order or reliability of messages, which can be advantageous for applications that require speed and efficiency over reliability,

58

such as streaming services, online gaming, and VoIP.

- **Raw Sockets:** These afford direct access to lower-layer proto-cols, allowing applications to manipulate headers for fields like IP. Raw sockets serve specialized purposes, such as testing new protocol implementations, network monitoring, or conducting security assessments.

- **Sequenced Packet Sockets (SOCK_SEQPACKET):** Com-bining features from both SOCK_STREAM and SOCK_DGRAM, they provide a neutral ground offering reliable packet sequencing through a connection-oriented service.

The lifecycle of a socket entails a series of well-defined operations per-formed in sequence. Understanding this lifecycle is crucial for imple-menting socket-based communications correctly:

- **Socket Creation:** The initial step involves creating a socket using the socket system call, which requires defining the proto-col family (usually AF_INET for IPv4 or AF_INET6 for IPv6), the socket type, and the protocol. For instance, creating a TCP stream socket in C++ for IPv4 might look like:

```
int socket_fd = socket(AF_INET, SOCK_STREAM, 0);
if (socket_fd < 0) {
    perror("Error creating socket");
}
```

- **Binding:** Associating a socket with a specific port and IP ad-dress on the local machine is achieved through the bind call. This process assigns a specific communication endpoint to the socket within the local network interface, making it recognizable when data arrives.

```
struct sockaddr_in server_address;
server_address.sin_family = AF_INET;
server_address.sin_port = htons(8080);
server_address.sin_addr.s_addr = INADDR_ANY;

if (bind(socket_fd, (struct sockaddr*)&server_address, sizeof(
    server_address)) < 0) {
    perror("Binding failed");
}
```

- **Listening:** Primarily relevant for server-side applications, the socket is set to accept incoming connections. The listen function sets the maximum number of queued connections:

```
if (listen(socket_fd, 5) < 0) {
    perror("Error on listen");
}
```

- **Accepting Connections:** Specifically for server implementations, a socket is instantiated for each client connection, created as a result of the accept system call. This provides a dedicated communication channel:

```
int client_socket = accept(socket_fd, (struct sockaddr*)&client_address, &
    client_length);
if (client_socket < 0) {
    perror("Accept failed");
}
```

- **Data Transmission:** The core function where data packets are sent and received via established sockets, using send and recv:

```
int n = send(client_socket, buffer, sizeof(buffer), 0);
if (n < 0) {
    perror("Error sending data");
}

n = recv(client_socket, buffer, sizeof(buffer), 0);
if (n < 0) {
    perror("Error receiving data");
}
```

- **Termination:** The socket is closed once communication is complete, freeing resources:

```
close(socket_fd);
close(client_socket);
```

Sockets also incorporate a set of parameters that dictate their behavior during communications, such as socket options that can be configured using the setsockopt function, including options like TCP_NODELAY, SO_REUSEADDR, and SO_LINGER. These options alter how data is buffered, how connections are reused, and the handling of unfinished communications.

Understanding socket communication further involves grasping several critical considerations:

- **Concurrency Control:** Because sockets are a shared resource and communications occur asynchronously, concurrent connections may lead to complex intertwining of communications unless managed appropriately. This often necessitates concurrent programming mechanisms, such as multithreading or asynchronous input/output operations.

- **Network Byte Order:** Networks sometimes require consistency in data representation. To facilitate this, conversion functions like htonl (host to network long), ntohl (network to host long) ensure correct byte order across different architectures. This is particularly important when exchanging binary data between heterogeneous systems.

- **Non-blocking and Blocking IO:** By default, sockets operate in blocking mode, which can pause process execution until operations complete. Non-blocking IO allows for function calls to return immediately, preventing the program from stalling and enabling efficient event-driven programming.

Advanced socket operations encompass integrating with technologies such as Secure Sockets Layer (SSL) to encrypt communications, critical for secure data exchange over public networks. Libraries like OpenSSL provide APIs that abstract these complexities, allowing developers to secure their socket communications without delving into cryptographic detail.

Sockets' versatility and ubiquity have made them a foundation for numerous network applications, not only limited to web servers but also in database communications, multimedia applications, and distributed systems. Whether through a simple local communication between processes or an extensive multi-tiered network, sockets simplify the programmer's task.

Developing a robust understanding of sockets aids markedly in designing systems that are efficient, scalable, and adaptable to future networking protocols and standards. Mastering both the syntactic foundations and conceptual intricacies of socket programming opens a pathway for creating intricate and highly responsive networked applications.

61

3.2 Creating a Socket in C++

Creating a socket in C++ marks the initial step toward enabling network communication between different programs or devices across a network. The socket serves as a cornerstone of networked application development, providing a communication endpoint for sending and receiving data. This section delivers a comprehensive guide to creating sockets in C++ using relevant libraries, with an emphasis on practicality and detailed explanations of underlying processes.

Sockets in C++ are facilitated via system calls wrapped in the POSIX (Portable Operating System Interface) API, which encompasses a suite of standardized operating system interfaces. This makes socket programming highly portable across various Unix-like systems. Windows environments, though similar, require slight deviations due to variations in system libraries and header files.

The implementation of sockets in C++ usually revolves around the inclusion of certain essential libraries, specifically the header <sys/socket.h> for socket calls, and <netinet/in.h> for handling internet addresses. To support these, additional headers like <arpa/inet.h> and <unistd.h> might be necessary for IP address functions and system calls, respectively.

A socket in C++ is essentially initialized using the socket system call, creating an unbound socket in a specified communication domain:

```
int socket(int domain, int type, int protocol);
```

- **Domain:** Specifies the family of protocols to be used with the socket. Typically, AF_INET is employed for IPv4 networks and AF_INET6 for IPv6 networks. This parameter defines the address format and protocol family for the socket. Other domains include AF_UNIX for local socket communication.

- **Type:** Dictates the communication semantics of the socket. Common values include:

  - SOCK_STREAM: For a reliable, connection-oriented TCP transportation.

- SOCK_DGRAM: Supports connectionless UDP communication.

- SOCK_RAW: Ensures raw socket implementation for direct network layer access.

- **Protocol:** Usually set to 0, allowing the operating system to select the appropriate protocol based on the domain and type provided. This parameter can facilitate specification when multiple protocols exist under a single domain.

Socket Creation Example

To create a socket utilizing TCP with IPv4, the invocation of the socket function looks as follows:

```
#include <sys/socket.h>
#include <netinet/in.h>
#include <arpa/inet.h>
#include <unistd.h>
#include <iostream>
#include <cstring>

using namespace std;

int main() {
    int sockfd;
    sockfd = socket(AF_INET, SOCK_STREAM, 0);
    if (sockfd < 0) {
        cerr << "Error opening socket" << endl;
        return 1;
    }
    cout << "Socket created successfully" << endl;

    close(sockfd);
    return 0;
}
```

The code above:

- Includes necessary header files for standard input/output and socket-related functions.

- Declares an integer variable sockfd to store the socket descriptor returned by the socket function. This descriptor is analogous to a file handle used when engaging with files.

- Initializes the socket using AF_INET, SOCK_STREAM, and protocol 0.

63

- Implements basic error handling that checks if the socket descriptor is negative, signaling socket creation failure.

- Closes the socket using the close system call. Closing a socket is essential for releasing allocated resources.

Detailed Error Handling

Robust error handling is paramount in socket operations. Functions like perror or strerror(errno) can be used to obtain human-readable error messages:

```
#include <cerrno>
#include <cstdio>

sockfd = socket(AF_INET, SOCK_STREAM, 0);
if (sockfd < 0) {
    perror("socket failed");
    return 1;
}
```

The use of perror provides insights into errors relating to insufficient resources, permission issues, or unsupported configurations, helping distinguish between transient and persistent issues.

IPv4 vs. IPv6 Sockets

Modern networks often necessitate support for both IPv4 and IPv6 addressing schemes. Sockets tailored for IPv6 employ AF_INET6:

```
int sockfd = socket(AF_INET6, SOCK_STREAM, 0);
if (sockfd < 0) {
    perror("socket failed");
    return 1;
}
```

An IPv6 socket can typically handle an IPv4-mapped IPv6 address, bridging compatibility gaps. This harmonization streamlines applications that must operate across both addressing paradigms without extensive refactoring.

Socket Options and Optimization

Socket performance and behavior can be subtly adjusted using socket options manipulated via setsockopt. These options might include:

- **Address Reusability:** SO_REUSEADDR allows binding a socket to an address that may be presently in use, avoiding common startup delays.

- **Linger Options:** SO_LINGER determines the socket's closing behavior, specifying how long the socket remains in an active state as it finishes sending pending data.

- **Non-blocking Mode:** fcntl can toggle the socket into non-blocking mode, beneficial for asynchronous event-driven models.

Example setting a socket into non-blocking mode:

```
#include <fcntl.h>

int flags = fcntl(sockfd, F_GETFL, 0);
fcntl(sockfd, F_SETFL, flags | O_NONBLOCK);
```

Blocking vs. Non-blocking Sockets and IO Multiplexing

The blocking nature of sockets implies that certain operations pause progress until data is fully sent or received. While straightforward, blocking sockets inhibit responsive design in high-concurrency environments, leading to potential inefficiencies as threads wait idle. Non-blocking sockets ameliorate this by allowing an operation's continuation, even if data remains in transit.

To effectively manage multiple socket requests, IO multiplexing approaches like select, poll, or epoll help respond dynamically to varying network demands. These methods allow a single thread to monitor numerous sockets, adapting as data read or write requirements evolve.

Windows Variations

While POSIX API dominantly features in Unix-like operating systems, Windows employs Winsock for socket operations, leading to minor deviations involving header files, library linking, and initialization requirements. A Windows-centric example involves initializing the Winsock library:

```
#include <winsock2.h>
#include <ws2tcpip.h>

WSADATA wsaData;
int iResult = WSAStartup(MAKEWORD(2,2), &wsaData);
if (iResult != 0) {
```

```
    cout << "WSAStartup failed: " << iResult << endl;
    return 1;
}
SOCKET sockfd = socket(AF_INET, SOCK_STREAM, IPPROTO_TCP);
if (sockfd == INVALID_SOCKET) {
    cout << "Socket creation failed" << endl;
    return 1;
}

closesocket(sockfd);
WSACleanup();
```

Here, WSAStartup and WSACleanup manage Winsock's lifecycle, and the inclusion of <winsock2.h> adapts socket-based code to the Windows environment.

Conclusion

Creating a socket in C++ represents more than just opening a channel for information exchange; it is a crucial part of designing efficient networked applications. The flexibility afforded by sockets enables developers to encapsulate the complexity of underlying networks, focusing instead on safe and reliable data transmission. By setting foundational groundwork in socket creation, further processes—including connecting, binding, and communicating—are made approachable, streamlining the journey towards mastering robust and scalable network applications in C++.

3.3 Binding, Listening, and Accepting Connections

In socket programming, the transition from socket creation to actively handling communication demands a sequence of steps that include binding, listening, and accepting connections. These steps prepare a socket to receive incoming requests, effectively setting the stage for robust client-server interactions. This section meticulously explores each of these processes in a C++ programming context, offering insight into implementation nuances and best practices.

The workflow for binding, listening, and accepting connections revolves around a server socket, which acts as the initial point of contact in client-server architecture. By effectively managing these processes, a server becomes capable of managing multiple clients, delivering efficient communication handling, and ensuring system stability under varying load conditions.

Binding a Socket

Binding a socket is the process of associating it with a specific IP address and port number on the local machine. This association defines a unique endpoint through which data can be transmitted and received.

The bind function accomplishes this task, taking three primary arguments: the socket descriptor, a pointer to the address structure (such as struct sockaddr_in for IPv4), and the size of the address structure. A typical binding operation with error checking:

```cpp
#include <sys/socket.h>
#include <netinet/in.h>
#include <arpa/inet.h>
#include <iostream>
#include <cstring>

using namespace std;

int main() {
    int sockfd;
    struct sockaddr_in server_addr;

    sockfd = socket(AF_INET, SOCK_STREAM, 0);
    if (sockfd < 0) {
        cerr << "Error opening socket" << endl;
        return 1;
    }

    memset(&server_addr, 0, sizeof(server_addr));
    server_addr.sin_family = AF_INET;
    server_addr.sin_addr.s_addr = INADDR_ANY; // Bind to any available network
        interface
    server_addr.sin_port = htons(8080); // Convert port number to network byte
        order

    if (bind(sockfd, (struct sockaddr*)&server_addr, sizeof(server_addr)) < 0) {
        perror("Bind failed");
        close(sockfd);
        return 1;
    }

    cout << "Socket successfully bound to port 8080" << endl;
    close(sockfd);
    return 0;
}
```

Key concepts:

- **Port Number and IP Address:** The bind function associates a socket with a port and IP address. A port number is crucial, serving as an access point for incoming messages, while the IP address confirms the network interface on which the server listens. The use of INADDR_ANY allows the server to listen on all available interfaces.

- **Address Family:** The AF_INET constant indicates IPv4 usage. Extended implementations might involve struct sockaddr_in6 for IPv6.

- **Network Byte Order:** Utilizing htons ensures correct byte ordering of the port number, essential for cross-platform interaction given the differences in endianness across systems.

Listening for Connections

Once a socket is bound, it must be put into listening mode to prepare it for incoming connections. This is done using the listen system call, which designates the socket's role as a passive listener and establishes a backlog queue to hold pending connections:

```
if (listen(sockfd, SOMAXCONN) < 0) {
    perror("Listen failed");
    close(sockfd);
    return 1;
}
```

Breakdown:

- **Backlog Queue:** The second parameter to listen defines the number of active, unaccepted connections that can be queued, waiting for service. The SOMAXCONN constant allows the system to manage the queue size dynamically.

- **Passive Role:** Listen mode transforms the socket into a passive one, incapable of initiating data exchange until a connection is accepted. This is crucial for handling incoming client-server dialogues effectively, preventing premature shutdowns or excessive resource utilization.

68

Accepting Connections

The final step in preparing a server to handle active connections involves accepting client requests through the accept function. This function creates a new, dedicated socket for the connection with each client, thereby isolating communications:

```
struct sockaddr_in client_addr;
socklen_t client_len = sizeof(client_addr);
int client_sockfd = accept(sockfd, (struct sockaddr*)&client_addr, &client_len);
if (client_sockfd < 0) {
    perror("Accept failed");
    close(sockfd);
    return 1;
}
cout << "Connection established with client" << endl;
```

Highlights:

- **Connection Acquiescence:** The accept blocks until a connection request occurs, creating a new socket for client-server communication. This establishes a unique channel, enabling concurrent communication across multiple sockets created for different clients.

- **Client Address Storage:** The client_addr structure collects the respective properties of connected clients. With each accepted connection, client identifiers—such as IP address and port number—are obtainable, adding a layer of control and readability for server administration.

- **Concurrency Management:** By handling each client request with a distinct socket, the architecture fosters efficient multi-client scenarios using strategies such as forked processes or threads. Accepting non-blocking communication through select or poll enhances responsiveness and throughput.

Concurrent Server: Multi-client Handling

Addressing simultaneous client connections necessitates leveraging concurrent processing strategies. A fork/multi-threaded server example:

69

```
#include <pthread.h>

void* handle_client(void* arg) {
    int client_sockfd = *((int*)arg);
    char buffer[1024];

    // Communicate with the client
    recv(client_sockfd, buffer, sizeof(buffer), 0);
    cout << "Client message: " << buffer << endl;

    // Echo message back to the client
    send(client_sockfd, buffer, sizeof(buffer), 0);

    // Client connection ending
    close(client_sockfd);
    return NULL;
}

pthread_t client_thread;
// Inside the main accept loop
int client_sockfd = accept(sockfd, (struct sockaddr*)&client_addr, &client_len);
if (pthread_create(&client_thread, NULL, handle_client, (void*)&client_sockfd) != 0)
    {
    cerr << "Failed to spawn thread" << endl;
    close(client_sockfd);
}
pthread_detach(client_thread);
```

With threading:

- **Thread Creation and Management:** Each connection spawns a new thread that manages client-specific interactions, thereby decoupling connection logic from the main thread and augmenting scalability through parallel processing.

- **Thread Detachment:** The pthread_detach ensures that resources are properly freed once threads have completed execution, preventing memory leaks or undue resource accumulation.

An alternative approach utilizing the fork mechanism is particularly applicable when protocol separation or improved security is required, albeit at the cost of higher overhead compared to threading:

```
#include <unistd.h>

pid_t pid = fork();
if (pid < 0) {
    perror("fork failed");
} else if (pid == 0) {
    // In child process to handle client
```

```
    close(sockfd);
    handle_client(client_sockfd);
    exit(0);
} else {
    // In parent process, close client socket
    close(client_sockfd);
}
```

Lessons and Best Practices:

- **Resource Management:** Ensuring that sockets and resources are released and utilized judiciously avoids lingering resource allocation and server degradation.

- **Security Considerations:** Implementing authentication mechanisms or firewalls restrict unauthorized access, thus thickening defense against vulnerabilities exploited over open networks.

- **Load Balancing:** Employ load balancers to distribute incoming requests across multiple servers, improving response rates and system reliability.

In binding, listening, and accepting connections, mastery of these foundational networking concepts provides the framework needed to build responsive and robust network applications, each capable of handling high demand and dynamic requests seamlessly. A pragmatic understanding of these processes fueled by insightful code and best practices leads to superior application agility, allowing developers to innovate and provision concurrent network solutions adapted to evolving technological landscapes.

3.4 Establishing Client-Server Communication

The essence of socket programming lies in the successful establishment of client-server communication, an architecture that forms the backbone of numerous networking applications. This section outlines the steps and considerations involved in crafting a reliable client-server communication model in C++. Through detailed code examples and analysis, we explore how two distinct entities—a client and a server—exchange data seamlessly over a network.

Client-Server Model Overview

The client-server architecture operates on a fundamental principle where the server provides resources, services, or data, and the client consumes these services. This separation of concerns allows clients to make requests to the server and the server to respond accordingly. Such a model is not only pivotal for web services but also for applications like email, file transfer, and database access.

In a typical client-server communication lifecycle:

- **Server Initialization:** The server starts by creating a socket, binding it to a port, and listening for incoming client connections.

- **Client Connection:** The client initiates contact with the server by creating a socket and attempting to connect to the server's IP address and port.

- **Data Exchange:** Once the connection is established, data is exchanged through send and receive operations.

- **Connection Termination:** Both client and server terminate the connection gracefully once data exchange is complete.

Server Implementation

The server's responsibility is to be available for communication with any incoming client connections. Below is a detailed server-side implementation that encompasses socket creation, binding, listening, accepting connections, and handling client-server communication within a thread to maintain simultaneous interactions.

```
#include <sys/socket.h>
#include <netinet/in.h>
#include <arpa/inet.h>
#include <unistd.h>
#include <iostream>
```

```cpp
#include <cstring>
#include <pthread.h>

using namespace std;

const int PORT = 8080;

void *handle_client(void *client_socket) {
    int client_fd = *(int *)client_socket;
    char buffer[1024];
    int bytes_received;

    // Receive data
    bytes_received = recv(client_fd, buffer, sizeof(buffer), 0);
    if (bytes_received < 0) {
        cerr << "Error in receiving data" << endl;
    } else {
        buffer[bytes_received] = '\0';
        cout << "Client message: " << buffer << endl;

        // Send response
        const char *response = "Message received";
        send(client_fd, response, strlen(response), 0);
    }
    close(client_fd);
    pthread_exit(NULL);
}

int main() {
    int server_fd, client_fd;
    struct sockaddr_in server_addr, client_addr;
    socklen_t client_len = sizeof(client_addr);

    server_fd = socket(AF_INET, SOCK_STREAM, 0);
    if (server_fd < 0) {
        perror("socket failed");
        return -1;
    }

    memset(&server_addr, 0, sizeof(server_addr));
    server_addr.sin_family = AF_INET;
    server_addr.sin_addr.s_addr = INADDR_ANY;
    server_addr.sin_port = htons(PORT);

    if (bind(server_fd, (struct sockaddr *) &server_addr, sizeof(server_addr)) < 0) {
        perror("bind failed");
        close(server_fd);
        return -1;
    }

    if (listen(server_fd, 10) < 0) {
        perror("listen failed");
        close(server_fd);
        return -1;
    }

    cout << "Server is listening on port " << PORT << endl;
```

73

```
while (true) {
    client_fd = accept(server_fd, (struct sockaddr *) &client_addr, &client_len);
    if (client_fd < 0) {
        perror("accept failed");
        continue;
    }

    cout << "Accepted connection from client" << endl;

    pthread_t client_thread;
    pthread_create(&client_thread, NULL, handle_client, &client_fd);
    pthread_detach(client_thread);
}

close(server_fd);
return 0;
}
```

Client Implementation

The client's task is to connect to the server and initiate data exchange. Below is a typical client-side implementation in C++ that establishes a connection to the server, sends messages, and receives responses.

```
#include <sys/socket.h>
#include <netinet/in.h>
#include <arpa/inet.h>
#include <unistd.h>
#include <iostream>
#include <cstring>

using namespace std;

const int PORT = 8080;
const char *SERVER_IP = "127.0.0.1";

int main() {
    int sockfd;
    struct sockaddr_in server_addr;
    char buffer[1024] = "Hello, Server!";

    sockfd = socket(AF_INET, SOCK_STREAM, 0);
    if (sockfd < 0) {
        perror("Socket creation failed");
        return -1;
    }

    memset(&server_addr, 0, sizeof(server_addr));
    server_addr.sin_family = AF_INET;
    server_addr.sin_port = htons(PORT);

    if (inet_pton(AF_INET, SERVER_IP, &server_addr.sin_addr) <= 0) {
        cerr << "Invalid server address" << endl;
```

```
        close(sockfd);
        return -1;
    }

    if (connect(sockfd, (struct sockaddr *) &server_addr, sizeof(server_addr)) < 0) {
        perror("Connection to server failed");
        close(sockfd);
        return -1;
    }

    cout << "Connected to the server" << endl;

    // Send a message to the server
    send(sockfd, buffer, strlen(buffer), 0);

    // Receive a response from the server
    int bytes_received = recv(sockfd, buffer, sizeof(buffer)-1, 0);
    if (bytes_received > 0) {
        buffer[bytes_received] = '\0';
        cout << "Server reply: " << buffer << endl;
    } else {
        cerr << "Server response failed" << endl;
    }

    close(sockfd);
    return 0;
}
```

Key Components and Considerations

- **Socket Creation:** Both client and server create a socket with the `socket` function, choosing IPv4 (`AF_INET`) and TCP (`SOCK_STREAM`) as the protocol. The error handling ensures that any problems in socket creation are promptly identified and addressed.

- **IP Address and Port Handling:** The server binds to a port specified by `htons(PORT)`. The client specifies the server's address using `inet_pton`, which converts the textual IP address to the appropriate form. Such conversions are critical for ensuring compatibility across different platforms and network architectures.

- **Connection Management:** The server's use of the `accept` function creates a dedicated socket for each client connection, maintaining isolation of communication streams. The client establishes a connection using the `connect` function, effectively initiating the communication pathway.

75

- **Data Transmission and Reception:** The send and recv functions facilitate data exchange between client and server. Proper buffer management—including setting null terminators for strings—ensures data integrity and meaningful communication.

- **Concurrency and Threading:** Server-side threading permits multiple client connections to be managed concurrently, crucial for responsive and scalable systems. This threading model is versatile, supporting high-request environments effectively with minimal performance degradation.

- **Error Handling and Resource Management:** Comprehensive error checking across socket operations, binding, listening, and accepting connections safeguards against operational failures. Closing socket descriptors ensures released resources and prevents leaks, maintaining server and client stability over time.

Advanced Considerations

- **Security Enhancements:** To safeguard communication, integrating TLS (Transport Layer Security) via libraries like OpenSSL offers encryption. Securing transmitted data guards against interception and spoofing.

- **Non-blocking Sockets:** Leveraging non-blocking I/O operations or using asynchronous patterns (e.g., select, poll) can further enhance performance in high-load scenarios by allowing other operations to execute while waiting for I/O completion.

- **Load Balancing and Fault Tolerance:** Employing load balancers distributes client requests across multiple servers, optimizing response times and providing resilience against individual server failure. Architectural considerations such as stateless server design aid in scaling and failover operations.

- **Protocol Design:** Designing the data exchange protocol for client-server interaction requires careful consideration, including serialization methods (e.g., JSON, XML) and error-checking mechanisms for data consistency and transaction reliability.

76

Successfully establishing client-server communication isn't a mere exchange of data; it involves crafting robust, efficient, and secure pathways that accommodate the needs of varying application domains. Mastering these techniques enables the creation of sophisticated network services, placing developers at the forefront of distributed system innovations. The knowledge gained through adept management of client-server interactions serves as a foundational element for building complex systems that underpin modern computational tasks and services.

3.5 Sending and Receiving Data

Sending and receiving data are fundamental procedures in socket programming, forming the essence of network communication. Once a connection is established between a client and a server, the exchange of data becomes the primary mode of interaction. This section provides an in-depth exploration of the techniques and nuances involved in sending and receiving data over networks using sockets in C++. Through extensive examples, we delineate various data transfer methods and address both theoretical and practical aspects.

Understanding Data Transmission

At the core of data transmission is the reliable exchange of bytes, achieved using functions like send and recv for stream-based (TCP) sockets, or sendto and recvfrom for datagram-based (UDP) sockets. These functions form the building blocks that enable the flow of information across networked systems.

Basic Usage of Send and Receive

The send function transmits data across a connected socket. For a stream socket, it accepts parameters including the socket descriptor, a data buffer, the length of the data to be sent, and flags to modify the behavior of the function.

```
#include <sys/socket.h>
```

```cpp
#include <unistd.h>
#include <cstring>
#include <iostream>

using namespace std;

int sendData(int socket_fd, const char* message) {
    int total_sent = 0;
    int bytes_left = strlen(message);
    int bytes_sent;

    while (total_sent < bytes_left) {
        bytes_sent = send(socket_fd, message + total_sent, bytes_left, 0);
        if (bytes_sent == -1) {
            perror("send failed");
            return -1;
        }
        total_sent += bytes_sent;
        bytes_left -= bytes_sent;
    }
    return total_sent;
}
```

- **Reliability and Completeness:** Due to potential network variability, the loop continues until all bytes are sent. This ensures message integrity and completeness by handling partial sends—a common occurrence with the send function where fewer bytes are sent than requested.

- **Flags:** The MSG_DONTWAIT flag, for instance, allows for non-blocking operations, which is vital in high-performance situations where waiting for I/O hampers responsiveness.

On the receiving end, the recv function corresponds to reading data from the socket, with similar parameters—socket descriptor, buffer, buffer length, and flags.

```cpp
int receiveData(int socket_fd, char* buffer, int size) {
    int bytes_received = recv(socket_fd, buffer, size - 1, 0);
    if (bytes_received < 0) {
        perror("receive failed");
        return -1;
    } else if (bytes_received == 0) {
        cout << "Connection closed by peer" << endl;
        return 0;
    }
    buffer[bytes_received] = '\0'; // Null-terminate string
    return bytes_received;
}
```

- **Connection State Awareness:** A return of 0 indicates a gracefully closed connection from the peer, which is essential information when ensuring proper shutdown procedures and resource management.

Advanced Techniques and Considerations

While the basic usage of these functions provides a framework for data exchange, several advanced considerations must be addressed to achieve a robust communication model.

Buffer Management and Size Considerations

Efficient buffer management mitigates memory-related issues and optimizes throughput. Buffer size should be adjusted based on message size expectations and available network bandwidth. Larger buffers can reduce the number of send and receive calls, enhancing efficiency.

```
const int BUFFER_SIZE = 4096; // Example buffer size

void processData() {
    char buffer[BUFFER_SIZE];
    // Receiving and processing data
}
```

- **Dynamic Buffering:** Adapting buffer allocation based on runtime data size analysis ensures that applications remain agile across varied workload conditions.

Handling Large Data Transfers

Transferring large datasets demands segmentation into manageable chunks, ensuring each is transmitted and received correctly.

```
void sendLargeData(int socket_fd, const char* large_data, size_t size) {
    size_t bytes_sent = 0;
    while (bytes_sent < size) {
        size_t segment_size = min(size - bytes_sent, BUFFER_SIZE);
        int sent = send(socket_fd, large_data + bytes_sent, segment_size, 0);
        if (sent < 0) {
            perror("Error in sending large data");
            break;
```

79

```
        }
        bytes_sent += sent;
    }
}
```

Message Framing and Protocol Design

Implementing a framing protocol is vital when designing network applications to delimit pieces of data clearly. This aids in the correct interpretation and reconstruction of messages.

- **Fixed-Length Framing:** Each frame has a predefined size, reducing complexity at the cost of potential overhead.

- **Delimiter-based Framing:** Using character sequences (e.g., newlines) to signify frame boundaries.

- **Length-Field Framing:** Incorporates a header indicating the size of the subsequent data payload.

```
// Length-field framing example
void sendFramedMessage(int socket_fd, const char* message) {
    uint32_t length = htonl(strlen(message));
    send(socket_fd, &length, sizeof(length), 0);
    send(socket_fd, message, strlen(message), 0);
}
```

Here, the header encodes the message length, ensuring that the receiver extracts exactly the intended bytes.

Event-Driven Data Transfer

Using event-driven or asynchronous I/O improves responsiveness by allowing application processing to continue while waiting for data operations to complete.

Select, Poll, and Epoll

Using select, poll, or epoll, developers can monitor multiple file descriptors to determine when I/O is possible without blocking.

```
#include <sys/select.h>

void handleIOSelect(int server_fd) {
    fd_set read_fds;
    struct timeval timeout;
    FD_ZERO(&read_fds);
    FD_SET(server_fd, &read_fds);

    timeout.tv_sec = 5;
    timeout.tv_usec = 0;

    if (select(server_fd + 1, &read_fds, NULL, NULL, &timeout) < 0) {
        perror("Select error");
    } else if (FD_ISSET(server_fd, &read_fds)) {
        // Ready to accept connections or read data
    }
}
```

The select function allows checking readiness across multiple sockets, facilitating simultaneous client management and improving performance by reducing latency in request handling.

Protocol-Specific Considerations

For applications dependent on specific protocols beyond basic TCP/IP, additional considerations are essential:

- **Binary Data Handling:** Consider systems with varying endianness—e.g., converting multibyte integers with htonl or ntohl.

- **Data Encryption:** Integrating encryption libraries such as OpenSSL secures data transfers, protecting content from unauthorized access.

- **Compression:** Applying compression (e.g., Zlib) lessens bandwidth impacts by reducing message size.

```
// Example encryption using OpenSSL
#include <openssl/ssl.h>

// Assume ssl is an initialized SSL* pointer
void encryptedSend(SSL *ssl, const char *message) {
    SSL_write(ssl, message, strlen(message));
}
```

81

Conclusion

The complexity of sending and receiving data through sockets requires a nuanced understanding of network dynamics and communication paradigms. Through careful consideration of buffering, framing, concurrency, and protocol requirements, developers can design efficient and robust systems that satisfy varied communication needs. Mastery of these techniques enables the construction of scalable, resilient network applications, capable of facilitating dynamic interactions across diverse computing environments. As such, a profound comprehension of these elements is indispensable for professionals aiming to harness the power of network communications within modern software ecosystems.

3.6 Error Handling in Socket Programming

Error handling in socket programming is a crucial aspect in ensuring the robustness and reliability of network applications. Network environments can be unpredictable, with various factors contributing to potential points of failure. These can range from resource limitations and network interruptions to software bugs. Effective error management involves detecting errors, responding appropriately, and implementing strategies to mitigate repeated issues.

Importance of Error Handling

Error handling provides a safety net, allowing programs to fail gracefully without losing data or becoming unresponsive. It facilitates debugging, enhances user experience, and ensures system stability. By anticipating possible failures and implementing robust handling routines, developers can design applications that are resilient to the unpredictabilities of network environments.

Common Sources of Errors

Errors in socket programming can be broadly categorized into three main areas:

- System Resource Constraints: Limitations in memory, file descriptors, or other resources can impede socket operations.

- Network Issues: Packet loss, latency, or disconnection can disrupt communication channels.

- Code and Logic Errors: Bugs or incorrect logic in code may lead to unexpected behavior or crashes.

Implementing Error Handling

Error handling in socket programming typically involves the use of return values, examination of the global errno variable, and application-specific logging or notification systems.

Standard Error Reporting Mechanism

Most socket functions return a negative value or -1 upon encountering an error, commonly accompanied by setting errno to a specific error code. For instance:

```
int sockfd = socket(AF_INET, SOCK_STREAM, 0);
if (sockfd == -1) {
    perror("Error opening socket");
    return -1;
}
```

In this example, perror maps errno to a descriptive text string, providing immediate feedback on the nature of the failure.

Common errno Values

- **EACCES:** Permission denied.

- **EADDRINUSE:** Address already in use.

83

- **EAFNOSUPPORT:** Address family not supported.

- **ECONNRESET:** Connection reset by peer.

- **ENOMEM:** Insufficient memory available.

- **ETIMEDOUT:** Connection timed out.

Handling Specific Error Scenarios

Each stage of socket communication involves potential errors that require tailored handling strategies.

Socket Creation Errors

Creating a socket might fail due to lack of resources, requiring fallback mechanisms or user notifications to address the failure.

```
int sockfd = socket(AF_INET, SOCK_STREAM, 0);
if (sockfd == -1) {
    switch(errno) {
        case EACCES:
            cerr << "Permission denied" << endl;
            break;
        case EMFILE:
            cerr << "Too many file descriptors in use" << endl;
            break;
        default:
            cerr << "Socket creation failed: " << strerror(errno) << endl;
    }
    return -1;
}
```

Connection Errors

Establishing a connection, particularly in client-side applications, is prone to timeouts or unreachable network paths.

```
int status = connect(sockfd, (struct sockaddr *)&server_addr, sizeof(server_addr));
if (status == -1) {
    if (errno == ECONNREFUSED) {
        cerr << "Connection refused by server" << endl;
    } else if (errno == ETIMEDOUT) {
        cerr << "Connection timed out" << endl;
    } else {
```

84

```
        cerr << "Unknown connection error: " << strerror(errno) << endl;
    }
    close(sockfd);
}
```

Data Transmission Errors

Even during established connections, sending and receiving data can
face issues due to network anomalies, requiring retries or alternative
actions.

```
int bytes_sent = send(sockfd, message, message_length, 0);
if (bytes_sent == -1) {
    if (errno == EINTR) {
        cerr << "Operation interrupted, retrying" << endl;
        // Retry logic here
    } else {
        cerr << "Data send error: " << strerror(errno) << endl;
    }
    close(sockfd);
}
```

Enhancing Error Handling

- **Use of Exceptions:** While C++ exceptions are less common in
  socket programming due to the traditionally C-based APIs, they
  can encapsulate errors and streamline complex error propagation.

  ```
  class SocketException : public std::runtime_error {
  public:
      explicit SocketException(const std::string &message)
          : std::runtime_error(message) {}
  };

  void sendData(int socket_fd, const char* message) {
      if (send(socket_fd, message, strlen(message), 0) == -1) {
          throw SocketException(strerror(errno));
      }
  }
  ```

- **Logging and Monitoring:** Implement robust logging systems
  to capture detailed error information, providing critical insights
  during development and operations.

  ```
  #include <fstream>
  ```

85

```
void logError(const std::string &error_message) {
    std::ofstream log_file("socket_errors.log", std::ios_base::app);
    log_file << error_message << std::endl;
}
```

- **Using Back-off Strategies:** Particularly for network operations, applying exponential back-off strategies in retries helps
  in managing transient network issues without overwhelming the
  system.

```
int retry_count = 0;
while (retry_count < MAX_RETRIES) {
    int result = connect(sockfd, (struct sockaddr *)&server_addr, sizeof(
        server_addr));
    if (result == 0) {
        break;
    }
    int backoff_time = pow(2, retry_count);
    sleep(backoff_time);
    retry_count++;
}
if (retry_count == MAX_RETRIES) {
    cerr << "Max retries reached, connection failed" << endl;
    close(sockfd);
}
```

- **Graceful Degradation:** Design interfaces and services to handle failures gracefully, notifying users of issues without application or service crashes.

Distributed and Advanced Network Environments

For applications in distributed systems or utilizing advanced technologies such as cloud services and IoT, error handling requires adaptability and coordination between multiple components.

- **Failover and Redundancy:** Implementing system
  redundancy ensures continued operation despite individual
  component failures, crucial in cloud-based applications.

- **Fault Tolerance:** Design systems with fault-tolerant protocols
  that can dynamically reroute communications or manage partial
  failures without total collapse.

86

- **Alert Systems:** Integrate alerting mechanisms that inform administrators of critical errors in real-time, allowing for rapid response to mitigate adverse effects.

Conclusion

Effective error handling in socket programming is not an afterthought but a fundamental part of software design and development. By understanding potential error sources and implementing robust handling strategies, developers can build resilient applications that handle failures gracefully and continue to function under adverse conditions. This mastery of error management not only extends application longevity but also enhances user confidence and satisfaction. Through diligent error tracking, adaptive response strategies, and efficient use of resources, socket-based applications can maintain high availability and performance standards even in complex and unpredictable network environments.

Chapter 4

TCP/IP Protocol Suite

This chapter examines the TCP/IP protocol suite, the foundational architecture for modern internet communication. It explores the structural layers of the TCP/IP model, detailing the functionalities and interactions of critical protocols such as IP, TCP, and UDP. Emphasizing their distinct roles, the chapter also addresses application layer protocols like HTTP and FTP, highlighting their integration within the suite. Additionally, it discusses networking tools and utilities essential for analyzing and troubleshooting TCP/IP-based networks, providing a comprehensive understanding of these vital communication protocols.

4.1   Structure of the TCP/IP Model

The TCP/IP model, or the Internet Protocol Suite, is a conceptual framework used to understand and configure network protocols. It draws its roots from the Department of Defense's ARPANET project, leading to a robust model for large-scale network protocol design. Unlike the OSI model, which contains seven layers, the TCP/IP model is traditionally composed of four layers: the Link Layer, the Internet Layer, the Transport Layer, and the Application Layer. This structure guides how data is transmitted across diverse networks and encompasses all processes involved in networking, from hardware to application software.

The core philosophy of the TCP/IP model is to divide the network functions into a set of layers, with each layer focusing on specific tasks. This separation allows engineers to modify one layer without affecting the others, facilitating scalable, flexible development. Furthermore, the TCP/IP model operates with a 'bottom-up' approach, starting from physical network operations (in the Link Layer) up to user applications (in the Application Layer). Below, we discuss each of these layers in greater detail, elucidating their roles and the protocols operating within them.

Link Layer

The Link Layer is the foundation of the TCP/IP model; it is responsible for the physical transmission of data packets. Operating on the boundary between tangible, physical hardware and abstract networking layers, it governs how data is physically sent over various types of media. Specific tasks include framing, addressing, and managing the Medium Access Control (MAC) layer protocols.

Protocols such as Ethernet, Wi-Fi (IEEE 802.11), and others fall under this category. These protocols define how devices within the same network segment communicate. They handle error correction of data, synchronize devices and media, and ensure collision-free transmission through various techniques like Carrier Sense Multiple Access with Collision Detection (CSMA/CD) or Carrier Sense Multiple Access with Collision Avoidance (CSMA/CA).

Essential control components such as network interface cards (NICs) operate within the Link Layer to control and interface with the physical transmission medium of a network (e.g., optics or copper cabling).

```
# An illustration of Access Control in Ethernet using CSMA/CD
while transmitting:
    if channel is quiet:
        transmit frame
        wait for acknowledgment
    elif collision occurs:
        stop transmission
        wait a random time interval
# Retry
```

Internet Layer

Situated above the Link Layer, the Internet Layer is pivotal for laying out the communication path across networks by handling the logical addressing of hosts and managing data packet routing through interconnected networks. It is primarily focused on forming the Internet's backbone structure, interlinking multiple networks together on the global scale.

The most prominent protocol in this layer is the Internet Protocol (IP), with its two versions: IPv4 and IPv6. IP handles both addressing and fragmenting data packets to traverse different networks and reassemble them appropriately.

IP addresses are unique identifiers for network devices, allowing packets to find their destination. Routing protocols such as the Routing Information Protocol (RIP), and more advanced methods like Open Shortest Path First (OSPF) and Border Gateway Protocol (BGP), work in the Internet Layer to determine the most efficient routing path for packets through networks.

```
# Simple Python script demonstrating conversion of IPv4 address
import socket

hostname = 'www.example.com'
ip_address = socket.gethostbyname(hostname)
print(f'The IP address of {hostname} is {ip_address}')
```

The Internet Layer also accommodates the Internet Control Message Protocol (ICMP), whose primary uses involve error reporting and diagnostics such as in the widely used 'ping' command.

```
> ping www.example.com
Pinging example.com [93.184.216.34] with 32 bytes of data:
Reply from 93.184.216.34: bytes=32 time=56ms TTL=56
```

Transport Layer

The Transport Layer, crucial for maintaining robust end-to-end communication, is responsible for the reliability and control of message transmission between hosts. It establishes, maintains, and terminates communication sessions. Two key protocols dominate this layer: the Transmission Control Protocol (TCP) and the User Datagram Protocol (UDP).

91

TCP provides a connection-oriented service, ensuring reliable data transmission with error detection, packet ordering, and flow control. It is suitable for applications where data integrity and order are vital (e.g., web browsing using HTTP, email via SMTP).

```
# Pseudocode for a simple TCP Client
def tcp_client():
    create socket
    connect to server
    send data
    receive response
    close connection
```

UDP, on the other hand, offers a connectionless service with low overhead by forgoing reliability guarantees; it is used for applications requiring fast data transmission without error correction, such as video streaming or online gaming.

```
# Pseudocode for a UDP Client
def udp_client():
    create socket
    bind to address
    send data to destination
    receive response
    close socket
```

The choice between TCP and UDP depends on the application's requirements regarding speed, reliability, and overhead.

Application Layer

The Application Layer sits at the apex of the TCP/IP model and integrates all protocols and technologies developed for specific communication tasks, providing necessary interfaces for network services. Protocols include Hypertext Transfer Protocol (HTTP), File Transfer Protocol (FTP), Simple Mail Transfer Protocol (SMTP), Domain Name System (DNS), among others.

HTTP, a foundational protocol in web communications, facilitates the retrieval of web resources and operates on a client-server principle. A typical HTTP transaction involves a client sending a request for resources and a server responding with the desired resource, often alongside an HTTP status code.

```
# Example of HTTP GET request using Python's requests library
import requests

response = requests.get('https://www.example.com')
```

```
print(response.content)
```

Similarly, FTP offers a protocol for transferring files over networks, while SMTP is crucial for the transmission of email messages. DNS translates human-readable domain names into machine-readable IP addresses, essential for locating and addressing devices on an IP network.

The Application Layer protocols inherently depend on the layers beneath them, illustrating intricate interrelationships between all layers of the TCP/IP model to facilitate comprehensive network communication.

Throughout the TCP/IP model, data encapsulation plays a critical role. As data travels from the upper layers down to the Link Layer, each layer encapsulates the data from the previous layer, adding its header information. Conversely, each layer on the receiving end interprets the incoming data, removing the header attached by its counterpart. This process is fundamental to understanding how network communications successfully traverse diverse network infrastructures.

Through its layered architecture, the TCP/IP model offers a resilient, adaptive framework that has stood the test of time, effectively meeting the demands of modern internet communications while allowing for innovations and advancements without necessitating a complete overhaul of each component part.

4.2 Internet Protocol (IP)

The Internet Protocol (IP) serves as a core protocol in the Internet Layer of the TCP/IP model, facilitating the routing of packets across network boundaries. It is the principal communications protocol responsible for delivering packets from the source host to the destination host based solely on their IP addresses. The protocol ensures that messages, known as datagrams, traverse various networks efficiently and arrive at the correct destination. IP is the linchpin of the Internet, allowing computers connected over diverse networks to communicate seamlessly. This section delves into the fundamental aspects of IP, including its architecture, addressing mechanisms, and routing

93

functions, as well as the distinctions between IP versions.

IP addressing is central to the functionality of the Internet Protocol, serving as a unique identifier for each device connected to a network. An IP address performs two primary roles: identifying the host or network interface and providing a location of the host in the network, thus facilitating the routing of traffic.

An IP address is typically a numerical label, intricately structured, to imbue distinct characteristics that aid in both network identification and routing. There are two principal types of IP addresses based on the version of the Internet Protocol: IPv4 and IPv6.

IPv4 Addresses IPv4, the first version of IP to be widely deployed, uses a 32-bit address scheme, yielding over 4 billion unique addresses. These addresses are conventionally expressed in dot-decimal notation, comprising four octets separated by periods, such as 192.168.1.1.

IPv4 addresses are categorized into classes (A, B, C, D, E) to accommodate networks of different sizes and purposes. Classful networking has largely become obsolete with the advent of Classless Inter-Domain Routing (CIDR), which allows more flexible allocation of IP addresses.

```
# Python demonstration for converting an IPv4 address to binary
ip = "192.168.1.1"
ip_as_binary = '.'.join([f"{int(octet):08b}" for octet in ip.split('.')])
print(f"The binary representation of {ip} is {ip_as_binary}")
```

CIDR notation, such as 192.168.100.0/24, specifies the number of bits in the address used for the network portion, enhancing address allocation efficiency and improving routing performance.

IPv6 Addresses The limitations of IPv4, particularly in address exhaustion, led to the development of IPv6, which uses a 128-bit address space, vastly expanding the available IP address pool to accommodate the growing number of internet-connected devices. An IPv6 address is typically represented in hexadecimal, separated by colons, like 2001:0db8:85a3:0000:0000:8a2e:0370:7334.

IPv6 introduces several enhancements, such as simplified address headers, improved support for extension headers, and native support for IPsec. The adoption of IPv6 is gradually increasing as organizations prepare for inevitable IPv4 depletion.

```
# Python code to demonstrate IPv6 address manipulation
import ipaddress

# Create an IPv6 address object
ip = ipaddress.IPv6Address('2001:0db8:85a3:0000:0000:8a2e:0370:7334')
print(f"The compressed form of the IPv6 address is {ip.compressed}")
```

IP routing is a crucial function of the Internet Protocol, responsible for deciding the path that data packets take from their source to their destination. This process involves directing packets through intermediary nodes, known as routers, which forward packets towards their eventual endpoints based on a pre-determined set of rules and routing protocols.

Routers build and maintain routing tables, using these to efficiently forward packets through networks. Routing protocols can be divided into two primary types: interior gateway protocols (IGPs) and exterior gateway protocols (EGPs). IGPs, such as RIP and OSPF, are used within a single administrative domain, while EGPs, particularly BGP, are used between domains.

```
# Pseudocode illustrating basic IP packet forwarding logic
while receiving packet:
    determine destination address
    lookup routing table for next hop
    if route found:
        send packet to next hop
    else:
        send ICMP destination unreachable message
```

Internet Control Message Protocol (ICMP) is an integral component of the IP protocol suite, primarily used for network diagnostics and error-reporting purposes. Routers and hosts use ICMP to communicate issues with IP packet processing. For instance, if a host is unreachable, ICMP might be employed to inform the sending host of the difficulty.

Common ICMP message types include echo request and echo reply (used by the 'ping' utility) and destination unreachable messages. ICMP messages serve as an essential network administrator tool, enabling troubleshooting and problem resolution.

```
> ping -6 www.google.com
Pinging www.google.com [2a00:1450:4009:802::200e] with 32 bytes of data:
Reply from 2a00:1450:4009:802::200e: time=30ms
```

95

Fragmentation occurs when IP packets exceed the maximum transmission unit (MTU) of the network path. IP handles fragmentation by breaking large packets into smaller units, or fragments, which are reassembled into the original packet at their destination.

This process happens transparently to higher-layer protocols, but its significance becomes apparent when ensuring data arrives intact across networks with varying MTUs.

```
# Pseudocode for basic packet fragmentation
if packet size > MTU:
    divide packet into fragments
    attach required header information
    for each fragment:
        send fragment
else:
    send packet
```

The Address Resolution Protocol (ARP) functions within the Internet Layer, helping resolve the IP addresses to MAC (Media Access Control) addresses. This capability is essential for communication within Ethernet networks. When a device wishes to communicate with another device on the same local network, it broadcasts an ARP request to retrieve the MAC address corresponding to the destination IP address.

ARP operates within the confines of the local network and ensures that devices can reliably establish direct communication lines essential for packet delivery.

```
# Example ARP request packet created using Scapy (Python library)
from scapy.all import ARP, send

arp_pkt = ARP(op=1, pdst='192.168.1.1')
send(arp_pkt)
```

Despite IP's critical role, the protocol faces several challenges. The eventual exhaustion of IPv4 addresses necessitated the transition to IPv6, requiring significant infrastructure overhaul and compatibility considerations. Security is another concern, as IP inherently lacks robust mechanisms to ensure data integrity and authenticity. This shortcoming makes it vulnerable to various attacks, such as IP spoofing.

Network professionals leverage IPsec, an additional suite of protocols that adds security to IP communications, providing authentication, integrity, and confidentiality.

Network Address Translation (NAT) is another adaptation to IP short-comings, particularly the scarcity of public IP addresses. NAT allows multiple devices on a local network to share a single public IP address. However, NAT can complicate direct peer-to-peer communication and may interfere with certain applications.

```
# Pseudocode for a simple NAT translation table lookup
for incoming packet:
    retrieve source and destination IP
    if match exists in NAT table:
        translate IPs as per header information
        forward packet
    else:
        drop packet or initiate new NAT entry
```

Internet Protocol stands as the backbone of modern networking, exhibiting a high degree of adaptability demonstrated by the transition from IPv4 to IPv6, the enhancement in routing efficiencies, and constant troubleshooting advancements through ICMP and related technologies. This expertise forms a foundation to explore further progress in computer networking, heralding seamlessly interconnected digital ecosystems.

4.3 Transmission Control Protocol (TCP)

The Transmission Control Protocol (TCP) is a core protocol of the Internet Protocol suite, vital for facilitating reliable communication over packet-switched networks. Positioned in the Transport Layer of the TCP/IP model, TCP offers a connection-oriented, error-checked, and retransmission-capable data delivery service. TCP empowers datagram transmission with the capability to reconstruct data streams reliably, making it indispensable for applications where data integrity and order are crucial. This section provides an exhaustive examination of TCP, elucidating its mechanisms, internal architecture, and significance in a practical networking context.

TCP distinguishes itself through several key features:

- Connection-Oriented: TCP establishes a connection between two endpoints prior to data transfer, known as a TCP session, ensuring readiness before communication begins.

- Reliable Data Transfer: Reliability is achieved through sequence numbers, acknowledgments, and retransmissions, ensuring data packets reach destinations error-free and in order.

- Flow Control: TCP manages data flow between sender and receiver to prevent overwhelming slower devices.

- Congestion Control: Techniques like slow start, congestion avoidance, and fast recovery optimize network performance by managing data flow during varying network conditions.

- Stream-Oriented: TCP views data as a continuous stream, contrasting UDP's discrete datagrams.

The coupling of these features empowers TCP to support varied applications, from web browsers to email clients, where orderly and reliable data delivery is non-negotiable.

Data is encapsulated into TCP segments, each comprising a header and payload. The TCP header, typically 20 bytes in standard form, includes fields vital for segment management and reliability assurance.

- Source and Destination Ports (16 bits each): Mark communication endpoints, allowing multiplexing of applications.

- Sequence Number (32 bits): Identifies the segment's ordinal range in the data stream, ensuring ordered assembly at the receiver.

- Acknowledgment Number (32 bits): Confirms received data range, prompting further data flow.

- Offset (4 bits): Indicates the start of data in the segment, indicating header length.

- Flags (9 bits): Control indicators, including SYN, ACK, FIN, RST, URG, to manage connection lifecycle and urgent data.

- Window (16 bits): Defines buffer size for flow control, indicating receiver readiness for additional data.

- Checksum (16 bits): Validates segment integrity, computed over both header and payload.

- Urgent Pointer (16 bits, optional): Offsets location of urgent data within the segment.

```
# Pseudocode to construct a basic TCP header
struct TCPHeader {
    unsigned short source_port;
    unsigned short dest_port;
    unsigned int sequence;
    unsigned int acknowledgment;
    unsigned short offset_and_flags;
    unsigned short window;
    unsigned short checksum;
    unsigned short urgent_pointer;
};
```

This structural foundation supports TCP's core reliability mechanisms, making it indispensable for many crucial network applications.

TCP's connection-oriented nature is embodied in the three-way handshake process, a critical protocol mechanism establishing a reliable session between two network hosts.

- SYN: The client initiates a connection by sending a SYN (synchronize) packet, encapsulating its initial sequence number.

- SYN-ACK: The server responds with a SYN-ACK (synchronize-acknowledge) segment, which acknowledges the client's SYN and announces its initial sequence number.

- ACK: The client sends an ACK (acknowledge) packet, acknowledging the server's sequence number, finalizing the connection setup.

```
# Python example using the Scapy library to simulate TCP SYN packet
from scapy.all import IP, TCP, send

src_ip = "192.168.1.2"
dst_ip = "192.168.1.1"
src_port = 1234
dst_port = 80

ip_packet = IP(src=src_ip, dst=dst_ip)
tcp_packet = TCP(sport=src_port, dport=dst_port, flags='S', seq=1000)
```

```
packet = ip_packet / tcp_packet
send(packet)
```

The three-way handshake establishes a full-duplex connection, ensuring both parties are synchronized for data exchange.

Data transmission within an established TCP connection relies on sequence numbers and acknowledgments to maintain reliability. TCP ensures data integrity and order through dependable mechanisms:

- Sliding Window Protocol: This dynamic window size dictates the number of bytes sent without waiting for acknowledgments, balancing sender pace with receiver readiness. The window size adjusts based on network conditions and receiver capability.

- Cumulative Acknowledgments: TCP sends cumulative ACKs, indicating all data up to a certain sequence number has been received correctly.

- Selective Acknowledgment (SACK): An optional extension allowing acknowledgment of specific data segments; particularly effective in high-latency connections or during packet loss.

- Retransmission Timers: TCP employs timers to detect lost packets, triggering retransmission if ACKs are not received within a specified timeframe.

```
# Example of TCP segment retransmission using pseudocode
set timer
send segment

while waiting for ACK:
    if timer expires:
        retransmit segment
        reset timer
    if ACK received:
        send next segment
        update sliding window
```

These features bolster TCP against network unreliability, maintaining data coherence across complex, potentially fickle environments.

TCP connection termination involves a controlled four-step process to safely release resources:

100

- FIN from Sender: The sender requests connection termination, sending a FIN (finish) packet.

- ACK from Receiver: The receiver confirms the FIN packet.

- FIN from Receiver: Upon transmitting remaining data, the receiver sends its FIN packet.

- ACK from Sender: The sender sends an ACK, allowing both parties to close the connection.

```
# Python example to close a TCP connection using Scapy
from scapy.all import TCP, IP, send

fin_packet = TCP(flags='FA', seq=1020, ack=1025)
ip_packet = IP(src="192.168.1.2", dst="192.168.1.1")
full_packet = ip_packet / fin_packet

send(full_packet)
```

Graceful connection termination prevents data loss and ensures proper resource deallocation, achieving completeness in communication.

Congestion control is imperative to TCP's reliability, aiming to optimize data flow across the network. Notable algorithms include:

- Slow Start: Initially increases the congestion window size exponentially to probe network capacity.

- Congestion Avoidance: Upon reaching a threshold, it shifts to linear growth, cautiously expanding the window.

- Fast Retransmit and Fast Recovery: Designed to respond swiftly to segment loss, executing accelerated retransmissions without entering slow start, stabilizing window size.

```
# Pseudocode for TCP congestion control in slow start
initialize congestion_window = 1
threshold = predefined_value

while data to send:
    if network condition is favorable:
        congestion_window *= 2
    else:
        threshold = congestion_window / 2
        congestion_window = 1
        enter congestion avoidance
```

TCP's congestion control mechanisms allow scalability, ensuring fair resource sharing and avoiding packet loss.

TCP's robust characteristics render it suitable for a variety of applications requiring reliability:

- Web Browsing (HTTP/HTTPS): Ensures HTML data integrity for consistent browsing experiences.

- Email (SMTP/IMAP/POP3): Supports error-free transmission of electronic mail, maintaining message completeness.

- File Transfer (FTP): Invokes orderly file exchange across networks, crucial for sensitive data transport.

Its integrated mechanisms provide a framework through which data-intense applications maintain functionality and reliability across volatile networks.

While TCP offers reliable data exchange, it inherently lacks security features, exposing it to vulnerabilities including:

- TCP Spoofing: Unauthorized data injection by impersonating legitimate packets.

- Man-in-the-Middle Attacks: Eavesdropping and potential alteration of communication.

- Denial-of-Service (DoS) and Distributed Denial-of-Service (DDoS) Attacks: Overwhelming a system through excessive traffic targeting.

To combat these, Internet Protocol Security (IPsec) or Transport Layer Security (TLS) can be overlaid to provide encryption, authentication, and integrity checks without altering the original framework from which TCP operates.

Through the comprehensive strength of its design, TCP represents a foundational element of Internet communications, accommodating diverse needs while maintaining robustness and flexibility. Its evolution represents efforts to adapt to new challenges while preserving its core principles of reliable, sequenced, and error-checked data transport.

4.4 User Datagram Protocol (UDP)

The User Datagram Protocol (UDP) is a fundamental communication protocol in the Internet Protocol suite, delivering a connectionless transport mechanism in the Transport Layer. Unlike the Transmission Control Protocol (TCP), UDP prioritizes simplicity and speed over reliability and order, making it a quintessential choice for applications where delay sensitivity is valued over data accuracy. This section delves into the structure, functionality, and applications of UDP, illustrating its strategic role in facilitating rapid communication across diverse networks.

UDP is defined by several distinct characteristics that differentiate it from TCP:

- **Connectionless Communication**: UDP does not establish a persistent session or connection between two endpoints; instead, it transmits data as discrete packets known as datagrams.

- **Minimal Overhead**: The absence of connection setup, sequencing, and acknowledgment phases results in low protocol overhead, enabling faster data transfer.

- **Best-Effort Delivery**: UDP does not guarantee delivery, order preservation, or error checking in the communication process, relying on higher-level applications to manage these concerns if necessary.

- **Broadcast and Multicast Support**: Unlike TCP, UDP supports broadcast and multicast transmissions, making it suitable for applications such as streaming media and gaming.

These characteristics render UDP advantageous in scenarios where rapid data transmission is vital and occasional data loss is tolerable.

UDP encapsulates data in units called datagrams. Each UDP datagram consists of a header and a payload. The simplicity of its header contributes to UDP's efficiency and performance.

- **Source Port (16 bits)**: Indicates the port number at the sender's end, assisting in application-specific communication.

- **Destination Port (16 bits)**: Specifies the recipient's port number, directing the datagram to the appropriate application.

- **Length (16 bits)**: Describes the total length of the datagram, including both header and payload, useful for determining message boundaries.

- **Checksum (16 bits)**: Provides a basic validation for data integrity; optional in IPv4 but mandatory for IPv6.

The UDP header's minimal complexity is vital for efficient processing, particularly in environments where computational resources or bandwidth are constrained.

```
# Pseudocode to create a basic UDP header
struct UDPHeader {
    unsigned short source_port;
    unsigned short destination_port;
    unsigned short length;
    unsigned short checksum;
};
```

The elegance of UDP's format facilitates expeditious handling of data, aligning with its design philosophy of simplicity and speed.

UDP's connectionless nature supports various communication models:

- **Unicast**: One-to-one communication between a single sender and receiver.

- **Broadcast**: Sending a message to all potential nodes within a network segment.

- **Multicast**: Targeted communication with multiple specific receivers, optimizing bandwidth by reducing redundant data packets.

These methodologies underpin UDP's utility in applications like DHCP (Dynamic Host Configuration Protocol), where initial device configuration can reach multiple clients simultaneously.

```
# Python code using socket library to send a UDP broadcast
import socket
```

```
broadcast_address = ('<broadcast>', 12345)
message = b'Hello, network!'

sock = socket.socket(socket.AF_INET, socket.SOCK_DGRAM)
sock.setsockopt(socket.SOL_SOCKET, socket.SO_BROADCAST, 1)
sock.sendto(message, broadcast_address)
```

UDP's flexibility grants developers the ability to tailor transmissions for specific network demands effectively.

UDP shines in scenarios where speed and efficiency are paramount, and minor packet loss is permissible:

- **Streaming Applications**: Video and audio streams use UDP to minimize latency. Protocols such as RTP (Real-time Transport Protocol) are layered over UDP to accommodate real-time media delivery.

- **Online Gaming**: Fast-paced games leverage UDP to reduce input lag and enhance responsiveness, conditions crucial for competitive play.

- **VoIP (Voice over IP)**: Real-time audio communication across networks benefits from UDP's low latency, enhancing call quality despite occasional audio packet loss.

- **DNS (Domain Name System)**: UDP supports rapid query-response cycles, essential for the quick resolution of domain names into IP addresses.

These applications illustrate UDP's versatility, addressing the need for immediacy in data transmission across global networks.

Despite its advantages, UDP has inherent limitations:

- **Lack of Reliability**: There are no assurances of packet delivery integrity; applications must implement their own error-checking mechanisms.

- **No Congestion Control**: UDP does not address network congestion issues, potentially leading to packet loss in heavily loaded networks.

- **Packet Duplication**: Due to its stateless nature, UDP does not inherently prevent duplicate datagrams.

Applications using UDP must integrate additional strategies to compensate for these shortcomings if correctness is imperative.

Socket programming offers a gateway for implementing network applications using UDP. Through the 'socket' library, developers can construct lightweight client-server models over UDP, capitalizing on its rapid, efficient protocol stack.

Here is an example of a basic UDP client-server communication schema:

```
# UDP Server using Python's socket library
import socket

server_address = ('localhost', 65432)
buffer_size = 1024

# Create a UDP server socket
server_socket = socket.socket(socket.AF_INET, socket.SOCK_DGRAM)
server_socket.bind(server_address)
print("UDP server up and listening")

while True:
    data, client_addr = server_socket.recvfrom(buffer_size)
    print(f"Received message: {data} from {client_addr}")
    server_socket.sendto(b"ACK", client_addr)
```

```
# UDP Client using Python's socket library
import socket

server_address = ('localhost', 65432)
message = b'Hello, UDP server!'

# Create a UDP client socket
client_socket = socket.socket(socket.AF_INET, socket.SOCK_DGRAM)

try:
    client_socket.sendto(message, server_address)
    data, server = client_socket.recvfrom(4096)
    print(f"Received message: {data}")

finally:
    client_socket.close()
```

This example demonstrates a simple UDP echo server, capturing data from clients and sending an acknowledgment, 'ACK', back. The intrinsic simplicity of UDP simplifies the application design, focusing purely on data exchange without connection management overhead.

UDP's lack of intrinsic security features poses challenges:

- **Packet Spoofing and Injection**: Attackers can insert malicious packets into a communication stream.

- **Amplification Attacks**: UDP's connectionless nature is exploited in reflection attacks, generating excessive response traffic to a target.

To mitigate such threats, developers often employ additional security protocols, like Datagram Transport Layer Security (DTLS), which provides data integrity, authentication, and confidentiality through encryption.

By incorporating these methods, applications can balance the speed and simplicity benefits of UDP with necessary security mechanisms to safeguard user data.

UDP's foundational simplicity offers significant benefits for applications prioritizing latency and simplicity over reliability and order assurance. Its operation forms the backbone of many mission-critical, latency-sensitive applications, empowering real-time data streaming, dynamic communications, and swift transactions across the vast expanse of the Internet. Despite inherent challenges concerning data reliability and security, UDP persists as an invaluable component of the modern networking tableau, sustaining innovations that revolutionize connectivity and interaction.

4.5 Application Layer Protocols

The Application Layer resides at the top of the TCP/IP model and is responsible for interacting directly with end-user software applications. It provides numerous protocols that define how applications communicate over a network. These protocols manage data exchange directly tied to particular application needs and functionalities, offering services such as file transfers, email delivery, and web browsing. This section explores key Application Layer protocols such as HTTP, HTTPS, FTP, SMTP, and DNS, explaining their functions, use cases, and impact on network communications.

HyperText Transfer Protocol (HTTP) HTTP is integral to the World Wide Web, facilitating the exchange of hypertext documents between web servers and clients (web browsers). Operating as a stateless protocol, HTTP functions upon request-response paradigms, where a client sends an HTTP request for a specific resource and the server responds with that resource, typically in the form of an HTML document.

HTTP Methods HTTP defines a set of request methods which indicate the desired action:

- GET: Retrieves data from a specified resource.

- POST: Sends data to a server to create or update resources.

- PUT: Updates a resource with the provided data.

- DELETE: Removes the specified resource.

Request and response headers further encapsulate metadata, including content type, encoding, and cache control, guiding data interchange specifics.

```
# Python example to perform an HTTP GET request using requests library
import requests

url = 'http://www.example.com'
response = requests.get(url)
print(f"Response status: {response.status_code}")
print(response.content)
```

HTTP/2 and HTTP/3 introduce enhancements in multiplexing requests, reducing latency, and improving performance, addressing the protocol's historical limitations concerning performance efficiency.

Security - HTTPS HTTPS, or HTTP Secure, elevates traditional HTTP by incorporating encryption using TLS (Transport Layer Security). HTTPS ensures confidentiality, integrity, and authentication of data between clients and servers, protecting communication against eavesdropping, man-in-the-middle attacks, and data integrity violations.

The secure transport provided by HTTPS is essential for sensitive transactions such as online banking, confidential communications, and secure commercial operations.

```
# Simple HTTPS request example using Python's requests library
url = 'https://www.secureexample.com'
response = requests.get(url)
print(f"Response secure status: {response.status_code}")
if response.ok:
    print(response.content)
```

File Transfer Protocol (FTP)   FTP offers a standard method to transfer files between systems over a network, enabling both file upload and download capabilities. Operating on a client-server model, FTP uses two separate connections: a control connection for transmitting commands and a data connection for actual file transfers.

FTP Commands   Core FTP commands offer control functionalities:

- USER: Provides a username for authentication.

- PASS: Supplies the password to complete login.

- LIST: Lists files in a directory.

- RETR: Downloads a file.

- STOR: Uploads a file.

FTP supports active and passive modes. Active mode uses server-initiated data connections, while passive mode, beneficial for firewall traversal, uses client-initiated connections.

```
# Python FTP example using ftplib to download a file
from ftplib import FTP

ftp = FTP('ftp.example.com')
ftp.login()
ftp.cwd('pub')
filename = 'example.txt'
with open(filename, 'wb') as file:
    ftp.retrbinary(f'RETR {filename}', file.write)
ftp.quit()
```

Security - FTPS and SFTP FTP, inherently insecure due to plain text data transmission, can be augmented with security enhancements:

- FTPS: Extends FTP with SSL/TLS for encrypted channels.

- SFTP: Employs Secure Shell (SSH) for both secure file transfer and control, offering robust security compared to its counterparts.

Simple Mail Transfer Protocol (SMTP) SMTP governs the transmission of emails across the Internet, facilitating communication between mail servers. It defines the process through which email messages are sent from a client to a recipient's mail server, subsequently delivering these to the appropriate mailboxes.

SMTP Commands SMTP communication utilizes text commands for message transfer:

- HELO: Identifies the client to the server.

- MAIL FROM: Identifies the sender's email address.

- RCPT TO: Specifies recipient addresses.

- DATA: Initiates the transfer of the email contents.

Compatibility with MIME (Multipurpose Internet Mail Extensions) allows SMTP to handle diverse formats beyond plain text, including attachments, images, and multimedia.

```
# Python example to send an email using smtplib
import smtplib
from email.mime.text import MIMEText

msg = MIMEText('This is the body of the email.')
msg['Subject'] = 'Test Email'
msg['From'] = 'sender@example.com'
msg['To'] = 'recipient@example.com'

with smtplib.SMTP('smtp.example.com') as server:
    server.login('username', 'password')
    server.sendmail(msg['From'], [msg['To']], msg.as_string())
```

Security Enhancements   SMTP's vulnerability to unauthorized access and eavesdropping can be mitigated using encryption protocols such as STARTTLS, providing both confidentiality and integrity.

Domain Name System (DNS)   DNS plays a crucial role in Internet functioning by translating human-readable domain names into IP addresses, essential for locating and routing data to web servers.

Components and Operation   DNS operates through hierarchical databases, consisting of domain names mapped to IP addresses. Its core components, including Domain Name Servers and resolvers, interact to fulfill queries and return corresponding IP addresses:

- **Root Nameservers**: Serve as the initial step in DNS resolution, directing queries to appropriate top-level domain (TLD) nameservers.

- **TLD Nameservers**: Direct requests to authoritative nameservers for specific domain hierarchies (e.g., com, org, net).

- **Authoritative Nameservers**: Provide direct IP address mappings for domain queries.

The DNS resolution process exemplifies distributed computing where cache mechanisms significantly enhance query performance by storing previous responses locally, reducing latency.

```
# DNS query example using Python's socket module
import socket

domain = 'www.example.com'
ip = socket.gethostbyname(domain)
print(f'The IP address for {domain} is {ip}')
```

Security - DNSSEC   DNS, initially designed without built-in security, is susceptible to spoofing attacks. DNS Security Extensions (DNSSEC) mitigate security vulnerabilities by employing digital signatures to ensure data integrity and authenticity.

Additional Application Layer Protocols   Beyond the heavily utilized protocols, the application layer embraces diverse protocols serving specific communication needs:

- Telnet: Allows remote command-line interface access to systems but lacks inherent security.

- SSH (Secure Shell): Grants secure command-line administration over networks, replacing Telnet with robust encryption.

- SIP (Session Initiation Protocol): Fundamental to real-time communication such as VoIP, enabling signaling and control over multimedia sessions.

- LDAP (Lightweight Directory Access Protocol): Facilitates accessing and maintaining distributed directory databases over an IP network.

Each protocol carries features tailored to its operations, enhancing network functionality and enriching user experiences.

Security Challenges and Considerations   Despite inherent challenges, application layer protocols contribute significantly to the vibrant ecosystem of interactive communications. Security remains a primary concern, demanding careful analysis and enhancements:

- **Data Encryption**: Ensures confidentiality and integrity of data exchanged between clients and servers.

- **Authentication Measures**: Verifies user identities before granting access to sensitive data or services.

- **Regular Updates**: Ensures protocol implementations address vulnerabilities, benefiting from the latest security research.

In integrating these protocols, network architects and developers strive to balance efficient data exchange against security imperatives, creating resilient systems poised to meet evolving demands. The constellation of protocols residing in the application layer forms the foundation upon which the Internet's wide-ranging services build, driving innovation and connectivity across the digital landscape.

4.6 Networking Tools and Utilities

In the domain of computer networks, tools and utilities play a crucial role in both the analysis and maintenance of networking environments. These tools assist network administrators and engineers in monitoring, diagnosing, and optimizing network performance and security. This section elaborates on the most significant networking tools and utilities, covering their functionalities, practical applications, and illustrating how they facilitate efficient network management.

Ping The tool ping is a fundamental network utility employed for testing connectivity between devices through ICMP (Internet Control Message Protocol) echo request and reply messages. It gauges whether a host is reachable over an IP network and measures round-trip time for messages sent to the destination.

Functionality and Use

- **Reachability Test**: Determines if a host is active on a network.

- **Latency Measurement**: Assesses the responsiveness and round-trip time to a remote host.

- **Packet Loss Detection**: Identifies any loss in data transmission, aiding in diagnosing network reliability.

```
# Example use of ping command in terminal
ping google.com
```

```
PING google.com (142.250.190.78): 56 data bytes
64 bytes from 142.250.190.78: icmp_seq=0 ttl=118 time=29.9 ms
```

Limitations While ping can confirm connectivity and delay metrics, it cannot diagnose nuanced network pathology or packet integrity. Firewalls might also obstruct ICMP packets, rendering the tool nonoperational in such guarded environments.

Traceroute and Tracert Traceroute (on UNIX-like systems) and tracert (on Windows) illustrate the pathway that packets take across a network. By revealing each hop's IP address, these utilities provide insights into the network's routing topology.

Functional Details

- **Path Discovery**: Identifies each router traversed along the path to a destination.

- **Latency Analysis**: Provides time data per hop, indicating where delays occur.

- **Network Troubleshooting**: Discerns where packets may be dropped or misrouted.

```
# Example use of traceroute command
traceroute example.com
```

```
traceroute to example.com (93.184.216.34), 30 hops max
 1  192.168.1.1 (192.168.1.1)  1.123 ms  1.211 ms  1.304 ms
 2  10.0.0.1 (10.0.0.1)  9.654 ms  10.332 ms  10.789 ms
```

Variability Across Networks Results from traceroute can vary due to dynamic routing algorithms, network congestion, and timeouts at different network hops. These variations necessitate multiple runs for reliable data collection.

Netstat The netstat utility provides comprehensive insights into the network connections and sockets on a device. It is indispensable in assessing network activity and diagnosing connectivity issues.

Capabilities and Usage

- **Active Connection Listing**: Displays both incoming and outgoing connections on a system, including protocol, local and foreign addresses, and connection state.

114

- **Routing Tables**: Outputs kernel routing tables, offering a glimpse into how packets are routed.

- **Interface Statistics**: Provides data traffic statistics for each network interface.

```
# Example use of netstat to display active connections
netstat -tuln
```

```
Active Internet connections (only servers)
Proto Recv-Q Send-Q Local Address      Foreign Address      State
tcp      0      0 0.0.0.0:80      0.0.0.0:*            LISTEN
udp      0      0 0.0.0.0:53      0.0.0.0:*
```

Diagnostic Benefits   Through its detailed output, netstat assists in identifying suspicious activities that may indicate security breaches, such as unexpected open ports or foreign addresses.

NSLookup   The nslookup tool queries the Domain Name System to obtain domain names or IP address mappings, facilitating domain diagnostics and resolution verification.

Functional Advantages

- **Domain Resolution**: Verifies that domain names correctly resolve to their respective IP addresses.

- **Server Query**: Directs queries to specific DNS servers, useful for troubleshooting DNS issues.

- **Mail Exchange Server Check**: Examines MX records to validate email server configuration.

```
# Example use of nslookup to query a domain
nslookup www.example.com
```

```
Server:     8.8.8.8
Address:    8.8.8.8#53

Non-authoritative answer:
Name:   www.example.com
Address: 93.184.216.34
```

115

Limitations and Considerations nslookup commands rely on the response of the DNS servers involved and might be influenced by caching, leading to variations in output over successive queries.

Wireshark Wireshark is a powerful network protocol analyzer that captures and decodes network packets, providing a microscopic view of network traffic.

Core Features

- **Real-Time Packet Capture**: Monitors live network data traffic across multiple interfaces.

- **Protocol Analysis**: Supports deep inspection of hundreds of protocols, aiding diagnostics of complex network issues.

- **Reassembly and Filtering**: Ability to reassemble fragmented traffic and apply packet filters to focus analysis.

```
# Basic command line invocation of Wireshark's command-line tool, 'tshark'
tshark -i eth0 -c 10
```

Capturing on 'eth0'
1 0.000000 192.168.1.2 -> 192.168.1.1 TCP 74 44350 > 80 [SYN] Seq=0 Win=65535 Len=0

Precautions and Ethical Usage Wireshark's ability to capture sensitive data mandates ethical use, with permissions secured prior to deployment, to avoid privacy violations and legal repercussions.

Curl curl is a versatile command-line tool that interacts with network protocols, primarily used to transfer data to or from a server using a broad range of supported protocols, including HTTP, HTTPS, FTP, and more.

Functional Scope

- **Data Transfer**: Moves data; supports file transfer with FTP, HTTP POST requests, and custom headers.

- **API Testing**: Verifies RESTful API endpoints, allowing for the execution of GET, PUT, DELETE actions directly from the console.

- **Automation Potential**: Supports scripting and automation of web interactions.

```
# Example of using curl to fetch data from a URL
curl -I http://www.example.com
```

```
HTTP/1.1 200 OK
Date: Mon, 01 Jan 2022 12:00:00 GMT
Server: ExampleServer/0.1
```

Advanced Scripting Capabilities Beyond manual operations, curl can be integrated into scripts for dynamic data processing, offering customizable options for headers, authentication, and more.

Nmap The nmap utility (Network Mapper) is renowned for its network discovery and security auditing capabilities, often employed to map networks and reveal security vulnerabilities.

Key Abilities

- **Network Discovery**: Efficiently scans large networks, providing insights into available hosts and services.

- **Port Scanning**: Identifies open ports and associated services on a system.

- **Vulnerability Assessment**: Offers extensions through nmap scripts to detect vulnerabilities within systems.

```
# Example nmap command to perform a comprehensible scan
nmap -A -T4 scanme.example.com
```

```
Starting Nmap 7.80 ( https://nmap.org ) at 2022-01-01 12:00 UTC
Nmap scan report for scanme.example.com (93.184.216.34)
Host is up (0.045s latency).
Not shown: 998 closed ports
PORT    STATE SERVICE VERSION
80/tcp  open  http    Apache httpd 2.4.1
```

117

Responsible Use and Regulatory Compliance   As with any robust network analysis tool, nmap should be utilized responsibly, ensuring compliance with network policies and regulations to mitigate unauthorized scans.

Implications and Strategic Use   The array of networking tools and utilities discussed enhances network management, troubleshooting, and security. The strategic deployment of these tools enables sophisticated insight into network behavior, facilitating informed decision-making in both operational and security contexts. Observing ethical guidelines and legal constraints is imperative to leverage their capacity effectively, ensuring networks are robust, responsive, and resilient against evolving challenges. These utilities provide the backbone for dynamic network oversight, empowering administrators to achieve balanced, secure, and high-performance networking environments.

Chapter 5

Asynchronous and Synchronous Communication

This chapter explores the fundamental differences between asynchronous and synchronous communication methods in network programming. It defines each communication type, highlighting their unique characteristics, advantages, and typical use cases. The chapter provides practical guidance on implementing both methods in C++ applications, along with a comparative analysis to assist in selecting the appropriate approach based on specific requirements. It also examines real-world scenarios and performance considerations, offering insights into the strategic application of these communication techniques in network software development.

5.1 Defining Synchronous Communication

Synchronous communication in computer science refers to a communication method where operations are executed in a predetermined sequence, with each operation waiting for the previous one to complete before initiating. This is particularly relevant in scenarios where immediate response is crucial, and it is necessary to ensure that data integrity or the order of operations is maintained.

A defining characteristic of synchronous communication is its reliance on time constraints for each interaction. Unlike asynchronous communication methods, which allow processes to operate independently and may lead to a state where operations continue without waiting for a response, synchronous communication entails a strict adherence to the operation order. This sequential handling makes it incredibly suited for tasks that require precision and certainty of response.

- **Blocking Nature:** Synchronous communications are blocking. A process that is in communication mode will not proceed to the next step until it has received a response. This blocking can simplify the logic of a program since the programmer does not have to manage complex states or check if an operation is complete.

- **Predictable Timing:** Since each operation must wait for the completion of the previous one, the timing in synchronous communication is predictable, a desirable feature in systems demanding high assurance levels, such as avionics or industrial systems.

- **Ease of Debugging:** Because operations proceed in a set order, debugging synchronous communication systems is generally simpler than their asynchronous counterparts. Each step can be traced sequentially, which makes identifying the source of a problem more straightforward.

- **Resource Utilization:** Synchronous communication can be resource-intensive, especially when network conditions are suboptimal since any delays affect the entire pipeline of operations.

In network communications, synchronous communication methods are implemented in protocols where direct and fast exchange of information is mandatory, such as HTTP/1.x where a request must receive a response before another request can be sent on the same connection.

Implementation in Real-World Systems

In real-world systems, synchronous communication is evident in many client-server models where operations proceed in a request-response fashion. Consider a traditional web browser communicating with a web server using the HTTP protocol. For each request, the client waits for an explicit response before sending another request.

```cpp
#include <iostream>
#include <cstring>
#include <sys/socket.h>
#include <arpa/inet.h>
#include <unistd.h>

int main() {
    int socket_desc;
    struct sockaddr_in server;
    char *message, server_reply[2000];

    // Create socket
    socket_desc = socket(AF_INET, SOCK_STREAM, 0);
    if (socket_desc == -1) {
        std::cout << "Could not create socket";
    }

    server.sin_addr.s_addr = inet_addr("74.125.235.20");
    server.sin_family = AF_INET;
    server.sin_port = htons(80);

    // Connect to remote server
    if (connect(socket_desc, (struct sockaddr *)&server, sizeof(server)) < 0) {
        std::cout << "connect error";
        return 1;
    }

    // Send some data
    message = "GET / HTTP/1.1\r\n\r\n";
    if (send(socket_desc, message, strlen(message), 0) < 0) {
        std::cout << "Send failed";
        return 1;
    }

    // Receive a reply from the server
    if (recv(socket_desc, server_reply, 2000, 0) < 0) {
        std::cout << "recv failed";
```

```
    }
    std::cout << "Reply received: " << server_reply;

    close(socket_desc);
    return 0;
}
```

This example demonstrates a simple synchronous communication model using sockets in C++. Here, the client establishes a connection to a server and waits for the server's response before proceeding further. The blocking nature of the 'recv' function ensures that the subsequent actions are only taken once a message is received from the server.

Advantages and Drawbacks

The advantages of synchronous communication mainly derive from its straightforwardness and predictability. In environments where it is crucial to have operations executed in a precise order and ensuring that feedback is immediately available from each operation, synchronous systems provide an excellent solution.

However, the blocking nature of synchronous communication can be inefficient, particularly in distributed systems where network latency can introduce significant delays. Additionally, because each operation must complete before the next can start, it can lead to increased waiting times and can be less scalable when the number of concurrent interactions grows.

Despite these drawbacks, synchronous communication remains a valuable approach in specific scenarios. Critical systems or those interacting with physical devices where precise timing is paramount often employ synchronous methods to maintain control flow integrity and reliability.

Application Domains

Synchronous communication is applied across a variety of domains where immediate acknowledgment and order maintenance are priority. Some notable applications include:

- **Telecommunications:** Traditional telephony systems where talk-spurt alternates between speaker and listener necessitating strict order.

- **Embedded Systems:** Such as industrial automation systems, which require precise control and feedback on each operation to ensure safety compliance.

- **Financial Transactions:** Especially in stock exchanges and banking transactions, where the flow of information is critically dependent on synchronous operations.

- **Command and Control Systems:** In military applications, where the response and the timing of command execution need to be predictable and reliable.

Synchronous Models in Application Development

In application development, synchronous methods are typically easier to implement when the transaction volume is manageable, and the structure of the communications follows a predictable pattern. This provides clear scalability limits and encourages disciplined coding practices.

```
std::string synchronousRequest(const std::string& url) {
    // Set up the request
    std::string response;
    CURL *curl = curl_easy_init();

    if(curl) {
        curl_easy_setopt(curl, CURLOPT_URL, url.c_str());
        curl_easy_setopt(curl, CURLOPT_WRITEFUNCTION, WriteCallback);
        curl_easy_setopt(curl, CURLOPT_WRITEDATA, &response);

        // Perform the request, res will get the return code
        CURLcode res = curl_easy_perform(curl);
        if(res != CURLE_OK) {
            std::cerr << "curl_easy_perform() failed: " << curl_easy_strerror(res) <<
                std::endl;
        }
```

```
    // Cleanup
    curl_easy_cleanup(curl);
  }
  return response;
}
```

In this C++ example, a synchronous HTTP request is made using the libcurl library. The simplicity of such an implementation is one of the main draws towards synchronous communication: setup, execution, and error handling are all neatly contained within a straightforward and easily monitorable pipeline.

Considerations for Synchronous Communication Design

When designing a system that employs synchronous communication, several factors must be considered:

- **Throughput Requirements:** Synchronous systems can restrict throughput, as operations are inherently serialized. In systems with high throughput requirements, alternative asynchronous or multi-threaded approaches may be recommended.

- **Fault Tolerance:** Since operations are closely coupled, a failure in one component can halt the process chain, making fault tolerance and error recovery critical design elements.

- **Latency Sensitivity:** The system must be capable of tolerating network-induced latencies without significant performance degradation or blocked processes.

- **Network Reliability:** The communication channel's reliability directly impacts the effectiveness of synchronous communication. High packet loss or erratic transmission speeds can introduce inefficiencies.

By understanding these factors, developers can effectively weigh synchronous communication's merits against its limitations, ensuring a well-informed decision tailored to the specific application context. Ultimately, synchronous communication remains a pivotal technique in the vast landscape of networked systems, its disciplined and linear approach indispensable in certain scenarios demanding an absolute order and clarity of operations.

5.2 Defining Asynchronous Communication

Asynchronous communication is a method that allows operations to occur independently from one another, enabling processes to progress without waiting for a response or completion of prior commands. This decoupling makes asynchronous communication a powerful technique, particularly in networked systems where latency and variable response times are inherent challenges.

A defining aspect of asynchronous communication is its ability to initiate multiple operations simultaneously, thereby optimizing resource utilization and enhancing system responsiveness. Unlike its synchronous counterpart, asynchronous communication does not follow a strict order of operations completion, offering flexibility in how tasks are managed and scheduled.

Characteristics of Asynchronous Communication

Asynchronous communication is marked by several distinguishing attributes:

- **Non-blocking Operations:** Operations in asynchronous communication are initiated without waiting for the prior operation to finish, allowing the system to continue its processes and manage other tasks simultaneously.

- **Concurrency:** Asynchronous communication supports concurrent operations, where multiple tasks are engaged in processing at the same time, improving the system's overall throughput and capabilities.

- **Scalability:** Asynchronous systems are inherently more scalable. They can handle a larger volume of operations simultaneously due to their non-blocking nature.

- **Complexity in Implementation:** Coding asynchronous systems requires more sophisticated constructs such as callbacks, promises, and future objects, which can add complexity to application development.

These features make asynchronous communication particularly well-suited for modern applications, including web services, where client expectations for speed and responsiveness are high.

Implementation in Real-World Systems

In practical applications, asynchronous communication is evident across various domains where independent task processing enhances efficiency. One clear use case is in the development of non-blocking server architectures, such as Node.js, which ensures high throughput and efficient resource utilization.

```cpp
#include <iostream>
#include <future>
#include <chrono>

int performAsyncTask(int duration) {
    std::this_thread::sleep_for(std::chrono::seconds(duration));
    return duration;
}

int main() {
    std::future<int> result = std::async(std::launch::async, performAsyncTask, 5);

    std::cout << "Processing other tasks while waiting for asynchronous task." << std
        ::endl;

    // Simulate doing other work here
    std::this_thread::sleep_for(std::chrono::seconds(2));

    int value = result.get(); // This will block if the task is not done yet
    std::cout << "Async task completed with duration: " << value << std::endl;

    return 0;
}
```

This example demonstrates the use of asynchronous operations using C++'s 'std::async'. Here, the 'performAsyncTask' function runs independently of the main thread, allowing other processes to execute concurrently. This ability to manage tasks concurrently without impeding the execution flow is a significant advantage of asynchronous communication models.

Advantages and Drawbacks

The advantages of asynchronous communication lie primarily in its ability to enhance responsiveness and maximize the efficiency of system resource utilization. Systems employing asynchronous techniques can handle more operations simultaneously, reducing wait times and increasing throughput.

However, the complexity associated with implementing asynchronous communication can pose significant challenges. Developers must manage concurrency-related issues such as race conditions and deadlocks, which requires a solid understanding of concurrency primitives and careful design planning.

The decoupled nature of asynchronous communication can also lead to challenges in maintaining data integrity and ensuring transactions complete successfully without interference, often necessitating additional mechanisms for handling failures and retries.

Application Domains

Asynchronous communication is highly applicable in environments where efficiency, speed, and scalability are critical. Prominent domains utilizing asynchronous methods include:

- **Web Development:** JavaScript and Node.js heavily rely on asynchronous calls to handle high volumes of requests efficiently without blocking the main execution thread.

- **Cloud Computing:** Cloud platforms frequently use asynchronous communication for operations that require rapid processing and high scalability potential.

- **Machine Learning Pipelines:** Distributing tasks and computations asynchronously maximizes computational resources and speeds up data processing pipelines.

- **Distributed Systems:** Distributed architectures often employ asynchronous protocols to communicate effectively over networks of independent nodes.

Asynchronous Models in Application Development

Developers use various models and structures to achieve asynchronous communication. Common patterns involve using callbacks, promises, and reactive programming paradigms that allow seamless integration of asynchronous tasks. Frameworks and languages offer diverse support for these models, enabling efficient, non-blocking application design.

```cpp
#include <iostream>
#include <future>

void doTask(std::promise<int>&& p) {
    std::this_thread::sleep_for(std::chrono::seconds(1));
    p.set_value(42); // Task completed
}

int main() {
    std::promise<int> promise;
    std::future<int> future = promise.get_future();

    std::thread taskThread(doTask, std::move(promise));

    std::cout << "Performing other operations while waiting for task result." << std::
        endl;

    auto status = future.wait_for(std::chrono::seconds(2));
    if (status == std::future_status::ready) {
        std::cout << "Received result: " << future.get() << std::endl;
    } else {
        std::cout << "Task is taking longer than expected." << std::endl;
    }

    taskThread.join();
    return 0;
}
```

This example uses 'std::promise' and 'std::future' to manage asynchronous operations, representing typical building blocks for asynchronous communication in C++. It illustrates how these constructs enable responses from asynchronous tasks to be awaited flexibly and provides a mechanism for determining task completion or ongoing status.

Considerations for Asynchronous Communication Design

Designing systems around asynchronous communication requires careful consideration of several factors:

- **Concurrency Control:** Proper use of synchronization mechanisms to manage operation overlap and resource contention should be considered.

- **Error Handling:** Asynchronous operations often require robust error handling strategies that can recover from partial failures naturally.

- **Performance Tuning:** Asynchronous systems should be designed with performance metrics in mind, ensuring that the benefits of concurrent processing outweigh overhead costs.

- **Scalability Arrangements:** The system should scale appropriately with the operation load, ensuring that system resources are adequately managed to sustain high concurrency levels.

As developers design asynchronous systems, they must understand the implications of breaking tasks into smaller, independently executable units and provide appropriate strategies for coordinating completed results. By acknowledging the inherent complexities yet substantial advantages, asynchronous communication remains a formidable tool in the arsenal for crafting advanced, responsive, and scalable networked systems.

5.3 Comparative Analysis of Communication Methods

Understanding the principles behind synchronous and asynchronous communication is crucial for the effective design and deployment of networked systems. These communication methods have unique attributes and serve different requirements based on system needs. An in-depth comparative analysis helps in choosing the most fitting approach for specific application scenarios, ensuring optimized performance, reliability, and scalability.

- **Operation Control:** Synchronous communication demands that each operation wait for the completion of the preceding one before proceeding. This is contrasted with the non-blocking structure of asynchronous communication, where operations can be initiated independently and executed out-of-order. This operational divergence significantly affects how systems are designed and optimized for task management and processing.

- **Response Manageability:** Synchronous systems are usually simpler to manage due to their predictable and linear control flow, where each step must be completed before the next one begins. In asynchronous systems, multiple operations run concurrently, complicating the tracking and synchronization of responses but enabling greater system throughput and efficiency.

Performance Considerations: Performance is a critical evaluation criterion when comparing communication methods. The blocking nature of synchronous communication can introduce latency into a system, particularly evident in networked environments where delays are common due to transmission time. In contrast, asynchronous communication thrives in environments where the system can continue processing other tasks while waiting for operations to complete, reducing idle time and improving overall system throughput.

```cpp
#include <iostream>
#include <thread>
#include <chrono>

// Simulate a blocking synchronous task
void synchronousTask() {
    std::this_thread::sleep_for(std::chrono::seconds(2)); // Simulate delay
    std::cout << "Synchronous task completed." << std::endl;
}

// Simulate an asynchronous task
void asynchronousTask() {
    std::this_thread::sleep_for(std::chrono::seconds(2)); // Simulate delay
    std::cout << "Asynchronous task completed." << std::endl;
}

int main() {
    std::cout << "Starting synchronous task..." << std::endl;
    synchronousTask();

    std::cout << "Starting asynchronous task..." << std::endl;
    std::thread taskThread(asynchronousTask);
    taskThread.detach();

    std::cout << "Main thread is free to perform other tasks." << std::endl;

    // Simulate doing other work
    std::this_thread::sleep_for(std::chrono::seconds(1));
    std::cout << "Main thread work completed." << std::endl;
```

```
    return 0;
}
```

In this C++ example, a comparison is drawn between synchronous and asynchronous tasks. The synchronous function blocks the main thread until completed, leading to potential inefficiencies. Conversely, the asynchronous task runs on a separate thread, allowing the main thread to execute other tasks concurrently, thus demonstrating enhanced parallelism and resource utilization.

- **Synchronous Communication:** Typically finds its place in systems where operation order integrity and immediate response are critical, such as legacy systems and tightly coupled transactional systems in finance where atomic transactions need assured sequential completion.

- **Asynchronous Communication:** Excels in environments where parallelism and scalability are paramount, such as modern web servers and cloud-based applications, which must efficiently handle numerous concurrent requests without bottlenecks.

```python
import asyncio

async def handle_request(reader, writer):
    data = await reader.read(100)
    message = data.decode()
    addr = writer.get_extra_info('peername')

    print(f"Received {message} from {addr}")

    print("Send: %s" % message)
    writer.write(data)
    await writer.drain()

    print("Closing the connection")
    writer.close()

async def main():
    server = await asyncio.start_server(
        handle_request, '127.0.0.1', 8888)

    async with server:
        await server.serve_forever()

asyncio.run(main())
```

Asynchronous communication technologies like Python's 'asyncio' are commonly used in web servers to handle many connections concurrently without the need for multi-threading, showcasing how asynchronous communication can enable efficient, scalable service architectures.

Ease of Debugging and Maintainability: Synchronous communication offers an easier debugging experience due to its straightforward, linear execution model. Tracking the execution path and identifying points of failure is substantially more amenable in a predictable, step-by-step process flow.

Asynchronous systems, due to their non-linear and often concurrent nature, require more sophisticated debugging strategies, potentially involving logging and performance profiling tools capable of managing concurrency issues such as deadlocks and race conditions. Nevertheless, though challenging, frameworks and libraries provide constructs to improve both traceability and maintainability in asynchronous applications.

Resource Management and Scalability: Scaling synchronous systems often requires significant resource allocations because of the blocking operations that tie up resources, waiting for replies before moving forward. In contrast, asynchronous systems can efficiently manage resources by continuing operations while waiting, thus enabling better scalability in distributed and heavily loaded environments.

For network protocols, implementing an asynchronous communication scheme can greatly reduce latencies and increase throughput, particularly where the network round trip time (RTT) is variable. By allowing other operations to progress while waiting for network responses, systems can maintain high responsiveness to user requests.

Security Implications: Security considerations also play a role in the choice between synchronous and asynchronous communications. Synchronous systems, with their sequential operation, naturally limit the concurrency-related security issues but must handle blocking-related vulnerabilities, such as denial of service (DoS) attacks where processes are lodged indefinitely waiting for network responses.

Asynchronous systems require more careful consideration of security issues related to concurrency, such as resource access violations arising from unprotected shared data and ensuring the integrity and confidentiality of data that may linger in transit or in-memory caches between asynchronous executions.

Summary of Comparative Implications: Having explored synchronous and asynchronous communication's core attributes, it is essential for engineers and developers to consider specific use-cases and balance the advantages. The choice between these methods should be driven by the application's requirements regarding process synchronization, resource allocation, and performance objectives.

Aspect	Synchronous Communication
Operation Mode	Blocking and sequential execution.
Scalability	Limited by blocking operations' resource holding.
Responsiveness	Predictable timing but can delay other tasks.
Debugging	Easier due to linear control flow.
Security	Fewer concurrency-related issues but susceptible to DoS vulnerabilities.

Aspect	Asynchronous Communication
Operation Mode	Non-blocking and concurrent execution.
Scalability	Superior with efficient resource utilization.
Responsiveness	Maximized throughput but potentially complex to manage.
Debugging	Complex due to non-linear events and concurrency issues.
Security	Requires handling data integrity during concurrency operations.

Both synchronous and asynchronous communication techniques possess distinct benefits and trade-offs; careful consideration is necessary to determine their suitability in specific contexts requiring different levels of transaction control, response time, and cost-efficiency tuning. This careful analysis serves as a guide for professionals when architecting systems designed to achieve both reliability and scalability in various domains.

5.4 Implementing Synchronous Communication in C++

The implementation of synchronous communication in C++ is crucial in a multitude of use cases where operation order integrity and immediacy are imperative. This section delves into various techniques and constructs within C++ that facilitate synchronous communication, adhering to the language's standard libraries and capabilities. In C++, synchronous communication is typically characterized by blocking operations that follow a sequential execution flow.

One of the fundamental applications of synchronous communication is in network programming, particularly using sockets. TCP/IP socket programming is inherently a synchronous operation, providing guarantees on message ordering and delivery acknowledgment.

To establish a synchronous TCP connection using C++, the standard socket API is the primary gateway. The following C++ example establishes a simple synchronous connection to a server using sockets.

```cpp
#include <iostream>
#include <cstring>
#include <sys/socket.h>
#include <arpa/inet.h>
#include <unistd.h>

int main() {
    int sock;
    struct sockaddr_in server;
    char message[1000], server_reply[2000];

    // Create socket
    sock = socket(AF_INET, SOCK_STREAM, 0);
    if (sock == -1) {
        std::cerr << "Could not create socket" << std::endl;
        return 1;
    }
    std::cout << "Socket created" << std::endl;

    server.sin_addr.s_addr = inet_addr("192.168.1.1");
    server.sin_family = AF_INET;
    server.sin_port = htons(8888);

    // Connect to remote server
    if (connect(sock, (struct sockaddr *)&server, sizeof(server)) < 0) {
        std::cerr << "Connection failed" << std::endl;
        return 1;
    }
    std::cout << "Connected" << std::endl;

    // Send some data
    strcpy(message, "GET / HTTP/1.1\r\n\r\n");
    if (send(sock, message, strlen(message), 0) < 0) {
        std::cerr << "Send failed" << std::endl;
        return 1;
    }
    std::cout << "Data sent" << std::endl;

    // Receive a reply from the server
    if (recv(sock, server_reply, 2000, 0) < 0) {
        std::cerr << "Receive failed" << std::endl;
```

```
      return 1;
   }
   std::cout << "Reply received:\n" << server_reply << std::endl;

   close(sock);
   return 0;
}
```

In the example above, a socket is created using the POSIX socket API, which blocks the client application until a connection is successfully established with the server. The program waits for a response to each block, achieving the critical sequential execution characteristic of synchronous communication.

In C++, synchronous communication is not limited to network programming but extends to various other areas such as file I/O operations, where data is read or written in a blocking manner. The standard C++ I/O library provides classes like fstream for such operations.

```cpp
#include <iostream>
#include <fstream>

int main() {
    std::ofstream outfile("example.txt");

    if (!outfile.is_open()) {
        std::cerr << "Error opening file for writing" << std::endl;
        return 1;
    }

    outfile << "This is a line.\n";
    outfile << "This is another line.\n";

    outfile.close();
    std::cout << "File written successfully" << std::endl;

    std::ifstream infile("example.txt");
    if (!infile.is_open()) {
        std::cerr << "Error opening file for reading" << std::endl;
        return 1;
    }

    std::string line;
    while (std::getline(infile, line)) {
        std::cout << line << std::endl;
    }

    infile.close();
    return 0;
}
```

This example illustrates synchronous file handling, where fstream operations ensure that writing to and reading from a file occur sequentially and completely before proceeding to the next statement. The synchronous sequences guarantee that data consistency and temporal ordering are appropriately preserved.

Synchronous communication also plays a vital role in IPC, where processes communicate through mechanisms such as pipes or shared memory. In such settings, data is typically exchanged in a blocking manner to maintain coordination.

```
#include <iostream>
#include <fcntl.h>
#include <unistd.h>
#include <sys/stat.h>

int main() {
    const char* pipeName = "/tmp/testpipe";
    mkfifo(pipeName, 0666);

    pid_t pid = fork();
    if (pid == 0) { // Child process
        int readFd = open(pipeName, O_RDONLY);
        char buffer[100];
        read(readFd, buffer, sizeof(buffer));
        std::cout << "Child process received: " << buffer << std::endl;
        close(readFd);
    } else { // Parent process
        int writeFd = open(pipeName, O_WRONLY);
        char message[] = "Hello from parent!";
        write(writeFd, message, sizeof(message));
        close(writeFd);
    }

    // Remove the named pipe after use
    unlink(pipeName);
    return 0;
}
```

In this code, both parent and child processes engage in a synchronous exchange over a named pipe (/tmp/testpipe). The read and write operations are blocking, requiring each party to wait for the respective operation to complete, typifying synchronous communication within IPC.

In environments with concurrent threads, synchronization primitives are necessary to ensure ordered execution through mutual exclusion and condition variables. These primitives help maintain the systematic exchange between threads to avoid race conditions.

```
#include <iostream>
```

```cpp
#include <thread>
#include <mutex>
#include <condition_variable>

std::mutex mtx;
std::condition_variable cv;
bool ready = false;

void print_id(int id) {
    std::unique_lock<std::mutex> lock(mtx);
    cv.wait(lock, []{ return ready; });
    std::cout << "Thread " << id << std::endl;
}

void set_ready() {
    {
        std::lock_guard<std::mutex> lock(mtx);
        ready = true;
    }
    cv.notify_all();
}

int main() {
    std::thread threads[10];
    for (int i = 0; i < 10; ++i) {
        threads[i] = std::thread(print_id, i);
    }

    std::this_thread::sleep_for(std::chrono::seconds(1));
    std::cout << "Setting ready state." << std::endl;
    set_ready();

    for (auto &t: threads) {
        t.join();
    }
    return 0;
}
```

In this example, the std::mutex and std::condition_variable work together to synchronize threads, ensuring that all threads wait for the ready condition. This synchronization enforces a specific order of operations, critical in applications requiring controlled access to shared resources in synchronous communication schemes.

Implementing synchronous communication in C++ requires careful consideration of potential pitfalls such as deadlocks in multi-threaded environments and the impact of blocking operations on application responsiveness. The design of synchronous systems should consider factors such as:

- **Deadlock Avoidance:** Ensuring that resources are acquired and released in a consistent order can prevent deadlock scenarios.

- **Timeouts:** Introducing time limitations on blocking operations can mitigate adverse effects such as liveness issues or long wait times.

- **Error Handling:** Robust error handling mechanisms are crucial, especially in network communications where latency and transmission errors might affect synchronous operations.

- **Performance Impacts:** Awareness of the performance trade-offs involved in blocking operations is necessary to select appropriate techniques based on application needs.

Synchronous communication in C++ provides a reliable means for order-dependent communication tasks, offering simplicity in coding logic best suited for applications where predictability and process simplicity are prerequisites. Through careful implementation and consideration of the pros and cons of synchronous models, developers can effectively exploit C++ capabilities to design solutions tailored to specific operational demands that adhere to the synchronous approach.

5.5 Implementing Asynchronous Communication in C++

Asynchronous communication is integral to the design of modern software systems, allowing for efficient resource use through concurrent operation execution. In C++, implementing asynchronous communication leverages a range of features and libraries allowing developers to design systems that are responsive and capable of handling large volumes of tasks in parallel.

- C++11 introduced several features that provide native support for asynchronous programming. These include threads, futures, promises, and the standard asynchronous library, providing a foundation for constructing complex, non-blocking communications.

- Threads are the building blocks of concurrent applications where multiple paths of execution occur simultaneously. The std::thread library in C++ enables developers to manage asynchronous tasks and improve application performance through parallel processing.

```
#include <iostream>
#include <thread>

void computeTask(int duration) {
    std::this_thread::sleep_for(std::chrono::seconds(duration));
    std::cout << "Task duration: " << duration << " seconds completed." << std::
        endl;
}

int main() {
    std::thread t1(computeTask, 3);
    std::thread t2(computeTask, 5);

    std::cout << "Main thread continues execution..." << std::endl;

    t1.join();
    t2.join();

    std::cout << "All tasks completed." << std::endl;
    return 0;
}
```

In this example, two asynchronous tasks are spawned using threads, allowing the main program to continue its execution while waiting for these tasks to finish. This approach ensures optimal use of multiple processors.

- Futures and promises provide a mechanism to work with deferred computations and handle the results once tasks complete. They allow initiating asynchronous operations and later retrieving their results without blocking the main execution flow.

```
#include <iostream>
#include <thread>
#include <future>

int asyncComputation(int value) {
    std::this_thread::sleep_for(std::chrono::seconds(value));
    return value * 2;
}

int main() {
    std::promise<int> prom;
```

139

```
        std::future<int> fut = prom.get_future();

        std::thread t([&prom]() {
            prom.set_value(asyncComputation(5));
        });

        std::cout << "Waiting for the result..." << std::endl;
        std::cout << "Result: " << fut.get() << std::endl;

        t.join();
        return 0;
}
```

Using a promise, we encapsulate a long-running computation. A future is used to obtain the result when it becomes available. This approach abstracts the asynchrony and provides a straightforward way to wait for computations without locking the main thread.

- The std::async function template is part of the C++ standard library used to asynchronously run a function. std::async manages thread creation and workload distribution, offering the benefit of launching tasks asynchronously or synchronously based on the launch policy.

```
#include <iostream>
#include <future>

int performCalculation(int x) {
    std::this_thread::sleep_for(std::chrono::seconds(3));
    return x * x;
}

int main() {
    std::future<int> result = std::async(std::launch::async, performCalculation, 10);

    std::cout << "Main continues, waiting for the result..." << std::endl;
    std::cout << "Calculation result: " << result.get() << std::endl;

    return 0;
}
```

The std::async facilitates the operation of performCalculation in a non-blocking manner, where the main program can perform other tasks while waiting for the result. The result is retrieved through a future, allowing the result to be processed once ready.

- In addition to standard threading and concurrency utilities, specialized libraries provide enhanced capabilities for asynchronous network programming. Libraries such as Boost.Asio enable developers to structure non-blocking communication applications efficiently.

- Boost.Asio is a cross-platform C++ library for network and low-level I/O programming that emphasizes asynchronous operations. Manifesting through a strong async model, Boost.Asio allows sophisticated asynchronous system designs.

```cpp
#include <iostream>
#include <boost/asio.hpp>
#include <boost/bind/bind.hpp>

using boost::asio::ip::tcp;

void connectHandler(const boost::system::error_code& ec) {
    if (!ec) {
        std::cout << "Connection established successfully." << std::endl;
    } else {
        std::cerr << "Failed to connect: " << ec.message() << std::endl;
    }
}

int main() {
    boost::asio::io_context io_context;

    tcp::socket socket(io_context);

    tcp::resolver resolver(io_context);
    auto endpoints = resolver.resolve("example.com", "80");

    boost::asio::async_connect(socket, endpoints, connectHandler);

    io_context.run();
    return 0;
}
```

Here, the connection process is initiated asynchronously using async_-connect, providing a connectHandler callback to handle the completion signal. The io_context.run() executes the operations associated with the io_context until the work is done.

- Successfully building asynchronous applications requires understanding design patterns and best practices that govern this non-linear execution model.

- The event-driven model is foundational to creating asynchronous systems. It enables applications to react to events or messages

141

and execute corresponding callbacks without blocking operations.

```
#include <iostream>
#include <functional>

void asyncOperation(std::function<void(int)> callback) {
    std::cout << "Performing some operation..." << std::endl;
    std::this_thread::sleep_for(std::chrono::seconds(2));
    callback(42); // Trigger callback with result
}

void resultCallback(int result) {
    std::cout << "Operation completed with result: " << result << std::endl;
}

int main() {
    asyncOperation(resultCallback);
    std::cout << "Main function continues execution." << std::endl;
    std::this_thread::sleep_for(std::chrono::seconds(3)); // Keep the main thread alive
        for asynchronous completion
    return 0;
}
```

This example demonstrates an asynchronous operation that invokes a callback function once the task completes. The main function continues execution during this asynchronous operation, illustrating effective decoupling.

- Asynchronous systems require thoughtful error handling methods. Whether using try-catch blocks within task threads or leveraging features like exceptions in futures, robust error management is critical to maintaining system stability.

```
#include <iostream>
#include <future>

int riskyComputation() {
    std::this_thread::sleep_for(std::chrono::seconds(3));
    throw std::runtime_error("An error occurred in computation!");
}

int main() {
    std::future<int> result = std::async(std::launch::async, riskyComputation);

    try {
        int value = result.get();
        std::cout << "Computation result: " << value << std::endl;
    } catch (const std::exception &e) {
        std::cerr << "Caught exception: " << e.what() << std::endl;
```

142

```
    }
    return 0;
}
```

In this code, std::async is used to manage a risky calculation, where exceptions are anticipated and caught when retrieving the result from the future, preventing the application from terminating unexpectedly.

- Implementing asynchronous communication in C++ extends beyond mere multithreading. It envelops the complete asynchronous paradigms, ranging from task parallelism to network I/O and event-driven patterns. C++ provides a robust toolset to create non-blocking applications, ensuring high responsiveness and throughput. Proper application design to adhere to asynchronous strategies, coupled with judicious use of C++ features and libraries like std::async and Boost.Asio, results in systems that are both scalable and efficient. Understanding the intricacies, pitfalls, and best practices of asynchronous programming equips developers to create sophisticated, high-performance applications suited to the demands of modern software infrastructure.

5.6 Use Cases and Performance Considerations

The decision to employ synchronous or asynchronous communication models in software systems is heavily influenced by specific use cases and the performance objectives to be achieved. Each model's characteristics render them more suitable for certain applications based on network conditions, resource availability, scalability requirements, and user expectations. It is essential to perform a thorough analysis of these aspects to create systems capable of meeting both operational and performance standards.

- **Real-world Use Cases**

- **Synchronous Communication Use Cases**

1. **Transaction Processing Systems:** In financial services, transaction processing demands high integrity and sequential consistency. Systems such as online banking, stock trading platforms, and payment gateways often rely on synchronous communication to ensure that operations like fund transfers and order placements occur in a well-defined sequence, avoiding anomalies like double spending.

```cpp
#include <iostream>
#include <mutex>

int accountBalance = 1000;
std::mutex balanceMutex;

void performTransaction(int withdrawalAmount) {
    std::lock_guard<std::mutex> lock(balanceMutex);
    if (accountBalance >= withdrawalAmount) {
        accountBalance -= withdrawalAmount;
        std::cout << "Transaction successful, new balance: " <<
            accountBalance << std::endl;
    } else {
        std::cout << "Insufficient balance for transaction." << std
            ::endl;
    }
}

int main() {
    performTransaction(200);
    performTransaction(500);
    return 0;
}
```

In the code above, mutexes enforce synchronous access to shared resources, ensuring transaction integrity.

2. **Command and Control Systems:** In military or critical infrastructure applications, operations rely on precise control of commands executed in a strict order. Such applications prioritize immediate processing and confirmation before executing subsequent commands, emphasizing reliability and predictability.

3. **Collaborative Software and Interactive Applications:** Applications that feature real-time collaboration, for example, multiplayer games and virtual meetings, often utilize synchronous communication to maintain a consistent state across all participants, reducing latency in response to user actions.

144

- **Asynchronous Communication Use Cases**

  1. **Web and Network Servers:** Modern web servers such as Nginx and Node.js leverage asynchronous communication to handle a multitude of client connections simultaneously, optimizing performance and resource utilization without the need for multithreading.

     ```
     const http = require('http');

     const server = http.createServer((req, res) => {
         res.writeHead(200, {'Content-Type': 'text/plain'});
         res.end('Hello, World!\n');
     });

     server.listen(3000, '127.0.0.1');
     console.log('Server running at http://127.0.0.1:3000/');
     ```

     The non-blocking model allows the server to continue accepting new connections while handling active requests.

  2. **Background Processing and Tasks:** Applications like email servers, web crawlers, or data pipelines often offload intensive computations or I/O-bound tasks to asynchronous processes, enabling continued system responsiveness without waiting for task completion.

  3. **Microservices:** Asynchronous communication is prevalent in microservice architectures, where services are loosely coupled, and communication often occurs through message brokers or event-driven patterns. This enhances fault tolerance and scalability, as services can operate independently and asynchronously handle failures or latency.

- **Performance Considerations**

- **1. Latency and Throughput**

  - **Synchronous Communication:** Latency in synchronous systems is typically determined by the round-trip time required for each operation to complete. The sequential execution process commonly accumulates delays, impacting throughput and overall system responsiveness if unforeseen network latencies arise.

145

```
Processing Order:
[Request 1] -> [Response 1]
[Request 2] -> [Response 2]
(increased latency with dependency on prior completion)
```

– **Asynchronous Communication:** Asynchronous systems excel in environments where latency is variable, as tasks can be processed concurrently without the need for preliminary completion. This architecture results in higher throughput and resource efficiency as tasks complete independently.

```
Processing Order:
[Request 1] -------\
[Request 2] ----> (processes complete independently)
```

- **2. Resource Utilization**

  – **Synchronous Systems:** The blocking nature of synchronous communication often results in inefficient resource use, as active resources are held indefinitely while waiting for operations to complete.

  – **Asynchronous Systems:** Resources are utilized more efficiently due to non-blocking operations. Systems can serve multiple requests simultaneously without the fixed overhead of waiting for results, optimizing CPU and I/O resources.

- **3. Complexity and Maintenance**

  – **Synchronous Communication:** Offers a straightforward implementation with linear control flow, simplifying maintenance and reducing potential points of failure. The lack of concurrency-related complexity facilitates easier debugging and issue resolution.

  – **Asynchronous Communication:** Demands a more intricate implementation due to concurrency and potential race conditions. Designing non-blocking architectures introduces additional complexity but enhances adaptiveness to diverse performance criteria.

146

- **Design Considerations**

  1. **Choosing the Right Model:** The determination between synchronous and asynchronous designs must consider application requirements, such as data integrity, response time expectations, and processing volume. Applications demanding real-time interactions and immediacy might favor synchronous models, whereas those demanding scalability and high throughput might prefer asynchronous.

  2. **Error Handling and Reliability:** Asynchronous systems necessitate robust error-handling mechanisms, including retries, message logging, and compensatory transactions to address incomplete or failed operations.

  3. **System Scalability:** Asynchronous systems are inherently more scalable due to their capacity to independently handle tasks without the need for sequential dependencies.

  4. **Development Complexity:** The complexity of managing concurrent operations in asynchronous systems must be weighed against the benefits of enhanced performance and responsiveness.

- **Conclusion on Use Cases and Performance**

The decision to adopt synchronous or asynchronous communication models hinges upon the detailed analysis of specific use cases and performance considerations. Understanding the unique characteristics of each method allows for efficient system design, aligning with application objectives and optimizing for critical criteria. Synchronous communication ensures reliability and order, fitting scenarios where immediate response and determinism are paramount. In contrast, asynchronous communication excels in scalability and performance optimization, catering to environments demanding high throughput and concurrency. As developers and architects navigate these paradigms, balancing complexity with desired outcomes paves the path for designing systems apt for today's diverse computational environments.

Chapter 6

Multithreading in Network Applications

This chapter delves into the use of multithreading to enhance the performance and efficiency of network applications. It begins by elucidating the importance of multithreading and how it can handle multiple tasks concurrently. Readers will learn to create and manage threads using C++, focusing on synchronization techniques to prevent race conditions. The chapter also covers shared data management and how to optimize network I/O through threading. Common challenges such as deadlocks are discussed, along with strategies to avoid them, equipping developers to build robust, high-performance network software.

6.1 Understanding Multithreading

Multithreading is a fundamental concept in modern computing that allows multiple threads of execution within a single process. Each thread shares the process's resources, including memory and open files, which facilitates efficient communications and task handling. The relevance of multithreading lies in its capability to enhance the performance of applications by enabling concurrent execution of tasks. This is particularly important in network applications, where multiple operations often need to be handled simultaneously, such as sending and receiving data over a network, processing requests, and interacting with databases.

The core advantage of multithreading is its potential to improve the responsiveness of applications. In scenarios where tasks are CPU-bound, threads can exploit multiple cores in a processor for parallel processing, significantly reducing the time required to complete computationally intensive tasks. In I/O-bound situations, such as network communication, multithreading allows tasks that are waiting for network responses to relinquish the CPU to other tasks, thereby improving application responsiveness and resource utilization.

To appreciate how multithreading can be utilized effectively, it is first necessary to understand the concept of a thread. A thread can be considered the smallest unit of processing that an operating system can schedule. It typically contains a unique thread ID, a program counter, a register set, and a stack. Threads within the same process share resources, but each operates independently, executing individual sequences of instructions.

The implementation of multithreading varies across operating systems, but the underlying principles remain consistent. In Unix-like systems, the pthreads (POSIX Threads) library provides a robust framework for multi-threading applications, while Windows employs its own threading API. C++ provides a standardized library to create and manage threads, making it easier to write portable and efficient multithreading code.

```cpp
#include <iostream>
#include <thread>

// Function that will be executed by the thread
void threadFunction() {
    std::cout << "Hello from the thread!" << std::endl;
}

int main() {
    // Create a thread and start it
    std::thread t(threadFunction);

    // Wait for the thread to finish
    t.join();
```

```
    return 0;
}
```

In the code above, we define a simple thread in C++. The std::thread object t is initialized with the function threadFunction, which it executes in parallel with the rest of the program. The t.join() method is used to make the main thread wait for the thread t to complete its execution, ensuring that all threads are synchronized before the program exits.

The main target of multithreading is to improve application performance through parallel execution of tasks. However, effective multithreading demands careful management of shared resources to avoid issues such as race conditions, deadlocks, and resource contention. A race condition occurs when multiple threads modify shared resources concurrently, leading to unpredictable and erroneous behavior. In such scenarios, thread synchronization mechanisms must be employed to ensure that only one thread accesses the shared resource at a time.

The following example illustrates a race condition:

```
#include <iostream>
#include <thread>
#include <vector>

int counter = 0;

void incrementCounter() {
    for (int i = 0; i < 1000; ++i) {
        ++counter;
    }
}

int main() {
    std::vector<std::thread> threads;

    // Create 10 threads that increment the counter
    for (int i = 0; i < 10; ++i) {
        threads.push_back(std::thread(incrementCounter));
    }

    // Wait for all threads to finish
    for (auto& t : threads) {
        t.join();
    }

    std::cout << "Final counter value: " << counter << std::endl;
    return 0;
}
```

The expected outcome of the code is for the counter to reach a value of

10,000. However, due to the race condition, the actual value may be less. This demonstration shows how unsynchronized access to shared variables can result in incorrect values. To mitigate this, thread synchronization is required, as explored in subsequent sections.

Using mutexes and locks is the standard approach to synchronizing threads, ensuring atomic access to shared resources. The C++ Standard Library provides mechanisms such as std::mutex and std::lock_guard to facilitate thread-safe operations. Implementing these tools prevents threads from simultaneously entering critical sections of code that access shared data.

```cpp
#include <iostream>
#include <thread>
#include <mutex>
#include <vector>

int counter = 0;
std::mutex counterMutex;

void incrementCounter() {
    for (int i = 0; i < 1000; ++i) {
        // Lock the mutex before modifying the counter
        std::lock_guard<std::mutex> guard(counterMutex);
        ++counter;
    }
}

int main() {
    std::vector<std::thread> threads;

    // Create 10 threads that increment the counter
    for (int i = 0; i < 10; ++i) {
        threads.push_back(std::thread(incrementCounter));
    }

    // Wait for all threads to finish
    for (auto& t : threads) {
        t.join();
    }

    std::cout << "Final counter value: " << counter << std::endl;
    return 0;
}
```

This modified example incorporates a std::mutex to lock access to the counter variable, ensuring that only one thread can increment it at a time. Applying a std::lock_guard guarantees that the mutex is released as soon as the guard falls out of scope, thus preserving program correctness and reducing the risk of deadlocks.

Multithreading's potential extends beyond local computations to network applications, where managing multiple connections and data streams efficiently is crucial. Threads can be employed so that each handles specific network tasks, such as listening for requests or sending responses. This promotes scalable and responsive applications capable of meeting the demands of high-throughput environments.

In a network server scenario, for instance, a multithreaded model can allow individual threads to address separate client connections concurrently. This prevents the server from becoming a performance bottleneck and ensures that client connections are served without undue delay, thereby enhancing user experience. A practical example is a multithreaded TCP server where each client connection is serviced by its own thread.

```cpp
#include <iostream>
#include <thread>
#include <vector>
#include <boost/asio.hpp>

using boost::asio::ip::tcp;

void clientSession(tcp::socket socket) {
    try {
        while (true) {
            char data[512];
            boost::system::error_code error;

            size_t length = socket.read_some(boost::asio::buffer(data), error);
            if (error == boost::asio::error::eof) {
                break; // Connection closed cleanly by peer
            } else if (error) {
                throw boost::system::system_error(error); // Other error
            }

            boost::asio::write(socket, boost::asio::buffer(data, length));
        }
    } catch (std::exception& e) {
        std::cerr << "Exception in thread: " << e.what() << "\n";
    }
}

int main() {
    try {
        boost::asio::io_context io_context;
        tcp::acceptor acceptor(io_context, tcp::endpoint(tcp::v4(), 1234));

        while (true) {
            tcp::socket socket(io_context);
            acceptor.accept(socket);
            std::thread(clientSession, std::move(socket)).detach();
        }
```

```
} catch (std::exception& e) {
    std::cerr << "Exception: " << e.what() << "\n";
}

return 0;
}
```

In this example, boost::asio is utilized to establish a TCP server that asynchronously accepts connections. Each new client connection initiates a thread running the clientSession function, which echoes data back to the client. By detaching the threads, we ensure resource deallocation once the client communication completes.

The correct application of multithreading requires balancing efficiency with complexity. The overhead introduced by context switching, synchronization delays, and potential deadlock scenarios can outweigh the benefits if not carefully managed. An understanding of the operating system's thread scheduling policies and the underlying hardware architecture is also essential to leverage fully the power of multithreading.

Furthermore, debugging multithreaded applications presents unique challenges due to their non-deterministic execution and the intricacies of parallel processes. Tools such as Valgrind, gdb, and specialized thread analyzers are indispensable in identifying and resolving concurrency-related issues.

The transition to multithreading should be guided by a clear rationale to enhance processing efficiency, not merely for its own sake. Applications with significant computational loads or I/O interactions stand to gain the most. In every case, cautious consideration of data sharing and the judicious use of locks can minimize contention and unlock the full potential of multithreading in network applications.

6.2 Creating Threads in C++

Creating threads in C++ involves leveraging the Standard Library's threading capabilities, introduced in C++11, which enable the development of concurrent programs in a more straightforward and structured manner. C++ integrates thread support through the <thread> header, providing a platform-independent interface that allows developers to initiate and manage threads effectively.

A thread in C++ is instantiated from the std::thread class, which represents a single thread of execution. Each std::thread object begins executing a callable object, which could be a function, a lambda expression, or a callable object obtained from the std::function template. Employing std::thread abstracts away the complexities of platform-specific threading APIs, granting the programmer a cohesive and streamlined approach to multithreading.

```cpp
#include <iostream>
#include <thread>

// Defining a simple function to be executed by a thread
void simpleFunction() {
    std::cout << "Thread is executing simpleFunction." << std::endl;
}

int main() {
    // Creating a thread to execute simpleFunction
    std::thread t1(simpleFunction);

    // Waiting for the thread to complete
    t1.join();

    std::cout << "Main thread finished." << std::endl;
    return 0;
}
```

In this example, the simpleFunction is executed in a separate thread. The std::thread object t1 is initialized with simpleFunction, starting its execution concurrent to the main program. The t1.join() method ensures that the main thread waits for t1 to complete, which is crucial for synchronizing thread execution and avoiding premature termination of the main thread.

The lifecycle management of threads is critical in C++ multithreading. Threads can either be joined or detached. If the join member function is called, the calling thread waits for the execution of the individual thread to end. Conversely, a detached thread operates independently, releasing its resources upon completion without necessitating a corresponding join call. Detaching is useful when the thread execution time is independent and doesn't affect the primary execution flow.

```cpp
#include <iostream>
#include <thread>
#include <chrono>

// Function that executes independently
void independentFunction() {
    std::this_thread::sleep_for(std::chrono::seconds(2));
```

```
    std::cout << "Independent function executed." << std::endl;
}

int main() {
    // Create a thread and detach it
    std::thread t(independentFunction);
    t.detach(); // Detaching the thread

    std::cout << "Thread detached, continuing main execution." << std::endl;
    std::this_thread::sleep_for(std::chrono::seconds(1));
    return 0;
}
```

Detaching a thread, as illustrated, allows the main thread to continue execution without waiting for the independent function to finish. As such, the main program might complete and exit before the detached thread, demonstrating its asynchronous nature.

Moreover, it's vital to handle thread ownership correctly. A std::thread object holds ownership of a thread of execution. If it is destroyed without being joined or detached, the program calls std::terminate. This could lead to undefined behavior and is thus crucial to ensure that all threads are properly managed before their std::thread objects go out of scope.

The flexibility of the std::thread constructor enables different methods to set the initial function. It can start executing a free function, a member function, a lambda function, or even a functor. We explore each option below, illustrating their syntax and application.

Threads with Lambdas:

Lambdas, introduced in C++11, provide a convenient way to define inline functions. They are especially valuable in multithreading for defining thread tasks without the overhead of additional function definitions.

```
#include <iostream>
#include <thread>

int main() {
    // Lambda function executed by a thread
    std::thread t([] {
        std::cout << "Thread executing lambda function." << std::endl;
    });

    t.join();

    std::cout << "Main thread finished." << std::endl;
    return 0;
```

156

```
}
```

This example illustrates how a lambda can be directly passed to a std::thread constructor, providing concise syntax for defining thread behavior.

Threads with Member Functions and Functors:

C++ threads can also execute member functions and functors. However, when invoking a member function, the corresponding object must be passed—either as a pointer or a reference—and the member function to be executed should be publicly accessible.

```cpp
#include <iostream>
#include <thread>

class Worker {
public:
    void doWork() {
        std::cout << "Thread executing member function doWork of Worker." << std::
            endl;
    }
};

int main() {
    Worker w;

    // Thread executing a member function
    std::thread t(&Worker::doWork, &w);

    t.join();

    std::cout << "Main thread finished." << std::endl;
    return 0;
}
```

In this instance, the member function doWork within class Worker is executed in a new thread, with the object instance w being passed to the thread constructor.

Alternatively, functors—or objects that act like functions—can be leveraged within a thread like so:

```cpp
#include <iostream>
#include <thread>

class Functor {
public:
    void operator()() const {
        std::cout << "Thread executing functor." << std::endl;
    }
};
```

```
int main() {
    Functor f;

    // Thread initiated with a functor
    std::thread t(f);

    t.join();

    std::cout << "Main thread finished." << std::endl;
    return 0;
}
```

The functor here is the class Functor with an overloaded operator().
When passed to the std::thread constructor, it runs seamlessly as any
callable object.

Passing arguments to threads can be achieved through the std::thread
constructor. The arguments are passed after specifying the function
and are automatically forwarded using std::forward semantics.

```
#include <iostream>
#include <thread>

// Function that takes parameters
void parameterizedFunction(int x, const std::string& message) {
    std::cout << "Received: " << x << ", " << message << std::endl;
}

int main() {
    // Starting a thread with parameters
    std::thread t(parameterizedFunction, 42, "Hello, multithreading!");

    t.join();

    std::cout << "Main thread finished." << std::endl;
    return 0;
}
```

In cases like this, parameterizedFunction is provided with integer and
string parameters, which the thread processes upon execution. Since
arguments are copied into the new thread's scope, it's essential to ensure that data marshaling adheres to application requirements, especially with instances of complex data types or large amounts of data.

Lastly, adopting the C++ future and promise mechanisms can facilitate
asynchronous operations and value passing between threads safely.
Combined with std::async, this paradigm avoids explicit thread management, optimizing code clarity and efficiency.

```cpp
#include <iostream>
#include <future>

// Task executed asynchronously
int asyncTask() {
    return 42;
}

int main() {
    // Launch task asynchronously
    std::future<int> result = std::async(std::launch::async, asyncTask);

    std::cout << "Waiting for result..." << std::endl;

    // Get the result of the asynchronous task
    int value = result.get();

    std::cout << "Received result: " << value << std::endl;

    return 0;
}
```

Executing tasks asynchronously using std::async abstracts thread creation while enabling futures to encapsulate potential results, thereby simplifying how multithreading can be effectively employed in C++ network applications.

Thread creation in C++ opens possibilities for richer application architecture and performance optimization. It enables leveraging multicore systems for parallel computations and responsiveness, crucial in crafting modern network software and services. As seen, std::thread and complementary constructs like lambdas, promises, and futures provide a robust framework for developing advanced multithreaded applications. Multithreading demands meticulous resource and synchronization management to harness its full potential, ensuring threads work collaboratively without conflicts or inefficiencies.

6.3   Thread Synchronization Techniques

Thread synchronization is a critical aspect of multithreaded programming where threads in a process need to access shared resources without conflicts. Synchronization ensures the correct sequencing of thread execution, avoiding race conditions, data corruption, and unpredicted behavior. In C++, several synchronization constructs provided by the Standard Library can be utilized, such as mutexes, locks,

159

condition variables, and others. Examining these constructs furnishes an understanding of their configurations, use cases, and impact on concurrent programming paradigms.

A race condition occurs when the timing or scheduling of thread execution affects the program outcomes. This issue is prevalent when multiple threads are allowed to write data concurrently without appropriate synchronization mechanisms. In C++, the mutex (std::mutex) is a primary tool to serialize access to shared resources, thereby eliminating race conditions.

```cpp
#include <iostream>
#include <thread>
#include <vector>

int sharedCounter = 0;

void incrementCounter() {
    for (int i = 0; i < 10000; ++i) {
        ++sharedCounter;
    }
}

int main() {
    std::vector<std::thread> threads;

    // Launch multiple threads that increment the counter
    for (int i = 0; i < 10; ++i) {
        threads.emplace_back(incrementCounter);
    }

    for (auto& t : threads) {
        t.join();
    }

    std::cout << "Final shared counter: " << sharedCounter << std::endl;
    return 0;
}
```

In this example, without synchronization, the value of sharedCounter is uncertain, demonstrating a classic race condition. To mitigate this, tools like mutexes can be implemented for thread synchronization.

- A mutex (short for mutual exclusion) is employed to protect the critical section of code, allowing only one thread to execute the guarded section at any time. In C++, std::mutex provides basic locking and unlocking functionality. A common practice is employing std::lock_guard which ensures mutexes are unlocked automatically when they go out of scope, enhancing exception safety.

```
#include <iostream>
#include <thread>
#include <mutex>
#include <vector>

int protectedCounter = 0;
std::mutex counterMutex;

void incrementProtectedCounter() {
    for (int i = 0; i < 10000; ++i) {
        std::lock_guard<std::mutex> lock(counterMutex);
        ++protectedCounter;
    }
}

int main() {
    std::vector<std::thread> threads;

    // Launch multiple threads that increment the protected counter
    for (int i = 0; i < 10; ++i) {
        threads.emplace_back(incrementProtectedCounter);
    }

    for (auto& t : threads) {
        t.join();
    }

    std::cout << "Final protected counter: " << protectedCounter << std::endl;
    return 0;
}
```

In this instance, utilizing std::lock_guard along with counterMutex secures each increment operation of protectedCounter, preventing race conditions. The lock_guard automatically manages the mutex state, locking it upon instantiation and unlocking it upon destruction. This reduces human error in explicitly managing lock and unlock states, simplifying complex multi-threaded logic.

- std::recursive_mutex allows a single thread to acquire the mutex multiple times without causing a deadlock, enabling reentrant locking necessary when a function calls itself recursively.

```
#include <iostream>
#include <thread>
#include <mutex>

std::recursive_mutex recursiveMutex;
```

```cpp
void recursiveFunction(int depth) {
    if (depth <= 0) return;

    std::lock_guard<std::recursive_mutex> lock(recursiveMutex);
    std::cout << "Recursion depth: " << depth << std::endl;

    recursiveFunction(depth - 1);
}
int main() {
    std::thread t(recursiveFunction, 5);
    t.join();

    return 0;
}
```

Here, the std::recursive_mutex facilitates safe recursion by allowing the same thread to lock the mutex multiple times, supporting programs with recursive critical sections.

- std::timed_mutex provides additional functionality, allowing threads to attempt locking with a timeout. This is particularly beneficial in systems where waiting indefinitely for a lock might be undesirable.

```cpp
#include <iostream>
#include <thread>
#include <mutex>
#include <chrono>

std::timed_mutex timedMutex;

void tryLockWithTimeout() {
    if (timedMutex.try_lock_for(std::chrono::seconds(1))) {
        std::this_thread::sleep_for(std::chrono::seconds(2));
        std::cout << "Locked and working on the resource." << std::endl;
        timedMutex.unlock();
    } else {
        std::cout << "Could not lock the mutex. Timeout reached." << std::endl;
    }
}

int main() {
    std::thread t1(tryLockWithTimeout);
    std::thread t2(tryLockWithTimeout);

    t1.join();
    t2.join();

    return 0;
}
```

162

Using std::timed_mutex in the example, each thread endeavors to acquire the lock within a specified duration. If unsuccessful, it proceeds without awaiting indefinitely, improving application responsiveness in certain scenarios.

- Condition variables enable threads to communicate and synchronize by signaling state changes across threads. They are especially useful when a thread needs to wait for another thread to perform an operation or reach a certain state before continuing execution.

```cpp
#include <iostream>
#include <thread>
#include <mutex>
#include <condition_variable>

std::mutex cvMutex;
std::condition_variable cv;
bool ready = false;

void waitForWork() {
    std::unique_lock<std::mutex> lock(cvMutex);
    cv.wait(lock, [] { return ready; });
    std::cout << "Worker thread is proceeding." << std::endl;
}

void setReady() {
    std::lock_guard<std::mutex> lock(cvMutex);
    ready = true;
    std::cout << "Main thread sets ready to true." << std::endl;
    cv.notify_one();
}

int main() {
    std::thread worker(waitForWork);
    std::thread producer(setReady);

    worker.join();
    producer.join();

    return 0;
}
```

In the example above, a thread waiting for ready to become true uses cv.wait() in conjunction with a std::unique_lock. Upon the setReady() function setting ready to true and notifying the condition variable, the waiting thread detects the state change and continues execution. This pattern promotes effective synchronization, ensuring thread-safe interactions around shared data.

- C++ offers concurrent data structures with built-in synchronization, like std::atomic, which manage variables shared among threads guaranteeing atomic operations. These wrappers eliminate the need for explicit locking when performing uncomplicated operations.

```
#include <iostream>
#include <thread>
#include <atomic>
#include <vector>

std::atomic<int> atomicCounter(0);

void incrementAtomicCounter() {
    for (int i = 0; i < 10000; ++i) {
        ++atomicCounter;
    }
}

int main() {
    std::vector<std::thread> threads;

    // Launch multiple threads that increment the atomic counter
    for (int i = 0; i < 10; ++i) {
        threads.emplace_back(incrementAtomicCounter);
    }

    for (auto& t : threads) {
        t.join();
    }

    std::cout << "Final atomic counter: " << atomicCounter.load() << std::endl;

    return 0;
}
```

The std::atomic variable atomicCounter efficiently handles concurrent thread increments without supplementary synchronization. Atomic variables offer operations like load and store, designed to facilitate synchronization of simple data types without external locking mechanisms.

While mutexes and locks are foundational to thread synchronization, these must be used judiciously to avoid deadlocks—a situation where two or more threads wait indefinitely for resources to be released. Circular wait conditions, hold and wait, and other deadlock elements should be eliminated applying deadlock prevention tactics such as lock ordering, resource allocation strategy revisions, and thread identification methods to break dependency cycles.

Thread synchronization in C++ aims to balance resource protection with performance efficiency, applying mutexes, locks, and atomic operations to allocate safe simultaneous data access. Condition variables further enable handling complex thread operations necessary in network applications and large-scale systems. Skilled application of these techniques allows developers to craft robust, high-performance multithreaded programs harnessing optimal system concurrency potential.

6.4 Shared Data and Resource Management

Shared data and resource management in multithreaded applications is crucial for maintaining consistency, ensuring performance, and preventing resource contention. When multiple threads access shared resources like memory, files, or devices concurrently, carefully structured strategies are needed to avoid data races, deadlocks, and performance bottlenecks. This section delves into techniques and best practices for managing shared data in C++, with a particular focus on locking mechanisms, protected access patterns, and resource-sharing strategies.

Mutexes are fundamental to protecting shared data in multithreaded programs. They prevent multiple threads from concurrently accessing critical sections of code where shared data might be modified. Though simple, mutexes enforce mutual exclusion, ensuring that once a thread has locked a resource, others can only access it after the initial thread releases the lock.

The appropriate use of mutexes involves understanding the balance between locking granularity and contention. Fine-grained locks limit the lock scope to the smallest data set possible, resulting in higher complexity but reduced waiting times. However, coarse-grained locks simplify code logic but may lead to increased competition among threads, potentially causing performance issues.

```
#include <iostream>
#include <thread>
#include <mutex>
#include <vector>
```

```
std::vector<int> sharedVector; // Shared data structure
std::mutex vectorMutex; // Mutex for protecting the vector

void addToVector(int value) {
    std::lock_guard<std::mutex> lock(vectorMutex); // Lock the mutex
    sharedVector.push_back(value);
    std::cout << "Added " << value << " to vector." << std::endl;
}

int main() {
    std::thread t1(addToVector, 1);
    std::thread t2(addToVector, 2);

    t1.join();
    t2.join();

    std::cout << "Vector size: " << sharedVector.size() << std::endl;

    return 0;
}
```

In the example, vectorMutex guarantees that only one thread modifies sharedVector at any given time. Employing std::lock_guard abstracts manual mutex handling, automatically unlocking it when the lock object goes out of scope, enhancing the exception safety and correctness.

Standard mutexes allow exclusive access, making them unsuitable for scenarios where reads outweigh writes. Reader-writer locks come into play when it is permissible for multiple threads to read shared data simultaneously, though exclusive access is essential for writing operations. std::shared_mutex, introduced in C++17, embodies this concept, enabling concurrent read access while locking writers.

```
#include <iostream>
#include <thread>
#include <shared_mutex>
#include <vector>

std::vector<int> sharedNumbers;
std::shared_mutex sharedMutex;

// Function to read data
void readData() {
    std::shared_lock<std::shared_mutex> lock(sharedMutex); // Acquire shared lock
    if (!sharedNumbers.empty()) {
        std::cout << "Latest number: " << sharedNumbers.back() << std::endl;
    }
}

// Function to write data
void writeData(int number) {
    std::lock_guard<std::shared_mutex> lock(sharedMutex); // Acquire unique lock
    sharedNumbers.push_back(number);
```

166

```cpp
    std::cout << "Number added: " << number << std::endl;
}

int main() {
    std::thread writer1(writeData, 10);
    std::thread reader1(readData);
    std::thread writer2(writeData, 20);
    std::thread reader2(readData);

    writer1.join();
    reader1.join();
    writer2.join();
    reader2.join();

    return 0;
}
```

The substitution of std::mutex with std::shared_mutex enhances performance by allowing multiple concurrent readers, using std::shared_-lock for reading operations and std::lock_guard for write operations. This dual-locking strategy suits scenarios with a high ratio of reads to writes, optimizing throughput and reducing data access delays.

For specific data types and operations, atomic objects, provided by std::atomic, ensure thread-safe concurrent modifications without requiring explicit locks. Atomic operations are lock-free at the hardware level, making them very efficient for frequently accessed variables.

```cpp
#include <iostream>
#include <thread>
#include <atomic>
#include <vector>

std::atomic<int> atomicCounter(0);

void incrementAtomicCounter() {
    for (int i = 0; i < 10000; ++i) {
        ++atomicCounter;
    }
}

int main() {
    std::vector<std::thread> threads;

    for (int i = 0; i < 10; ++i) {
        threads.emplace_back(incrementAtomicCounter);
    }

    for (auto& t : threads) {
        t.join();
    }

    std::cout << "Final atomic counter: " << atomicCounter << std::endl;
```

```
    return 0;
}
```

std::atomic guarantees that each increment operation is processed atomically, which is suitable for simple, concurrent modifications of primitive types like counters or flags. This eliminates the need for locking, providing rapid execution and preventing potential contention issues.

- Immutable Data Structures:

    - Immutable objects, whose state cannot be altered post-creation, are inherently thread-safe. In functional programming, using immutable structures can completely avoid synchronization overhead caused by state changes.

- Avoid Global Shared Data:

    - Reducing the scope and the lifetime of shared resources minimizes exposure to race conditions, encouraging more localized and manageable data sharing patterns.

- Resource Ownership:

    - Implement resource ownership concepts, as in RAII (Resource Acquisition Is Initialization), where resource management responsibilities, such as locking, are scoped within object lifetimes. Smart pointers, for instance, automatically handle the lifecycle management of dynamically allocated resources.

- Thread-safe Libraries and Containers:

    - Utilize library-provided concurrent collections and tools to reduce duplication of complex concurrency logic. Libraries may offer containers with intrinsic support for concurrent actions, decreasing the developer's synchronization burden.

- Measure and Profile Concurrency:

    - Use profiling tools to identify contention hotspots, assess lock contention, and determine synchronization-induced delays. Optimizing these points contributes to enhanced application responsiveness.

- Design Patterns for Concurrency:

  - Patterns like the producer-consumer model, fork-join, or agent-based parallelism help structure multithreaded applications efficiently. For instance, using lock-free queues within a producer-consumer model effectively decouples data production and consumption phases, reducing wait times and boosting throughput.

- Fine-grained Locking:

  - Where applicable, prefer fine-grained locking or even lock-free strategies over coarse locks to limit thread waiting schemes amid accessing broader resources.

Complex shared objects, such as an interconnected data graph or hierarchical resources, require advanced synchronization strategies. Database transactions or logical isolation through transactions can ensure that operations on shared objects maintain integrity without ad hoc locking policies.

Consider cases like resource pools (e.g., thread pools, connection pools). Standard libraries may not suffice, prompting the need for custom synchronization code adopting specific application semantics and constraints. Often, such scenarios necessitate implementing context-specific locking policies ensuring thread safety and minimal resource wait times while considering system's performance characteristics and scalability expectations.

Multi-threaded programming in C++ offers significant computational advantages but also demands sophisticated data handling to maximize these benefits. Shared data and resource management are central to the reliable and performant operation of multi-threaded C++ programs. Employing mutexes, locks, and condition variables assiduously can prevent data races, safeguard resource integrity, and assure the correctness of concurrent programs. Furthermore, leveraging reader-writer locks, atomic operations, immutable structures, thread-safe libraries, and comprehensive design templates enrich the robustness of

C++ multi-threading, contributing to the construction of stable, high-performance network applications.

6.5 Multithreading and Network I/O

Multithreading plays a crucial role in improving the efficiency and responsiveness of network I/O operations. Network applications often require the handling of numerous I/O tasks concurrently, such as processing multiple client requests, managing data streams, and ensuring timely response handling. Leveraging threading alongside network I/O allows applications to utilize system resources intelligently, improving throughput, reducing latency, and enhancing overall performance.

Modern network applications frequently interact with multiple clients or services. A web server, for example, needs to manage numerous simultaneous connections, ensuring that requests are attended to promptly without causing undue delays due to blocked operations. The straightforward sequential handling approach cannot fulfill such requirements efficiently, particularly under heavy load, but multithreading offers viable strategies to parallelize operations and optimize processing.

A typical design pattern in networking is the concurrency model, where multiple threads handle separate connections or tasks. Each thread operates independently without blocking the others, facilitating better CPU utilization and lessening response wait times. Here's an illustration:

```
#include <iostream>
#include <thread>
#include <boost/asio.hpp>

using boost::asio::ip::tcp;

void handleClient(tcp::socket socket) {
    try {
        std::cout << "Connected to client." << std::endl;
        for (;;) {
            char data[512];
            boost::system::error_code error;
            size_t length = socket.read_some(boost::asio::buffer(data), error);

            if (error == boost::asio::error::eof) {
```

```
            break; // Connection closed
        } else if (error) {
            throw boost::system::system_error(error); // Some other error occurred
        }

        boost::asio::write(socket, boost::asio::buffer(data, length));
    }
} catch (std::exception& e) {
    std::cerr << "Exception in client handler: " << e.what() << std::endl;
}
}

int main() {
    try {
        boost::asio::io_context ioContext;
        tcp::acceptor acceptor(ioContext, tcp::endpoint(tcp::v4(), 1234));

        for (;;) {
            tcp::socket socket(ioContext);
            acceptor.accept(socket);

            // Create a thread for each client connection
            std::thread(handleClient, std::move(socket)).detach();
        }
    } catch (std::exception& e) {
        std::cerr << "Exception: " << e.what() << std::endl;
    }

    return 0;
}
```

In this server, each client connection is managed in a separate thread, allowing the server to concurrently handle multiple clients without blocking. Using std::thread::detach() permits each thread to execute independently, and upon completion, resources are automatically reclaimed without explicit joining.

Another approach to improving network application performance is using asynchronous I/O operations alongside threads. While typical multithreaded servers allocate a dedicated thread per client, asynchronous programming enables non-blocking operations, minimizing time spent waiting for I/O completion by allowing other computations or networking tasks to proceed.

Boost.Asio, a library for network and low-level I/O programming in C++, provides extensive support for asynchronous operations. Using asynchronous I/O in tandem with worker threads enables the handling of numerous simultaneous requests without close coupling between threads and client connections.

```cpp
#include <iostream>
#include <memory>
#include <thread>
#include <boost/asio.hpp>

using boost::asio::ip::tcp;

class Session : public std::enable_shared_from_this<Session> {
public:
    explicit Session(tcp::socket socket) : m_socket(std::move(socket)) {}

    void start() {
        doRead();
    }

private:
    void doRead() {
        auto self(shared_from_this());
        m_socket.async_read_some(boost::asio::buffer(m_data, maxLength),
            [this, self](boost::system::error_code ec, std::size_t length) {
                if (!ec) doWrite(length);
            });
    }

    void doWrite(std::size_t length) {
        auto self(shared_from_this());
        boost::asio::async_write(m_socket, boost::asio::buffer(m_data, length),
            [this, self](boost::system::error_code ec, std::size_t /*length*/) {
                if (!ec) doRead();
            });
    }

    tcp::socket m_socket;
    enum { maxLength = 1024 };
    char m_data[maxLength];
};

class Server {
public:
    Server(boost::asio::io_context& io_context, short port)
        : m_acceptor(io_context, tcp::endpoint(tcp::v4(), port)) {
        doAccept();
    }

private:
    void doAccept() {
        m_acceptor.async_accept(
            [this](boost::system::error_code ec, tcp::socket socket) {
                if (!ec) std::make_shared<Session>(std::move(socket))->start();
                doAccept();
            });
    }

    tcp::acceptor m_acceptor;
};

int main() {
    try {
```

172

```cpp
    boost::asio::io_context ioContext;

    Server server(ioContext, 1234);

    std::vector<std::thread> threads;
    for (unsigned i = 0; i < std::thread::hardware_concurrency(); ++i) {
        threads.emplace_back([&ioContext]() { ioContext.run(); });
    }

    for (auto& thread : threads) {
        thread.join();
    }
} catch (std::exception& e) {
    std::cerr << "Exception: " << e.what() << std::endl;
}

    return 0;
}
```

The server implemented with Boost.Asio demonstrates the use of asynchronous operations. The Session class employs asynchronous read and write operations to handle client requests without blocking threads, supported by a thread pool associated with the io_context object. This separation of concerns allows io_context.run() to handle I/O tasks while threads remain available to manage resultant operations effectively.

Thread pools are pivotal when repetitive tasks are performed frequently and unpredictably, like managing network connections. A thread pool maintains a group of pre-allocated threads ready to perform tasks, minimizing the overhead associated with creating and destroying threads continually. Using a thread pool is especially advantageous in network applications involving frequent connection requests and long-running network tasks.

```cpp
#include <iostream>
#include <thread>
#include <vector>
#include <boost/asio.hpp>
#include <boost/asio/thread_pool.hpp>

using boost::asio::ip::tcp;

void session(tcp::socket socket) {
    // Same handleClient functionality defined previously
}

int main() {
    try {
        boost::asio::io_context ioContext;
        tcp::acceptor acceptor(ioContext, tcp::endpoint(tcp::v4(), 1234));
```

```
boost::asio::thread_pool pool(std::thread::hardware_concurrency());

while (true) {
    tcp::socket socket(ioContext);
    acceptor.accept(socket);

    // Assign each client connection to a thread in the pool
    boost::asio::post(pool, [sock = std::move(socket)]() mutable {
        session(std::move(sock));
    });
}

pool.join();
} catch (std::exception& e) {
    std::cerr << "Exception: " << e.what() << std::endl;
}

return 0;
}
```

The introduction of boost::asio::thread_pool facilitates connection handling in the thread pool setup. With the post() function, tasks are efficiently distributed among the available threads in the pool, streamlining network requests and optimizing resource consumption.

The use of multithreading in network I/O presents challenges such as managing concurrent access to shared data, debugging asynchronous operations, and configuring optimal concurrency levels. Addressing these requires a nuanced understanding of system architecture, threading overhead, and network load characteristics.

- **Data Races and Synchronization:** Network I/O inevitably involves shared resources, making data race conditions a significant concern. Implementing appropriate synchronization mechanisms, like mutexes and atomic operations, ensures data consistency.

- **Error Handling and Thread Safety:** Asynchronous operations require meticulous error handling strategies. Unexpected network failures or connection drops demand robust recovery and retry mechanisms to maintain service reliability.

- **Optimizing Throughput and Latency:** Balance between latency and throughput is critical. Minimizing context switching and ensuring efficient request handling through the judicious use

174

of thread pooling and asynchronous I/O contribute to scalable network applications.

- **Load Balancing and Resource Allocation:** Configuring thread pools considering the system's capabilities and load patterns optimizes resource allocation, preventing both under- and over-utilization of server resources, ensuring optimal performance.

- **Monitoring and Profiling:** Continuous monitoring of network applications is essential for maintaining efficient operations. Profiling tools help identify bottlenecks, assess load distribution, and diagnose issues in the multithreading model.

Implementing multithreading and concurrent I/O operations significantly enhances network application efficiency. By structuring such applications with asynchronous I/O and thread pool strategies, developers can navigate complex scenarios while achieving higher throughput and responsiveness. Managing concurrent access and optimizing thread allocation are foundational to addressing the challenges that arise within these architectures.

6.6 Challenges in Multithreaded Network Applications

The development of multithreaded network applications holds significant potential for enhancing performance and scalability, yet it is not without its share of challenges. Addressing these challenges is crucial for designing resilient, efficient, and reliable software solutions. Understanding the nuances of concurrency, synchronization, resource management, and error handling is vital for overcoming the inherent complexities in such applications.

Concurrency and Race Conditions

Concurrency introduces potential issues where multiple threads operate on shared resources concurrently. Race conditions manifest when thread executions interleave unpredictably, leading to erratic data states and bugs that are complicated to trace and reproduce.

```cpp
#include <iostream>
#include <thread>
#include <vector>

int sharedResource = 0;

void incrementResource() {
    for (int i = 0; i < 1000; ++i) {
        ++sharedResource; // Potential race condition
    }
}

int main() {
    std::vector<std::thread> threads;

    for (int i = 0; i < 10; ++i) {
        threads.emplace_back(incrementResource);
    }

    for (auto& t : threads) {
        t.join();
    }

    std::cout << "Final shared resource value: " << sharedResource << std::endl;
    return 0;
}
```

The above code demonstrates a typical race condition scenario where increment operations might not execute atomically, leading to undefined final values of sharedResource. Solutions involve the use of mutexes or atomic variables to guard shared data.

```cpp
#include <iostream>
#include <thread>
#include <mutex>
#include <vector>

int safeResource = 0;
std::mutex resourceMutex;

void safeIncrement() {
    for (int i = 0; i < 1000; ++i) {
        std::lock_guard<std::mutex> lock(resourceMutex);
        ++safeResource;
    }
}

int main() {
    std::vector<std::thread> threads;

    for (int i = 0; i < 10; ++i) {
        threads.emplace_back(safeIncrement);
    }

    for (auto& t : threads) {
```

```
        t.join();
    }

    std::cout << "Final safe resource value: " << safeResource << std::endl;
    return 0;
}
```

By introducing a mutex, we ensure serialized access to the safeResource variable, eliminating the race condition and guaranteeing consistent results.

Deadlocks and Resource Management

Deadlocks, a persistent challenge in multithreaded applications, occur when two or more threads are waiting indefinitely for resources held by others, causing the application to stall. Avoiding deadlocks typically involves designing a strategy that ensures all locks are acquired atomically or applying lock ordering to minimize cyclical dependencies among resources.

```
#include <iostream>
#include <thread>
#include <mutex>

std::mutex mutex1, mutex2;

void taskA() {
    std::lock_guard<std::mutex> lock1(mutex1);
    std::this_thread::sleep_for(std::chrono::milliseconds(100)); // Simulate work
    std::lock_guard<std::mutex> lock2(mutex2);
    std::cout << "Task A executed." << std::endl;
}

void taskB() {
    std::lock_guard<std::mutex> lock2(mutex2);
    std::this_thread::sleep_for(std::chrono::milliseconds(100)); // Simulate work
    std::lock_guard<std::mutex> lock1(mutex1);
    std::cout << "Task B executed." << std::endl;
}

int main() {
    std::thread threadA(taskA);
    std::thread threadB(taskB);

    threadA.join();
    threadB.join();

    return 0;
}
```

The illustration above results in a deadlock, with taskA and taskB each holding a mutex and waiting for the other. To mitigate this, utiliz-

177

ing std::scoped_lock for mutual exclusion can prevent accidental dead-locks by acquiring multiple locks simultaneously.

```cpp
#include <iostream>
#include <thread>
#include <mutex>

std::mutex mutex1, mutex2;

void safeTaskA() {
    std::scoped_lock lock(mutex1, mutex2);
    std::cout << "Safe Task A executed." << std::endl;
}

void safeTaskB() {
    std::scoped_lock lock(mutex1, mutex2);
    std::cout << "Safe Task B executed." << std::endl;
}

int main() {
    std::thread threadA(safeTaskA);
    std::thread threadB(safeTaskB);

    threadA.join();
    threadB.join();

    return 0;
}
```

Using a scoped_lock ensures atomic locking, preventing cyclical lock waits and effectively averting deadlocks.

Handling Networking Errors and Exceptions

Network applications are susceptible to myriad run-time errors and exceptions, ranging from connection timeouts to broken pipes and in-complete data reads. Multithreading complicates these scenarios by dispersing error contexts across numerous execution flows, making di-agnostics and recovery demanding.

Effective strategies for managing networking errors involve:

- Comprehensive exception handling within threads, employing try-catch blocks to gracefully manage and log exceptions without compromising system integrity.

- Robust state management for connection sessions ensuring failed states are detectible and gracefully recoverable, often looped back into reconnection routines.

178

- Asynchronously retried operations for transient failures, leveraging exponential backoff techniques to prevent resource overuse.

```cpp
#include <iostream>
#include <thread>
#include <boost/asio.hpp>

using boost::asio::ip::tcp;

void clientSession(tcp::socket socket) {
    try {
        for (;;) {
            char data[512];
            boost::system::error_code error;
            size_t length = socket.read_some(boost::asio::buffer(data), error);

            if (error) {
                if (error == boost::asio::error::eof) {
                    std::cout << "Connection closed by client." << std::endl;
                } else {
                    std::cerr << "Read error: " << error.message() << std::endl;
                }
                break;
            }

            boost::asio::write(socket, boost::asio::buffer(data, length));
        }
    } catch (const std::exception& e) {
        std::cerr << "Session exception: " << e.what() << std::endl;
    }
}

int main() {
    try {
        boost::asio::io_context ioContext;
        tcp::acceptor acceptor(ioContext, tcp::endpoint(tcp::v4(), 1234));

        while (true) {
            tcp::socket socket(ioContext);
            acceptor.accept(socket);
            std::thread(clientSession, std::move(socket)).detach();
        }
    } catch (const std::exception& e) {
        std::cerr << "Server exception: " << e.what() << std::endl;
    }

    return 0;
}
```

The example demonstrates catching and handling networking exceptions inside the clientSession, ensuring individually restored or terminated sessions without affecting overall server operation.

Synchronization and Performance Trade-offs

179

Implementing synchronization mechanisms improves data safety but can weigh down application performance. Effects such as contention induced delays arise when extensive locking strategies prevent parallel execution. Therefore, it is essential to design concurrency models that maintain a balance between thread coordination and system throughput.

- **Fine-grained vs. Coarse-grained Locking:**

    - Obtain locks only on essential data segments to curtail contention and increase throughput.

    - Measure system performance with different locking granularities to optimize resource access models empirically.

- **Lock-free Strategies:**

    - Explore atomic operations and lock-free data structures for read-heavy scenarios or critically timed operations.

    - Consider non-blocking algorithms and eventual consistency models in distributed systems.

- **Maximizing Parallel Scalability:**

    - Utilize parallel processing capabilities offered by multicore processors.

    - Avoid thread oversubscription and manage task assignments judiciously to reduce choke points and unwarranted parallelism overhead.

Toolkit and Framework Considerations

Numerous libraries and frameworks are available to facilitate network multithreading, each offering unique abstractions beneficial to certain applications. Boost.Asio, for instance, delivers asynchronous and I/O multiplexing functionality. Similarly, Intel's Threading Building Blocks (TBB) provides algorithms and flow graphs for advanced parallel programming, emphasizing modularity and scalability.

Choosing the proper tools involves evaluating:

- Integration and compatibility with your application technology stack.

- Abstraction level required compared to raw socket programming.

- Community support, documentation, and ongoing maintenance ensuring long-term viability of tool adoption.

Security Considerations

Concurrent handling of network operations necessitates robust security practices:

- Implement secure communication protocols like TLS to protect data integrity and confidentiality.

- Leverage proper synchronization to avoid time-of-check to time-of-use (TOCTOU) vulnerabilities amidst concurrent processes.

- Monitor access controls meticulously to prevent unauthorized access across multithreaded workflows.

Multithreaded network applications promise enhanced performance capabilities; however, effectively developing and managing them is contingent upon addressing fundamental hurdles surrounding concurrency, resource coordination, error handling, synchronization efficiency, and ensuring extraordinary system and process security. Emphasizing these factors in architecture and implementation results in reliable, high-performing, and secure network services.

Chapter 7

Handling Data Streams and Serialization

This chapter focuses on the manipulation of data streams and the process of serialization in network communication. It explains the role of data streams in transmitting information across networks and the conversion of complex data structures into serial formats for efficient transmission. The chapter presents techniques for handling streams in C++, differentiates between binary and textual data representations, and discusses the use of custom serialization protocols like Protocol Buffers. Additionally, it addresses the importance of maintaining data integrity during transmission, providing techniques to ensure accurate and secure data handling.

7.1 Basics of Data Streams

Data streams are integral to network communication, providing a mechanism for transferring data between devices in a continuous and efficient manner. They are abstract representations of data in transmission, distinguished by their ability to facilitate real-time data exchange. Data streams are prevalent across various applications, from streaming media to IoT devices, and their understanding is crucial for developing networked systems.

A data stream is generally defined as a sequence of digitally encoded signals used to represent information in transit. These streams can be categorized into three main types: unidirectional, bidirectional, and multi-directional. Unidirectional streams allow data to flow in a single direction, typically from sender to receiver, as seen in streaming services like video or audio broadcasting. Bidirectional streams, on the other hand, facilitate two-way communication, enabling data to flow both to and from the sender and receiver; a common example of this is chat applications. Multi-directional streams are a more complex form, where multiple devices can communicate simultaneously, often utilized in conferencing systems where numerous participants can send and receive data concurrently.

The role of data streams in network communication is underscored by their ability to carry large volumes of data efficiently and with minimal latency. This makes them particularly advantageous for applications requiring immediate or continuous data transfer. Streams maintain a constant flow of data, reducing the need for batch processing and thus minimizing delays typically associated with waiting for data consolidation before transmission.

A fundamental concept in working with data streams is their representation through either byte streams or character streams, translating to binary or textual forms respectively. Byte streams handle raw binary data, ensuring a more compact and bandwidth-efficient means of transmission. This is particularly useful in environments constrained by bandwidth, or when transferring non-textual data like images, audio, and video, where using a binary representation significantly reduces the volume of data relative to a character representation. Character streams translate data into a readable text format, representing and transmitting characters using human-readable encoding schemes such as UTF-8 or ASCII. The choice between byte and character streams depends heavily on the nature of the data being transferred and the requirements of the application consuming the stream.

In programming, the implementation and management of data streams often involve utilizing specific libraries and APIs that abstract

184

the intricacies of stream management. Within the C++ programming environment, the Standard Library provides a suite of tools for handling streams through classes such as ifstream, ofstream, and iomanip. These classes facilitate file streaming, allowing for reading from and writing to files using familiar stream syntax similar to console input and output operations.

```cpp
#include <iostream>
#include <fstream>
#include <string>

int main() {
    // Creating an output file stream (write)
    std::ofstream outFile("data.txt");
    if (outFile.is_open()) {
        outFile << "This is an example of file streaming in C++." << std::endl;
        outFile.close();
    }

    // Creating an input file stream (read)
    std::ifstream inFile("data.txt");
    if (inFile.is_open()) {
        std::string line;
        while (getline(inFile, line)) {
            std::cout << line << std::endl;
        }
        inFile.close();
    }
    return 0;
}
```

The above example demonstrates basic file streaming in C++. It shows how to utilize ofstream to write to a file and ifstream to read from it, illustrating the principles of data stream manipulation in programming.

In network communication, streams are commonly managed over protocols such as TCP/IP (Transmission Control Protocol/Internet Protocol) or UDP (User Datagram Protocol). TCP/IP is known for providing reliable, ordered, and error-checked delivery of bytes between applications, capitalizing on its stream-oriented nature to ensure data integrity over the network. In contrast, UDP is a simpler, connectionless protocol that allows for faster, albeit potentially less reliable, data transfer. The choice between TCP and UDP affects the design and implementation of data streams, relating to the level of reliability and speed required by the application.

The design of data streams also involves consideration of their scale-out potential, particularly in distributed systems where data

185

is generated and processed by numerous nodes. These systems require efficient data routing and balancing techniques to maximize resource usage and maintain throughput. Tools and frameworks such as Apache Kafka and Apache Flink are popular in handling large-scale data streams. They provide robust APIs for managing stream elasticity, data partitioning, and fault tolerance, thus enabling scalable and resilient stream processing solutions.

```
from kafka import KafkaProducer

producer = KafkaProducer(bootstrap_servers='localhost:9092')

# Sending data to a Kafka topic
producer.send('quickstart-events', b'value=42')
```

The previous code snippet offers a straightforward overview of utilizing Apache Kafka's Python API to produce data streams. Kafka's design supports both the scalability and fault tolerance required for high-throughput stream applications by permitting efficient partitioning and replication of data across nodes.

Synchronous and asynchronous streaming operations provide a nuanced perspective on handling data streams. Synchronous streaming ensures that data is processed in a sequential manner, preserving the order of operations and guaranteeing consistency. Although this method is simpler and more predictable, it often sacrifices performance due to its blocking nature. Asynchronous streaming, in contrast, allows for non-blocking operations where data can be processed out of order or on separate threads. This approach boosts the efficiency of data streaming applications by allowing various tasks to proceed concurrently, reducing latency and improving throughput.

While designing software that handles data streams, it is essential to consider aspects like latency, throughput, and fault tolerance. Latency signifies the time delay experienced during data transfer, while throughput measures data volume processed over a period. Reducing latency and maximizing throughput are critical for applications requiring real-time data processing. Fault tolerance involves implementing strategies to ensure data integrity during power failures or network disruptions; this may include redundancy and checkpoints to recover or replay data streams.

Security is another critical element in the management of data streams,

186

particularly as they traverse public networks susceptible to interception and tampering. Ensuring the confidentiality, integrity, and authenticity of stream data requires encryption protocols, such as TLS (Transport Layer Security), alongside secure cryptographic methods like AES (Advanced Encryption Standard) for encrypting data before transmission. Encryption provides a mechanism for concealment and protection against unauthorized access, while digital signatures verify the identity of the data source. Additionally, hash functions assist in maintaining data integrity over the network by allowing recipients to confirm that the data has arrived unaltered.

```cpp
#include <openssl/ssl.h>
#include <openssl/err.h>
#include <iostream>

void InitializeSSL() {
    SSL_load_error_strings();
    OpenSSL_add_ssl_algorithms();
}

int main() {
    InitializeSSL();

    SSL_CTX *ctx = SSL_CTX_new(SSLv23_client_method());
    if (!ctx) {
        std::cerr << "SSL Context initialization failed." << std::endl;
        return -1;
    }

    // SSL connection and data streaming code goes here

    SSL_CTX_free(ctx);
    return 0;
}
```

The example illustrates initializing an SSL context using OpenSSL in C++, laying groundwork for encrypted data streams. Using secure libraries like OpenSSL in applications mitigating security threats is an essential step in protecting data during streaming.

Data streams, in their complexity, offer significant advantages in terms of efficient data communication, with applications spanning media broadcasting, real-time communication systems, and sensor network data transfer. Understanding the foundational aspects, methodologies for implementation, and potential challenges associated with data streams equips developers with the knowledge required to harness their power effectively.

7.2 Serialization and Deserialization

Serialization and deserialization are pivotal processes in data handling, allowing for the transformation of complex data structures into a format suitable for storage or transmission over a network, and vice versa. These processes facilitate data interoperability between different systems and programming languages by providing a standardized method to encode and decode data structures.

Serialization is the process of converting a data structure or object state into a format that can be stored in a file or memory buffer, or transmitted over a network connection link to be reconstructed later in the same or another computing environment. The resulting serialized format is typically a byte stream, which efficiently represents the essential information needed to reconstruct the original data. This process effectively flattens objects, potentially reducing the data size and preparing it for checkpointing, archiving, or inter-process communication.

Deserialization, conversely, is the process of converting a byte stream back into a copy of the original object or data structure. This requires a well-defined format that encodes type information and metadata alongside the serialized data to enable accurate reconstruction. The word 'serialization' encompasses a group of formatting strategies, varying from simple textual representations like JSON (JavaScript Object Notation) and XML (Extensible Markup Language) to complex binary formats such as Protobuf (Protocol Buffers) and Apache Avro. Selecting an appropriate serialization format is often contingent on the application requirements regarding data compactness, speed, and interoperability.

In different programming environments, serialization tools and frameworks encapsulate the intricacies of this process, allowing developers to focus on specifying which pieces of an object's state should be serialized or deserialized. In C++, the Standard Library does not provide built-in serialization support, unlike Java or C#, because C++ values flexibility and custom implementation over strict standardizations. However, C++ offers serialization through various libraries such as Boost.Serialization, Cereal, and Protobuf.

```cpp
#include <boost/archive/text_oarchive.hpp>
#include <boost/archive/text_iarchive.hpp>
#include <sstream>
```

```
class Sample {
public:
    int data;
    Sample() {}
    Sample(int d) : data(d) {}

private:
    friend class boost::serialization::access;
    template<class Archive>
    void serialize(Archive & ar, const unsigned int version) {
        ar & data;
    }
};

int main() {
    // Serializing object
    Sample s1(10);
    std::ostringstream oss;
    boost::archive::text_oarchive oa(oss);
    oa << s1;

    // Deserializing object
    Sample s2;
    std::istringstream iss(oss.str());
    boost::archive::text_iarchive ia(iss);
    ia >> s2;

    return 0;
}
```

The provided example demonstrates object serialization and deserialization using the Boost.Serialization library in C++. Serialization is carried out via an archive class, which transforms the object into a structured format. This serialized data can then be stored, transmitted, or used for later reconstruction. Deserializing creates a new instance of the object from the serialized data stream, thereby reconstructing the original state.

The architecture of serialization mechanisms typically involves two components: schema and encoding. A schema provides a blueprint that includes information about the data types and structure of the serialized objects, ensuring that deserialization is accurate and type-safe. Encoding, on the other hand, defines the format used to represent this information. In formats like XML and JSON, text-based encoding provides self-describing messages but can be verbose and not as storage-efficient. Binary formats such as Protocol Buffers condense this information into a more compact, byte-oriented format, lending themselves to applications where low overhead is critical.

Choosing between textual or binary serialization formats depends on various factors, such as human readability, size efficiency, speed of encoding/decoding, and compatibility with existing infrastructure. Text-based formats like JSON are beneficial when human intervention or inspection of data representation is necessary, offering ease of debugging and comprehension. In contrast, binary formats such as Protocol Buffers and Apache Avro are optimized for serialized data's size and parsing speed, making them suitable for performance-critical applications where reducing bandwidth consumption is essential.

```
{
  "name": "John Doe",
  "age": 30,
  "isStudent": false
}
```

The above JSON example illustrates a simple data structure represented in a human-readable format. JSON serialization is widely used in web communication due to its simplicity and ease of parsing across various programming languages.

```
syntax = "proto3";

message Person {
  string name = 1;
  int32 age = 2;
  bool isStudent = 3;
}
```

Using Protocol Buffers for the same data structure yields a compact binary representation, fundamentally enhancing the performance efficiency of serialization and deserialization, especially when scaling to large datasets or transmitting over limited bandwidth.

During serialization, one must acknowledge common pitfalls, such as handling circular references and distinguishing between shared and unique object instances. Failure to address these issues might result in data corruption or inefficient serialized output. Some serialization frameworks handle object identity and referential integrity automatically, while others might require explicit annotation or intervention by the developer.

Security considerations related to serialization emerge when deserialized data is not properly validated, leading to vulnerabilities such as code injection and return-oriented programming (ROP) attacks.

Therefore, it is paramount to ensure that deserialized data comes from a trusted source and incorporates adequate validation checks before it influences application state or behavior.

Object evolution and schema migration are critical topics when dealing with serialized data over long periods, especially in environments where binary compatibility with older-version data is essential. An advantage of schema-based serialization, such as Protocol Buffers and Apache Avro, is their robust support for versioning and backward compatibility—allowing schemas to evolve over time while maintaining compatibility with older serialized data. This accommodates fields that are added, deprecated, or extended without impacting the existing system infrastructure, thus sustaining the long-term integrity and usability of serialized data.

In distributed computing, serialization's role extends to enabling Remote Procedure Call (RPC) frameworks, deepening the interaction between disparate systems or languages. RPC systems, such as Apache Thrift and gRPC (which uses Protocol Buffers), rely heavily on efficient serialization mechanisms to serialize procedure calls and arguments, ensuring seamless and efficient methods communications across networks.

Serialization and deserialization provide the foundation for data interchange formats that are pivotal to the interactions of distributed and networked systems. Understanding and implementing these processes, while considering the diverse factors outlined, ensures effective communication and integration across different systems, helping facilitate the modern architecture of web services, cloud computing, and emerging technologies.

7.3 Techniques for Stream Handling in C++

C++ provides comprehensive support for stream handling through its rich Standard Library, designed specifically to facilitate input and output operations in diverse contexts. Stream handling is essential for reading from and writing to various sources, such as files, memory, and networks, empowering developers to manipulate data fluidly in applications.

At the core of C++ stream handling are the I/O stream classes, which encompass a hierarchy of classes enabling typed and type-safe input and output. These classes, such as iostream, ifstream, ofstream, and sstream, manage data streams using operator overloading, stream states, and exceptions, allowing for elegant and efficient I/O operations. Integrating these classes with the architecture of applications improves the manageability of data flows, optimizing processing speed and performance.

The fundamental concept of C++ stream handling is encapsulated within the iostream library, which provides a universal interface for data input and output across various devices. The iostream header comprises various basic stream classes, or base classes, which include istream for input streams and ostream for output streams. These classes are specifically designed to handle any generic type of data via operator overloading of the » and « operators, facilitating type-specific stream handling.

```
#include <iostream>
#include <string>

int main() {
    std::string inputString;
    std::cout << "Enter a string: ";
    std::getline(std::cin, inputString);

    std::cout << "You entered: " << inputString << std::endl;
    return 0;
}
```

The example demonstrates simple console I/O using the iostream library. Here, std::cin and std::cout are used to read from and write to the standard input and output streams, respectively. The getline function handles space-delimited input, emphasizing the flexibility in utilizing the istream class for varied input scenarios.

In C++, file handling is achieved through the fstream library, which provides ifstream and ofstream classes, subclassing istream and ostream, respectively. These classes facilitate file reading and writing in a manner consistent with console input and output, simplifying the transition between managing different data flows. File streams instantiate by passing the file name and mode flags to their constructors, specifying how the file is accessed.

```
#include <fstream>
#include <iostream>
#include <string>

int main() {
    std::ofstream outFile("example.txt");
    if (outFile.is_open()) {
        outFile << "C++ stream handling example." << std::endl;
        outFile.close();
    }

    std::ifstream inFile("example.txt");
    if (inFile.is_open()) {
        std::string line;
        while (std::getline(inFile, line)) {
            std::cout << line << std::endl;
        }
        inFile.close();
    }
    return 0;
}
```

The above code exemplifies basic file handling in C++, illustrating both writing and reading tasks using file streams. File state is managed using member functions such as is_open() to verify successful file operations.

A cornerstone of C++ stream handling is the use of stream manipulators to refine data presentation and behavior. Manipulators alter stream characteristics to dictate formatting—a valuable aspect when output results must meet specific criteria, such as in business applications that require currency formatting or precision alignment.

```
#include <iostream>
#include <iomanip>

int main() {
    double value = 1234.56789;

    std::cout << "Original value: " << value << std::endl;
    std::cout << "Fixed-point notation: " << std::fixed << value << std::endl;
    std::cout << "Scientific notation: " << std::scientific << value << std::endl;
    std::cout << "Hexadecimal representation: " << std::hexfloat << value << std::endl;
    std::cout << "Precision set to 2: " << std::setprecision(2) << value << std::endl;
    return 0;
}
```

This code snippet showcases stream manipulators, such as std::fixed, std::scientific, and std::setprecision, altering numerical format and precision. These tailored outputs are crucial for ensuring consistent presentation across varied data forms.

Stream handling in C++ is not statically bound, thus allowing for dynamic reconfiguration and simultaneous management of multiple streams. This enables developers to redirect input and output on-the-fly, useful in scenarios where application behavior is dependent on context, such as developing a logging system that shifts between console and file outputs under specific conditions.

Robust treatment of errors and state monitoring is crucial in stream handling, where abstractions around stream states such as good(), eof(), fail(), and bad() provide insights into stream health, empowering developers to preemptively address and correct issues.

```cpp
#include <fstream>
#include <iostream>
#include <string>

int main() {
    std::ifstream file("nonexistent.txt");
    if (!file) {
        std::cerr << "Error opening file!" << std::endl;
        return 1;
    }

    std::string content;
    while (file >> content) {
        std::cout << content << std::endl;
    }

    if (file.eof()) {
        std::cout << "Reached end of file." << std::endl;
    } else if (file.fail()) {
        std::cerr << "Reading error detected." << std::endl;
    }

    file.close();
    return 0;
}
```

This example outlines error handling and state monitoring in stream operations. It highlights the importance of checking stream states using conditionals on functions like eof() and fail() to navigate potential issues gracefully.

More advanced techniques in C++ involve utilizing stringstream, part of the sstream library, which acts as a flexible mechanism for parsing and generating formatted data strings. stringstream provides an in-memory string buffer, affording developers the ability to manipulate strings with stream interfaces instead of relying on low-level string operations.

```
#include <sstream>
#include <iostream>
#include <string>

int main() {
    std::string data = "123 456 789";
    std::stringstream ss(data);

    int a, b, c;
    ss >> a >> b >> c;
    std::cout << a << ", " << b << ", " << c << std::endl;

    std::stringstream out;
    out << "A:" << a << " B:" << b << " C:" << c;
    std::cout << out.str() << std::endl;

    return 0;
}
```

This snippet uses stringstream for both input and output operations, demonstrating how data can be flexibly parsed and formatted without altering the original source string—showcasing the practicality of leveraging stream-like interfaces in buffer management.

By thoroughly integrating and utilizing these C++ stream handling techniques, developers empower themselves to build highly adaptable, efficient applications capable of handling diverse data flows and sources. C++ stream handling not only ensures smooth data operations but also enhances error management, data parsing, and stream manipulation, creating an optimized platform for modern software design.

7.4 Binary and Textual Data Representation

Data representation stands as a fundamental aspect in computing, defining how information is structured, stored, and transmitted. Binary and textual data representation constitute two primary methodologies for encoding information, each offering distinct advantages and trade-offs in terms of efficiency, readability, and interoperability.

Binary data representation involves encoding information in a compact, efficient binary format, leveraging sequences of bytes to represent data structures and values. This format provides a highly efficient mechanism for storing and transmitting data, as it minimizes the footprint of the encoded information. Binary formats are particularly advantageous in network communication and storage, where optimally utilizing bandwidth and disk space is vital. Encoding data in binary form reduces redundancy and overhead, enabling faster parsing and processing.

Conversely, textual data representation involves encoding information in a human-readable format, typically using characters to describe data structures and contents. This format is grounded in text-based encoding schemes such as ASCII or UTF-8, providing an accessible mechanism for developers to inspect, debug, and manipulate data. Textual formats such as JSON, XML, and YAML are pervasive in configurations, web communications, and data interchange because they enable easy sharing and understanding across different platforms and languages.

Each representation's choice is influenced by the application's requirements, including the need for human readability, data size constraints, and encoding/decoding performance. These considerations guide developers to leverage the right balance of efficiency and usability.

Binary formats like Protocol Buffers, Avro, and MessagePack offer durable and compact mechanisms for data serialization. Protocol Buffers (Protobuf), for example, provide a flexible schema-based serialization mechanism, generating byte-efficient binary representations of structured data defined in a language-neutral schema file.

```
syntax = "proto3";

message Person {
  int32 id = 1;
  string name = 2;
  string email = 3;
}
```

The Protobuf schema defines a simple message structure, specifying data types and field indices for serialization. Once compiled, it generates classes for C++ or other languages that enable reading, writing, and processing the serialized binary data efficiently.

```cpp
#include <iostream>
#include "Person.pb.h" // Generated header for Person protocol buffers

int main() {
    Person message;
    message.set_id(123);
    message.set_name("Alice");
    message.set_email("alice@example.com");

    std::string binaryData;
    if (!message.SerializeToString(&binaryData)) {
        std::cerr << "Failed to serialize data." << std::endl;
        return -1;
    }

    Person deserializedMessage;
    if (!deserializedMessage.ParseFromString(binaryData)) {
        std::cerr << "Failed to parse data." << std::endl;
        return -1;
    }

    std::cout << "Deserialized Name: " << deserializedMessage.name() << std::endl;
    return 0;
}
```

In the C++ example, the Protobuf library is used to serialize and deserialize a Person message. The serialized output, represented as a binary string, is concise and efficient, minimizing the data footprint while preserving the ability to reconstruct the original object state identically.

Textual representations, by contrast, favor formats like JSON and XML due to their support for self-descriptive encoding. JSON, a lightweight data format, uses attribute-value pairs and array structures to encode data in a highly readable manner. JSON's syntax simplicity makes it suitable for APIs, configurations, and data interchange between client-server systems.

```json
{
  "id": 123,
  "name": "Alice",
  "email": "alice@example.com"
}
```

The JSON example shows a text-based counterpart of the Protobuf binary message, providing an intuitive and easily processed structure. However, JSON's verbosity compared to binary representation incurs higher storage and transmission costs.

Parsing and generating JSON in C++ is facilitated by libraries such as RapidJSON and nlohmann/json, enabling users to seamlessly integrate JSON processing within applications.

```cpp
#include <iostream>
#include <nlohmann/json.hpp>

int main() {
    nlohmann::json jsonObject = {
        {"id", 123},
        {"name", "Alice"},
        {"email", "alice@example.com"}
    };

    std::cout << jsonObject.dump(4) << std::endl;

    int id = jsonObject["id"];
    std::string name = jsonObject["name"];
    std::string email = jsonObject["email"];

    std::cout << "Name from JSON: " << name << std::endl;
    return 0;
}
```

The C++ example shows encoding a JSON object using nlohmann/json, reading and writing data with familiar operators, and presenting text string outputs formatted for readability.

The selection of binary versus textual data representation extends beyond development phase decisions to infrastructure impacts. Binary data is preferred in bandwidth-constrained or latency-sensitive environments, whereas textual data is used when human intervention or system heterogeneity necessitates transparency and accessibility.

A nuanced understanding of encoding techniques involves analyzing data types and metadata inclusion. For instance, binary formats often incorporate type safety checks and comprehensive schemas to validate and process data across platforms. Textual formats may necessitate embedding type information through conventions or additional descriptors, allowing for more dynamic data constructs but also incurring validation complexity.

The issue of cross-language serialization is also addressed through these formats. While textual formats naturally support language interoperability due to their universal readability, binary formats like Protobuf maintain compatibility through the use of language-specific libraries and generated code, ensuring that data integrity is preserved across diverse technological ecosystems.

Compression techniques also influence the decision-making process. Binary formats, being highly compact, typically require less additional compression after serialization. Textual formats often benefit from techniques such as Gzip, which reduce size significantly by compressing repeating sequences inherent in verbose structures.

Security considerations play a notable role, as data represented in text can be more exposed to vulnerabilities like injection attacks if improperly validated. Binary data formats afford obfuscation but necessitate additional security mechanisms to ensure safe transport and ingestion, such as encryption layers and robust checksum verification.

In practical application, hybrid models often emerge, where metadata or instructions may be encapsulated in a textual format for human accessibility while bulk payload data is serialized in binary form to maximize efficiency—such as in the case of HTTP headers with binary body implementations.

An architectural understanding of binary and textual data representation encompasses both immediate operational efficiencies and broader system impacts, ensuring that as data passes through serializations, transformations, and transmissions, its integrity, accessibility, and performance remain aligned with the system's goals.

7.5 Protocol Buffers and Custom Serialization

Protocol Buffers (Protobuf) stands as a powerful and efficient serialization framework developed by Google. It is designed to serialize structured data, facilitating both storage and network communication. Its widespread adoption is underpinned by its ability to define data structure schemas that are both language-neutral and platform-independent, ensuring the compatibility and integrity of data across diverse technology environments.

At its core, Protobuf uses a schema defined in a .proto file, which specifies the data structures and their type specifications. This file is compiled into language-specific code (such as C++, Java, or Python), providing classes and methods that developers utilize to serialize and deserialize data. The serialization process in Protobuf generates a compact binary format, which optimizes data size and enhances performance, especially beneficial in bandwidth-limited applications.

```
syntax = "proto3";

message AddressBook {
  message Person {
    string name = 1;
    int32 id = 2;
    string email = 3;
  }
  repeated Person people = 1;
}
```

The example above illustrates a .proto file for an AddressBook message. It defines a Person message nested within the AddressBook, showcasing how Protobuf allows for complex, hierarchical data structures, including the use of scalar types like strings and integers alongside composite types represented as nested messages.

Once defined, the .proto file is compiled with the protoc compiler:

```
protoc --cpp_out=. addressbook.proto
```

This command generates C++ source files, providing classes and methods corresponding to the schema's data structures. These generated files use optimized binaries to handle serialization and deserialization efficiently.

Protobuf's significant appeal lies in its ability to evolve schemas without sacrificing backward compatibility. Fields within messages are assigned unique tags, allowing new fields to be added without disrupting older versions that might still rely on the original schema. This feature supports seamless data evolution in applications that span multiple versions or undergo incremental feature additions.

In terms of incorporation into existing systems, Protobuf offers multiple benefits:

- Efficiency: Being binary, Protobuf encodings are significantly more compact than textual formats, allowing for reduced storage and quicker transmission times due to decreased payload sizes.

- Speed: The absence of metadata overhead compared to formats like XML or JSON leads to faster parsing of Protobuf-encoded data, making it a top choice for performance-critical applications.

- Scalability: Protobuf's streamlined data handling is well-suited for distributed systems and microservices, where resource efficiency and stringent performance metrics dictate operational success.

- Interoperability: Given Protobuf's ability to generate code for multiple languages, it fosters seamless communication across varied technology stacks within an ecosystem.

Developers often need to customize serialization processes to fulfill specific application requirements, be it through fine-grained control over data representation or circumventing limitations imposed by generic serialization frameworks. Custom serialization can be tackled by manipulating raw binary data; however, libraries like Protobuf simplify these cases by balancing control with convenience.

```cpp
#include <iostream>
#include <fstream>
#include "addressbook.pb.h"

void WriteToFile(const std::string& filename, const AddressBook& book) {
    std::ofstream ofs(filename, std::ios::binary);
    if (!book.SerializeToOstream(&ofs)) {
        std::cerr << "Failed to write address book." << std::endl;
    }
}

void ReadFromFile(const std::string& filename, AddressBook& book) {
    std::ifstream ifs(filename, std::ios::binary);
    if (!book.ParseFromIstream(&ifs)) {
        std::cerr << "Failed to parse address book." << std::endl;
    }
}

int main() {
    AddressBook addressBook;
    AddressBook::Person* person = addressBook.add_people();
    person->set_name("John Doe");
    person->set_id(123);
    person->set_email("john.doe@example.com");

    WriteToFile("addressbook.data", addressBook);

    AddressBook newAddressBook;
    ReadFromFile("addressbook.data", newAddressBook);
    std::cout << "Read " << newAddressBook.people_size() << " person." << std::
        endl;
    return 0;
}
```

The C++ code sample demonstrates writing and reading a serialized AddressBook to and from a file using Protobuf-generated methods. Implementing serialization alongside I/O operations ensures data integrity and encapsulation, leveraging language-specific runtime libraries for smooth handling of Protobuf data.

Custom serialization often necessitates handling specific edge cases where default serialization facilities fall short or when domain-specific performance optimizations are required. This may include creating bespoke binary formats or enhancing existing standards to align with specific constraints.

A pertinent consideration is always ensuring data validation and proper error handling during serialization and deserialization, as malformed data can impede operations or degrade security, leading to vulnerabilities such as buffer overflows or injection attacks. Complete control over the serialization process allows developers to introduce necessary checks and balances, enhancing resilience against malformed or malicious inputs.

Security aspects, such as confidentiality during data transmission, necessitate using cryptographic techniques layered atop serialization outputs, where Protobuf output might be coupled with protocols such as TLS to provide end-to-end data protection.

Ultimately, the judicious use and extension of Protobuf within custom serialization processes equip applications with robust data interchange capabilities. Understanding and effectively applying these tools, bolstered by an overarching strategy for versioning, validation, and security, fosters the development of resilient, interoperable software systems in an increasingly interconnected technological landscape.

7.6   Managing Data Integrity

Data integrity is a crucial component in the realm of data management and network communication. It refers to the accuracy, consistency, and reliability of data throughout its lifecycle. Ensuring data integrity involves implementing strategies and mechanisms that prevent corruption and unauthorized access, thereby maintaining the data's original characteristics from creation to transmission and storage.

Data integrity can be categorized into three primary aspects: physical integrity, logical integrity, and referential integrity. Physical integrity refers to protecting data from physical harm, such as hardware failures and environmental calamities. Logical integrity ensures that data accurately represents its real-world counterpart, maintaining its correctness, accuracy, and validity. Referential integrity asserts consistent relationships between different data sets, ensuring that references between entities, such as foreign keys in databases, remain valid and unbroken across operations.

In network environments, maintaining data integrity becomes especially challenging due to potential errors during transmission, such as data loss, duplication, or modification, whether accidental or malicious. Implementing robust methods to manage integrity involves employing checksums, cryptographic hashes, and error-detecting codes as preventive measures.

Checksums are numeric values calculated from a data block to detect errors induced during storage or transmission. Commonly used algorithms for calculating checksums include CRC (Cyclic Redundancy Check) and Adler-32. These algorithms compute fixed-size values from variable-length data, providing a simple yet effective way to detect errors in blocks of data.

```cpp
#include <iostream>
#include <fstream>
#include <zlib.h> // For crc32 function

unsigned long CalculateChecksum(const std::string &filename) {
    std::ifstream file(filename, std::ios::binary);
    if (!file.is_open()) {
        std::cerr << "Unable to open file." << std::endl;
        return 0;
    }

    file.seekg(0, std::ios::end);
    std::streamsize size = file.tellg();
    file.seekg(0, std::ios::beg);

    std::vector<char> buffer(size);
    if (!file.read(buffer.data(), size)) {
        std::cerr << "Error reading file." << std::endl;
        return 0;
    }

    uLong crc = crc32(0L, reinterpret_cast<const Bytef*>(buffer.data()), size);
    return crc;
}
```

```
int main() {
    std::string filename = "data.bin";
    unsigned long checksum = CalculateChecksum(filename);
    std::cout << "CRC32 Checksum: " << checksum << std::endl;
    return 0;
}
```

In this C++ example, the CRC32 checksum is calculated for a file to verify its integrity. By comparing checksums before and after transmission or storage, one can ascertain the data's status and detect errors if the values differ.

While checksums offer a basic layer of integrity verification, cryptographic hash functions such as SHA-256 (Secure Hash Algorithm) provide more robust security guarantees by producing significantly larger and more distinct hash values. This minimizes collision probability, effectively preventing unauthorized tampering or corruption.

```
#include <openssl/sha.h>
#include <iomanip>
#include <sstream>
#include <iostream>
#include <fstream>

std::string CalculateSHA256(const std::string &filename) {
    std::ifstream file(filename, std::ios::binary);
    if (!file) {
        throw std::runtime_error("Could not open file.");
    }

    SHA256_CTX sha256;
    SHA256_Init(&sha256);

    char buffer[8192];
    while (file.read(buffer, sizeof(buffer))) {
        SHA256_Update(&sha256, buffer, file.gcount());
    }
    if (file.gcount() > 0) {
        SHA256_Update(&sha256, buffer, file.gcount());
    }

    unsigned char hash[SHA256_DIGEST_LENGTH];
    SHA256_Final(hash, &sha256);

    std::stringstream ss;
    for (unsigned char c : hash) {
        ss << std::hex << std::setw(2) << std::setfill('0') << static_cast<int>(c);
    }
    return ss.str();
}

int main() {
    try {
```

```
    std::string filename = "data.bin";
    std::string sha256hash = CalculateSHA256(filename);
    std::cout << "SHA-256: " << sha256hash << std::endl;
} catch (const std::exception &e) {
    std::cerr << "Exception: " << e.what() << std::endl;
}

    return 0;
}
```

The C++ example shown uses OpenSSL to compute the SHA-256 hash of a file's contents. The computed hash can serve to verify data integrity by comparing it with a known, trusted hash value.

Beyond checksums and hashes, ensuring data integrity may involve using data integrity protocols embedded within transport layer protocols, such as TCP (Transmission Control Protocol). TCP provides integrity checks through error-detection mechanisms that handle packet acknowledgments, retransmissions, and sequence numbering to ensure reliable data delivery.

Complementary to traditional error-checking methods, modern practices include employing blockchain technology to achieve data immutability, an extended form of integrity assurance. In data storage systems like distributed ledgers, each block contains a cryptographic hash of the previous block, creating a chain of blocks inherently resistant to modification.

Maintaining data integrity also includes implementing defensive techniques such as redundancy, where multiple copies of data are maintained across different storage devices or network nodes. Platform-level strategies such as RAID (Redundant Array of Independent Disks) and consensus algorithms used in distributed databases like Paxos or Raft ensure data availability and consistency despite node failures or network partitions.

Consideration of data integrity is not limited to storage and transmission but extends to processing, where mechanisms such as atomic transactions become vital. Database management systems employ ACID (Atomicity, Consistency, Isolation, Durability) properties to preserve data integrity during transactions. In distributed systems, transactions spanning multiple nodes may leverage two-phase commit or other consensus protocols to prevent data inconsistencies arising from concurrent updates.

The challenge of managing data integrity is further intensified by scenarios like real-time data processing, where integrity must be maintained amidst low-latency and high-throughput constraints. Here, streaming frameworks such as Apache Kafka and Apache Flink use partitioning and stateful processing to balance speed with accurately maintaining sequence and consistency.

Security considerations form an integral part of data integrity, with access controls protecting against unauthorized access or manipulation. Implementing authentication protocols, secure key management, and leveraging encryption techniques ensures that only legitimate entities can access or alter data. Integrating multi-factor authentication and endpoint protection further reinforces the safeguarding of integrity.

Finally, data auditing and validation mechanisms capture the audit trail of data modifications and states over time, offering forensic capabilities and enhancing transparency. Mechanisms like blockchain's provenance tracking facilitate traceability, emphasizing integrity compliance for sensitive applications such as finance or healthcare.

Managing data integrity encompasses a wide domain covering both technical and operational considerations. Combining insights across these facets enables robust systems that prioritize the fidelity, accountability, and reliability of data, fostering trust and empowering businesses to operate efficiently in the digital age.

Chapter 8

Security in Network Communication

This chapter addresses the essential aspects of security in network communication, focusing on safeguarding data exchange and protecting networks from vulnerabilities. It outlines common threats such as eavesdropping and unauthorized access, and presents encryption techniques to secure data. The chapter also covers authentication protocols to verify identities and ensure secure communication channels. The implementation of SSL/TLS for data protection is discussed alongside best practices for secure programming. Readers will gain insights into creating resilient network applications capable of withstanding evolving cybersecurity threats.

8.1   Fundamentals of Network Security

Network security is a critical aspect of modern communication systems that encompasses a wide range of technologies, devices, and processes. Understanding the fundamentals of network security involves grasping the basic principles, objectives, and methodologies employed to protect network communication from unauthorized access, misuse, and various forms of attack. This section delves into these foundational concepts, providing both a theoretical framework and practical insights into implementing robust network protection.

At the core of network security are several guiding principles designed to maintain the confidentiality, integrity, and availability of data. These principles, often abbreviated as the CIA triad, form the cornerstone of any secure network system.

Confidentiality refers to the protection of data from unauthorized access and disclosure. It ensures that only authorized individuals or systems can view sensitive information. Encryption and access control mechanisms are commonly used to achieve confidentiality. Encryption techniques, discussed in more detail in subsequent sections, transform data into unreadable formats for unauthorized users. Access controls, on the other hand, restrict who can access information, specifying permissions based on the user's identity or role.

Integrity involves maintaining the accuracy and reliability of data over its lifecycle. It involves ensuring data has not been improperly altered, corrupted, or tampered with, either maliciously or accidentally. Integrity is typically ensured through hashing algorithms and checksum mechanisms. Hash functions generate a unique fixed-size string (hash value) from data input, which acts as a digital fingerprint for that specific data set. Comparing hash values helps detect unauthorized modifications.

Availability ensures that information and resources are accessible to those who need them when they are needed. This involves safeguarding against disruptions from attacks such as Denial of Service (DoS), and maintaining redundant systems to avert failures. It's crucial for systems to balance security measures without hindering legitimate access, thereby optimizing resource availability.

Network security aims not just to protect the third-party interception of data but also to devise architectures resilient to malicious intrusions. This involves comprehending the multiple layers through which an attacker may attempt to breach network security:

- *Physical Layer Security*: This includes securing physical devices and hardware. Methods include limiting physical access to network infrastructure, surveillance systems, and employing biometric controls for critical hardware devices.

- *Data Link Layer Security*: This layer addresses issues like MAC spoofing and ARP spoofing, employing protocols for secure link-level connectivity.

- *Network Layer Security*: Technologies like IPsec are used to encrypt data packets at the network layer, ensuring secure IP communications.

- *Transport Layer Security*: Implements protocols such as TLS to secure data during transmission, ensuring it is protected from eavesdropping or interception.

- *Application Layer Security*: Focuses on securing software applications that run on the network, using application firewalls, and intrusion detection systems.

The architecture of a network security system typically involves several integral components working in concert to ensure the protection of data and communications:

1. **Firewalls**: These are designed to filter and monitor incoming and outgoing network traffic based on predetermined security rules. Firewalls can be hardware, software, or a combination of both. Their main goal is to establish a barrier between a trusted internal network and untrusted external networks, such as the internet.

   ```
   # Sample IPTables Rule to Allow Incoming SSH Traffic
   iptables -A INPUT -p tcp --dport 22 -j ACCEPT
   ```

2. **Intrusion Detection and Prevention Systems (IDPS)**: These systems monitor network traffic for suspicious activity and known threats, sending alerts or taking action to block such threats. They can be integrated with firewalls to provide a more comprehensive security posture.

3. **Anti-malware Solutions**: These are essential to detect and neutralize malware, which can comprise viruses, worms, or ransomware. They typically use pattern recognition, heuristics, and

machine learning algorithms to identify and mitigate malware threats.

4. **Virtual Private Networks (VPNs)**: VPNs provide secure connections over public networks by encrypting data transmitted over the internet. They are critical in protecting the data integrity and confidentiality in remote communications.

5. **Network Segmentation and Isolation**: By dividing networks into smaller sections and controlling traffic between them, network segmentation limits the spread of attacks and enables better management of sensitive information.

Equally important to understanding these components is the role of policy and governance in network security. Policies define the framework within which network security is managed, assigning roles and responsibilities, establishing compliance requirements, and outlining protocols for incident response and management.

Security Policies are formalized documents that dictate how an organization intends to protect its information technology assets. These documents include acceptable use policies, access control policies, and incident response guidelines.

Access Control Mechanisms play a crucial role in enforcing security policies. Mechanisms such as Role-Based Access Control (RBAC) and mandatory access control systems ensure that users are granted permissions based on their roles within an organization. RBAC simplifies management by linking roles to certain permissions, delivering uniform security controls across the network.

```
# Example of Role-Based Access Control Configuration
role {
  name: "Administrator",
  permissions: [
    "read:*",
    "write:*",
    "delete:*"
  ]
}

user {
  name: "Alice",
  roles: [
    "Administrator"
  ]
}
```

Effective governance also involves conducting regular **security audits** and **compliance checks** to ensure adherence to these policies and to identify vulnerabilities. Security audits should be comprehensive and encompass penetration testing, vulnerability assessments, and policy reviews.

In presenting the fundamentals of network security, it is essential to be aware of evolving technological trends and cyber threats. As technology advances, novel threats necessitate continuous adaptation and refinement of security measures. The importance of awareness and training cannot be overstated, as human errors frequently account for security breaches. Regular training sessions can keep staff informed about the latest security practices and threat scenarios.

By establishing a strong foundation in these basic principles, practices, and structures, a robust security framework can be built to protect an organization's network infrastructure. The integration of security architectures, policies, and tools fosters a defensive setup capable of sustaining operational integrity and mitigating evolving cyber threats. Understanding these fundamentals prepares for more technical aspects of network security, such as encryption techniques and authentication protocols, enriching the ability to design and maintain secure networks.

8.2 Common Threats and Vulnerabilities

In network security, identifying and understanding common threats and vulnerabilities forms a crucial component of safeguarding systems and ensuring the integrity, confidentiality, and availability of data. This section provides an in-depth analysis of prevalent security threats, detailing each threat's mechanism, potential impact, and methods of mitigation. The vulnerabilities that allow these threats to manifest are also explored, alongside strategies for vulnerability management.

Eavesdropping constitutes a significant threat in network communications. Often referred to as sniffing or snooping, eavesdropping involves unauthorized interception and listening to private communications over a network. Attackers can capture packets traversing a network, possibly extracting sensitive information such as passwords, credit card details, or personal identifiers. To carry out such attacks, adversaries use network monitoring software known as packet sniffers.

To defend against eavesdropping, encryption plays a pivotal role. Implementing robust encryption protocols, such as TLS for secure web communications or IPsec for securing IP packets, prevents unauthorized entities from interpreting intercepted data. Below is a sample configuration demonstrating how to enforce TLS in an Apache server, ensuring secure HTTPS connections:

```
<VirtualHost *:443>
  ServerName www.example.com
  SSLEngine on
  SSLCertificateFile "/path/to/cert.pem"
  SSLCertificateKeyFile "/path/to/key.pem"
  SSLCertificateChainFile "/path/to/chain.pem"
</VirtualHost>
```

Man-in-the-Middle (MitM) attacks are sophisticated forms of eavesdropping where the attacker inserts themselves in the middle of a conversation between two parties, impersonating both sides to secretly relay and potentially alter communication. Attackers might use MitM attacks to harvest credentials, inject malicious code into secure websites, or redirect traffic to fraudulent sites for further exploitation.

MitM attacks can be mitigated by deploying encryption to verify the parties involved in the communication, such as by using Public Key Infrastructure (PKI). Additionally, multi-factor authentication can reduce the risk of compromised credentials being used in such attacks.

Spoofing Attacks involve an adversary disguising themselves as a legitimate entity to gain an illegitimate advantage, such as unauthorized access or data exfiltration. Spoofing can occur at various layers, including IP address spoofing, where an attacker sends packets from a false IP address, and Email spoofing, where messages appear to originate from trusted sources.

Defending against spoofing requires a combination of techniques, such as employing packet filtering rules in firewalls and using Domain-based Message Authentication, Reporting & Conformance (DMARC) for emails to validate the authenticity of messages.

Denial of Service (DoS) and its distributed variant (DDoS) are attacks that aim to render systems or networks unavailable to users. In these attacks, the attacker floods the target system with excessive requests or data, overwhelming resources such as processor capacity or memory, leading to severe service disruptions. When executed in a distributed manner with multiple attacking sources, these attacks become even more challenging to mitigate.

Mitigation strategies for DoS and DDoS attacks include setting rate limits that restrict traffic to manageable levels, deploying content delivery networks (CDNs) that balance and distribute incoming traffic, and using anti-DDoS solutions that filter out malicious traffic before it reaches the target system.

Phishing constitutes a technique where attackers disguise themselves as trustworthy entities to deceive individuals into divulging sensitive information, commonly via email. Phishing can lead to compromised user accounts, financial loss, or unauthorized access to critical systems.

Phishing defenses emphasize awareness training to help users identify suspicious communications and report them. Implementing email filters that use machine learning to detect spoofed addresses, unusual content, or other indicators of phishing can also significantly reduce exposure to such attacks.

SQL Injection is an attack where malicious SQL statements are inserted into data input fields, allowing attackers to compromise databases underpinning applications. Through SQL injection, attackers can exfiltrate, alter, or delete sensitive information stored within the database. A typical SQL Injection vulnerability arises when user inputs are concatenated directly into an SQL query without proper sanitization.

Sanitizing inputs and using parameterized statements prevent SQL Injection. Here is an example of how parameterized queries can secure a database operation using prepared statements in Python:

```
import sqlite3

connection = sqlite3.connect('example.db')
cursor = connection.cursor()

# Using parameterized query to mitigate SQL Injection
user_id = input("Enter user ID: ")
cursor.execute("SELECT * FROM users WHERE id=?", (user_id,))
data = cursor.fetchall()
```

Cross-Site Scripting (XSS) involves injecting malicious scripts into web pages viewed by other users. These scripts may alter page content, steal session cookies, or redirect users to fraudulent sites. XSS vulnerabilities typically arise from unvalidated or improperly sanitized user inputs within web applications.

To prevent XSS attacks, inputs should be validated and sanitized. Employing Content Security Policy (CSP) headers also helps in mitigating the risk by restricting resources the web application is allowed to load.

Malware, an umbrella term encompassing viruses, worms, Trojans, and ransomware, poses severe security risks by compromising the integrity and availability of systems. Malware can inflict damage through data theft, system damage, or encryption of users' data for ransom (as seen in ransomware).

Deploying robust anti-malware solutions that offer real-time protection and regular updates are essential defenses against malware. Regular system and data backups ensure that critical information can be quickly restored following an attack.

Insider Threats present significant security challenges, as insiders typically have legitimate access to systems and data. Insider threats could involve employees or contractors who misuse their access, either maliciously or due to errors, leading to data breaches or information leaks.

Managing insider threats requires stringent access controls, comprehensive logging and monitoring for unusual activities, and fostering a culture of security awareness to detect and deter insider activities.

In analyzing these threats and vulnerabilities, one must recognize the underlying vulnerabilities that often facilitate them. Vulnerabilities are weaknesses or flaws in a system that can be exploited to carry out attacks. These may be due to inherent software bugs, misconfigurations, weak passwords, or outdated system components.

Vulnerability management involves identifying, classifying, remediating, and mitigating vulnerabilities. Regular patching ensures that known vulnerabilities are addressed promptly. Tools such as vulnerability scanners automate the detection of known vulnerabilities in systems, aiding administrators in identifying and prioritizing patches.

The dynamic nature of cyber threats necessitates a proactive security posture. Defense in depth, an approach that uses multiple layers of protection, ensures that if one layer fails, others remain to contain threats. Additionally, adopting a Zero Trust security model, which assumes that threats could originate from internal or external sources, ensures consistent and comprehensive access controls for all users and devices.

Through understanding these common threats and vulnerabilities, one develops a deeper awareness of both the tactics attackers employ and the effective strategies and defenses required to counteract them. This knowledge is foundational to embedding security practices within network design, operation, and policy development, equipping systems to resist increasingly sophisticated cyber threats.

8.3   Encryption Techniques

Encryption forms a fundamental pillar of securing data within network communications. It is the process of converting plaintext, which is understandable to humans, into ciphertext, a non-readable format, to prevent unauthorized access. Understanding encryption techniques is crucial for securing sensitive information as it traverses potentially vulnerable network channels. This section provides an in-depth exploration of encryption methodologies, types of encryption algorithms, and practical implementation strategies.

Encryption techniques are classified into two primary categories: symmetric encryption and asymmetric encryption. Each category has distinct characteristics, advantages, and use cases.

Symmetric Encryption involves the use of a single secret key for both encryption and decryption of data. The most significant advantage of symmetric algorithms is their efficiency; they require less computational overhead compared to asymmetric algorithms, making them suitable for scenarios requiring high throughput.

Common symmetric encryption algorithms include:

- *Data Encryption Standard (DES)*: Once a widely adopted encryption standard, DES uses a 56-bit key. Its key size is now considered too small, making it vulnerable to brute force attacks.

DES has been largely replaced by Advanced Encryption Standard (AES) and Triple DES (3DES).

- *Advanced Encryption Standard (AES)*: AES is the prevailing standard for encryption, approved by the National Institute of Standards and Technology (NIST). It employs key lengths of 128, 192, or 256 bits, providing a robust security level. AES is utilized in various applications, from encrypting sensitive data in databases to securing wireless networks.

- *Triple DES (3DES)*: An extension of DES, 3DES applies the DES algorithm three times to each data block, effectively increasing the key length and making it more secure than single DES.

Below is a Python code snippet demonstrating AES encryption using the PyCryptodome library:

```
from Crypto.Cipher import AES
from Crypto.Random import get_random_bytes
import base64

def encrypt_aes(plain_text, key):
    cipher = AES.new(key, AES.MODE_GCM)
    cipher_text, tag = cipher.encrypt_and_digest(plain_text.encode())
    return base64.b64encode(cipher.nonce + cipher_text).decode()

key = get_random_bytes(16)  # AES-128 requires a 16-byte key
plain_text = "Sensitive Data"
cipher_text = encrypt_aes(plain_text, key)
print(f"Encrypted: {cipher_text}")
```

The critical challenge with symmetric encryption is the secure exchange and management of encryption keys. If the secret key is intercepted or exposed, an adversary can decrypt the intercepted data. Therefore, the secure distribution of keys is essential and is often addressed through key exchange protocols or combined use with asymmetric encryption techniques.

Asymmetric Encryption utilizes a pair of keys—a public key and a private key—for the encryption and decryption processes. The public key encrypts data, and only the corresponding private key can decrypt it, facilitating more secure key exchange mechanisms. Asymmetric encryption is computationally more intensive than symmetric encryption and is typically used in smaller data sets where security is more critical than speed.

Prominent asymmetric encryption algorithms include:

- *RSA (Rivest-Shamir-Adleman)*: RSA is one of the first public-key cryptosystems, based on the difficulty of factoring large integers. It supports key sizes ranging from 1024 to 4096 bits. RSA is often used for encrypting small data blocks or keys for symmetric encryption.

- *Elliptic Curve Cryptography (ECC)*: ECC provides the same level of security as RSA but with shorter key lengths, enhancing efficiency. It is widely used in environments where processing power and memory are limited, such as mobile devices.

- *Diffie-Hellman Key Exchange*: Although primarily a key exchange algorithm, Diffie-Hellman allows two parties to derive a shared secret over an insecure channel, forming the basis for secure communications.

Below is a Python code example demonstrating RSA encryption:

```
from Crypto.PublicKey import RSA
from Crypto.Cipher import PKCS1_OAEP

# Generate RSA Key Pair
key = RSA.generate(2048)
private_key = key.export_key()
public_key = key.publickey().export_key()

# Encrypt a message with the public key
cipher_rsa = PKCS1_OAEP.new(RSA.import_key(public_key))
cipher_text = cipher_rsa.encrypt(b"Confidential Message")

# Decrypt the message with the private key
cipher_rsa = PKCS1_OAEP.new(RSA.import_key(private_key))
plain_text = cipher_rsa.decrypt(cipher_text)
print(f"Decrypted: {plain_text.decode()}")
```

The hybrid model of encryption often combines both symmetric and asymmetric techniques to harness the advantages of each. The typical approach involves using asymmetric encryption to securely exchange a symmetric key, which then encrypts and decrypts the bulk of data.

A noteworthy implementation leveraging this approach is TLS (Transport Layer Security), which uses asymmetric encryption for the key exchange and symmetric encryption for the actual data transmission, ensuring both security and efficiency.

Hash Functions, unlike encryption algorithms that assure the confidentiality of data, are widely used to verify the integrity and authenticity of information. Hashing generates a fixed-size output, called a hash value, from any input data. The hash is deterministic—each unique input produces a distinct hash value. Even a minor change in the input results in a drastically different hash, a feature known as the avalanche effect.

Well-known cryptographic hash algorithms include:

- *MD5 (Message Digest 5)*: Though traditionally popular, MD5 is not recommended for modern applications due to its vulnerability to collision attacks.

- *SHA-1 and SHA-2 (Secure Hash Algorithms)*: SHA-1 has similar weaknesses as MD5, leading to the replacement by SHA-2, which offers longer hash sizes (256, 384, or 512 bits) and is substantially more secure.

- *SHA-3*: The latest member of the Secure Hash Algorithm family, SHA-3 is based on a fundamentally different cryptographic principle (the Keccak sponge function). It is designed to withstand future advances in cryptanalysis.

Hash functions are integral in digital signatures and certificates to verify data integrity and authenticity. Here is an example of generating a SHA-256 hash of a message using Python:

```
import hashlib

message = "This is a secure message."
hash_object = hashlib.sha256(message.encode())
hash_digest = hash_object.hexdigest()
print(f"SHA-256 Hash: {hash_digest}")
```

Digital signatures further extend the concept of hashes to offer non-repudiation, ensuring that a message was sent by a legitimate sender. In practice, the private key is used to sign a message's hash, and the public key verifies it.

While encryption provides critical protection mechanisms, it also imposes necessary considerations and challenges:

- *Key Management*: Proper key management is paramount, involving securely storing, distributing, and periodically rotating keys to prevent unauthorized access. Infrastructure, such as Hardware Security Modules (HSMs) and Key Management Systems (KMS), can automate and secure these processes.

- *Performance Implications*: Especially for resource-constrained devices, computational overhead due to encryption can affect performance. Here, ECC is increasingly preferred due to its efficiency.

- *Quantum Computing*: Emerging threats like quantum computing could potentially break traditional cryptographic algorithms due to their computational power. Post-quantum cryptography aims to develop algorithms resistant to quantum attacks.

The continuous evolution of encryption techniques necessitates staying abreast of advancements in cryptography and revising methodologies accordingly. By leveraging state-of-the-art encryption and balancing performance with security, the protection of sensitive information across networks can be guaranteed, reinforcing the overall security posture against contemporary cyber threats.

8.4 Authentication Protocols

Authentication is a fundamental security process that verifies the identity of individuals or systems accessing resources. It ensures that only legitimate users can perform operations on protected systems and thereby prevents unauthorized access. The robustness of authentication protocols plays an essential role in securing network communications and safeguarding sensitive information.

Numerous authentication protocols exist, each with distinct methods, strengths, and context-specific use cases. This section explores several key authentication protocols, detailing their mechanisms, applications, and considerations for implementation.

Password-Based Authentication is the most traditional and widely used method where users provide a secret password to gain access to a system. While straightforward, this method relies heavily on the users selecting strong, unpredictable passwords to prevent unauthorized access.

Organizations enhance password-based authentication by adopting policies mandating complexity, length, and periodic changes in passwords. However, passwords alone often prove insufficient due to vulnerabilities such as phishing, brute force attacks, and password reuse.

Multi-Factor Authentication (MFA) seeks to augment security by requiring additional verification factors beyond the password. MFA leverages something the user knows (password), something the user has (security token or smartphone), and something the user is (biometrics) to verify identity.

A common implementation of MFA is Time-Based One-Time Passwords (TOTP), which generate time-limited codes based on a shared secret and the current time. Here's a Python example of generating a TOTP using the PyOTP library:

```
import pyotp

# Generate a TOTP secret key
secret = pyotp.random_base32()
totp = pyotp.TOTP(secret)
code = totp.now()

print(f"Current TOTP: {code}")
```

Implementing MFA adds a significant layer of security, making it much harder for adversaries to gain access through stolen or guessed credentials.

Certificates and Public Key Infrastructure (PKI) employ asymmetric encryption to authenticate users, machines, or even devices by using digital certificates. A central element of PKI is the Certificate Authority (CA), a trusted entity that issues certificates, verifying the holder's identity.

PKI is prevalent in securing web servers via SSL/TLS, enabling secure HTTP connections (HTTPS). When a user visits a secure website, the server presents its digital certificate to the user's browser. The browser verifies this certificate against a trusted root CA, ensuring the site's authenticity.

The process of deploying PKI for authentication involves creating a certificate signing request (CSR), having the CA verify the request, and issuing the certificate. Below is a Bash script example illustrating how to generate a CSR using openssl:

```
# Generate a private key
openssl genpkey -algorithm RSA -out private_key.pem

# Create a CSR
openssl req -new -key private_key.pem -out request.csr
```

Kerberos, a network authentication protocol developed by MIT, is designed to provide strong authentication using secret-key cryptography. Kerberos is extensively used in systems requiring cross-platform authentication and single sign-on capabilities.

Kerberos operates by issuing "tickets" that a client uses to prove their identity to services within the network. Key elements of Kerberos include the Key Distribution Center (KDC), which consists of the Authentication Server (AS) and the Ticket Granting Server (TGS).

After initially authenticating with the AS, the user is provided with a ticket-granting ticket (TGT). The TGT then allows the client to request service-specific tickets from the TGS without having to re-enter credentials, thus facilitating seamless access across multiple services.

However, Kerberos requires close synchronization among networked systems due to time-based ticket expiry, and it demands robust security to protect the KDC, as its compromise could lead to a widespread security breach.

OAuth 2.0 is an open standard for token-based authentication and authorization. It enables third-party applications to obtain limited access to web services on behalf of a user through access tokens without the need for sharing user credentials.

OAuth 2.0 supports multiple flows to facilitate various application scenarios, such as web server flows, client-side flows, and device flows. A typical flow involves the client application redirecting the user to the authorization server, obtaining an authorization code, exchanging it for an access token, and using this token to access the resources.

An example of an OAuth 2.0 authorization flow for a web server can be seen below in pseudocode:

```
# Step 1: Redirect user to authorization endpoint
redirect_uri = "https://authorization.server/auth"
client_id = "your_client_id"
redirect(user, redirect_uri + "?client_id=" + client_id + "&response_type=code")

# Step 2: User authorization and obtain an authorization code
authorization_code = receive_authorization_code() # User grants authorization

# Step 3: Exchange the authorization code for an access token
access_token = exchange_code_for_token(authorization_code, client_id,
    client_secret)
```

OAuth 2.0's stringent token issuance and scope limitations ensure that even if a token is compromised, the impact remains contained.

SAML (Security Assertion Markup Language) is an XML-based protocol that facilitates cross-domain authentication and single sign-on. It simplifies authentication processes by allowing users to log in once and gain interconnected service access.

SAML involves three roles: the user, the Identity Provider (IdP), and the Service Provider (SP). A user authenticates with the IdP once, which generates a SAML assertion to the SPs. The assertion contains the user's identity details, allowing SPs to establish authenticated sessions, thus eliminating the need for repeated logins.

SAML is especially beneficial in federated environments where organizations wish to enable trust relationships, reducing the complexities of managing multiple credentials.

Despite the robustness of authentication protocols, their effectiveness hinges on secure implementation, proper configuration, and the context of use. Authentication must consider usability and security balance, ensuring protection without hampering user convenience.

Biometric Authentication adds another layer by relying on individuals' unique physical traits, such as fingerprints, facial recognition, or iris patterns. Biometric systems use sensors to capture physical traits, which are then converted into data stored within the system's database.

A prominent example is the use of fingerprint or facial recognition in smartphones, facilitating quick identification with minimal input. Biometric systems must safeguard against spoofing attacks, and rely on precise yet non-intrusive sensors to maintain usability and accuracy.

While biometric authentication is appealing due to its security and convenience, it raises privacy concerns, necessitating stringent data protection and policy measures.

While deploying authentication protocols, a comprehensive security architecture must consider potential vulnerabilities such as replay attacks, man-in-the-middle threats, or session hijacking. Implementing countermeasures like using nonces, secure session management, and encryption of authentication channels enhances protection against such threats.

Authentication remains intricate, requiring constant evolution in response to technological advancements and emerging threats. An authentication protocol's choice depends on specific needs, risk levels, and technological infrastructure, aiming to achieve a resilient security system fostering trust in digital interactions.

8.5 Using SSL/TLS for Secure Communication

SSL (Secure Sockets Layer) and its successor, TLS (Transport Layer Security), are cryptographic protocols designed to furnish secure communication over a computer network. These protocols achieve privacy and data integrity by encrypting the data sent over the Internet and are integral to protecting sensitive information from interception and tampering.

SSL/TLS protocols provide security for a wide array of applications, notably securing web browsers and servers, delivering safe email communication, file transfers, and even secure VPNs. This section elucidates the operation, implementation, and best practices for using SSL/TLS in network communication.

SSL/TLS Protocol Structure centers on a layered construction consisting of two primary layers: the Record Protocol and the Handshake Protocol.

The SSL/TLS **Record Protocol** provides two services for higher-layer protocols: confidentiality and message integrity. It encapsulates application data into records, providing options for compression, encryption, and then hashing for message integrity.

The **Handshake Protocol** is pivotal to establishing the secure session. It authenticates and negotiates encryption parameters between the client and server. The handshake involves several steps:

1. **ClientHello**: The client sends a hello message to the server, containing TLS version, cipher suite options, and a random number, vital for session initialization.

2. **ServerHello**: On receiving the ClientHello, the server responds with a ServerHello message, selecting its preferred protocol version and cipher suite from those offered by the client, along with its provided random number.

3. **Server Certificate**: The server provides its digital certificate, issued by a trusted Certificate Authority (CA), which the client uses to authenticate the server's identity.

4. **Server Key Exchange**: If necessary, the server sends a key exchange message, particularly in Diffie-Hellman Key Exchange scenarios.

5. **Client Key Exchange**: The client generates a pre-master secret, encrypts it with the server's public key, and transmits it to the server.

6. **Finished Messages**: Both client and server compute a session key from the shared secrets and exchange encrypted Finished messages, verifying the handshake's success.

After this handshake, the client and the server utilize symmetric encryption with session keys for efficient and secure data exchange. A sample OpenSSL command sequence is shown below to create an SSL/TLS certificate, a crucial step in the setup process:

```
# Generate private key
openssl genpkey -algorithm RSA -out private_key.pem

# Create certificate signing request (CSR)
openssl req -new -key private_key.pem -out server.csr

# Self-sign the certificate (replace 'days' value with desired expiration period)
openssl x509 -req -days 365 -in server.csr -signkey private_key.pem -out server.crt
```

In practical terms, implementing TLS involves ensuring that web servers and client browsers are correctly configured to utilize these protocols. The Apache web server configuration example below illustrates enabling HTTPS with a TLS certificate:

```
<VirtualHost *:443>
  ServerName www.example.com
  DocumentRoot /var/www/html

  SSLEngine on
  SSLCertificateFile /etc/ssl/certs/server.crt
  SSLCertificateKeyFile /etc/ssl/private/private_key.pem
  SSLCACertificateFile /etc/ssl/certs/ca-chain.pem

  SSLProtocol all -SSLv2 -SSLv3
  SSLCipherSuite HIGH:!aNULL:!MD5
</VirtualHost>
```

TLS has evolved through several versions to improve security, with TLS 1.3 being the most current and secure version. TLS 1.3 offers improved security features, including forward secrecy, which ensures that the compromise of one session does not affect others, and a reduced number of round trips in the handshake, enhancing connection speed.

TLS Benefits and Use Cases extend beyond simply protecting web browsers. TLS provides a robust security layer for:

- **Email Traffic**: Encrypts emails in transit using protocols such as STARTTLS for SMTP, IMAP, and POP3, ensuring email content remains confidential and tamper-resistant.

- **Virtual Private Networks (VPNs)**: TLS facilitates secure point-to-point VPN connections, encapsulating data transmissions within an encrypted tunnel.

- **Internet of Things (IoT) Devices**: Protects data exchanged between IoT devices and central servers, vital for retaining data integrity and confidentiality in smart systems.

Implementing SSL/TLS should include adherence to best practices to ensure robust security. Recommended practices include:

- **Using Strong Cipher Suites**: Avoid weak cipher suites to thwart exploits; configure servers to insist on strong encryption

225

algorithms like AES and secure hashing algorithms like SHA-256.

- **Disabling Deprecated Protocols**: Deactivate SSL and older TLS versions (e.g., TLS 1.0 and 1.1) due to known vulnerabilities.

- **Enforcing HSTS (HTTP Strict Transport Security)**: This mechanism forces browsers to interact with web servers strictly over HTTPS, minimizing exposure to protocol downgrade attacks such as SSL stripping.

- **Regularly Updating Software**: Keep cryptographic libraries and systems updated to patch vulnerabilities that could be exploited by attackers.

```
# Enforcing HSTS via Apache
Header always set Strict-Transport-Security "max-age=63072000; includeSubDomains;
    preload"
```

Despite its efficacy, TLS comes with certain implementation challenges:

- **Certificate Management Complexity**: Proper deployment and management of certificates are vital. This complexity often involves updating certificates before expiration, checking for revocations, and handling multiple servers and domains.

- **Performance Overhead**: Encryption and decryption add computational overhead. However, modern hardware and optimizations, including session resumption and zero round trip time (0-RTT) in TLS 1.3, mitigate much of this.

- **Ensuring End-to-End Security**: While TLS secures data in transit, endpoint security remains critical to prevent attacks such as man-in-the-middle (MitM) within the device or rogue applications.

- **User Trust and Misconfigurations**: Interaction with users, such as erroneous certificates warnings, can lead to diminished trust. Comprehensive user education and correct configurations are essential.

Emerging technologies like Post-Quantum Cryptography aim to counter potential future threats posed by quantum computing to asymmetrical encryption used in TLS. As advancements continue, the commitment to evolving the protocol and continuous education about implementation challenges remains paramount.

Adopting and correctly implementing SSL/TLS protocols establish a robust security framework for safeguarding network communication. They form the backbone of digital trust, ensuring that personal, financial, and strategic data travels securely over networks, empowering a more secure digital ecosystem.

8.6 Best Practices for Secure Programming

Secure programming is a crucial practice in software development that involves designing and writing code resilient to attacks, ensuring that software behaves as intended even when faced with malicious inputs or unexpected usage patterns. The principles of secure programming aim to safeguard applications from exploitation and maintain data privacy, integrity, and availability.

A comprehensive understanding of vulnerabilities and mindful adherence to secure coding guidelines help mitigate common security issues. This section delineates key best practices for secure programming, providing insights and strategies necessary for developing resilient software applications, particularly focusing on the C++ programming language.

Input Validation and Sanitization are primary techniques for preventing vulnerabilities, such as SQL injection, buffer overflows, and cross-site scripting (XSS). Proper validation involves using rigorous checks and validation rules to ensure only legitimate inputs are processed by the application.

Inputs should always be treated as untrusted data. Performing input validation, as shown below, minimizes risk by confirming that input conforms to predefined constraints:

```
#include <iostream>
```

```
#include <regex>

bool isValidEmail(const std::string& email) {
    // Regex pattern for basic email validation
    const std::regex pattern("^[\\w.-]+@[\\w.-]+\\.[a-zA-Z]{2,}$");
    return std::regex_match(email, pattern);
}
```

In addition to validation, escaping or encoding inputs is necessary to eliminate special characters that might be interpreted in unexpected ways. Consider escaping operators in SQL queries to prevent injection:

```
#include <mysql/mysql.h>

void executeSafeQuery(MYSQL* conn, const std::string& userInput) {
    char query[512];
    mysql_real_escape_string(conn, query, userInput.c_str(), userInput.size());
    std::string executedQuery = "SELECT * FROM users WHERE name='" + std::
        string(query) + "'";
    mysql_query(conn, executedQuery.c_str());
}
```

Secure Authentication and Session Management are fundamental to protecting user accounts and session data. Implementing a strong authentication mechanism and securely managing session identifiers protect against unauthorized access and session hijacking.

Utilizing secure password storage mechanisms such as bcrypt or Argon2 ensures that stored passwords remain secure even if database infiltration occurs. Hashing algorithms designed for password security incorporate computational efficiency and adaptive cost factors, thwarting brute force attempts.

Implementing secure session management, such as using HttpOnly and Secure flags for cookies, enhances protection as demonstrated below:

```
// Secure cookie setup in HTTP headers
setcookie("sessionID", session.getID(), time() + 3600, "/", "example.com", true, true);
```

Memory Management and Buffer Safety consider the potential for buffer overflows and memory leaks, which can lead to unauthorized code execution and system crashes. This is particularly relevant in languages like C++ that offer low-level control over memory management.

While C++ features powerful constructs like the Standard Template Library (STL) designed to manage memory safely, managing raw point-

228

ers necessitates meticulous diligence. Employing modern C++ features, such as smart pointers (std::unique_ptr or std::shared_ptr), ensures automatic resource cleanup and minimizes memory leaks.

Here's an example of using smart pointers in C++:

```
#include <iostream>
#include <memory>

void processResource() {
    std::unique_ptr<int> ptr(new int(10)); // Unique ownership of resource
    std::cout << "Pointer value: " << *ptr << std::endl;
}
int main() {
    processResource(); // Automatic deallocation of memory when ptr goes out of
        scope
}
```

Access Control and Least Privilege assert that applications should grant the minimum levels of access necessary for users and processes to perform their functions. Adopting the principle of least privilege mitigates the risk of unauthorized access or accidental changes to sensitive data.

Fine-grained access control models, such as Role-Based Access Control (RBAC), attribute rights and permissions based on roles within an organization. This ensures predictable permission management across applications.

Implementing access controls programmatically may involve verifying user roles before granting access to sensitive features:

```
#include <iostream>
#include <string>

enum UserRole { GUEST, USER, ADMIN };

void accessFeature(UserRole role) {
    if (role == ADMIN) {
        std::cout << "Access granted to admin features." << std::endl;
    } else {
        std::cout << "Access denied." << std::endl;
    }
}
```

Data Encryption and Secure Communication ensure that sensitive data remains confidential during storage and transit. Encryption of sensitive information, such as personal identifiers and payment card details, is key to safeguarding data against unauthorized access and exposure.

In C++, standard libraries or third-party libraries like OpenSSL enable the incorporation of encryption into applications. This ensures secure data transmission by enabling TLS/SSL for network communications.

Below is a sample of how to encrypt files using OpenSSL:

```
#include <openssl/evp.h>
#include <openssl/aes.h>
#include <openssl/rand.h>
// Function prototypes and encryption logic
```

Error Handling and Logging focus on proper exception handling and comprehensive logging of events. Well-defined error management and logging strategies enhance security diagnostics, offering a means to audit activities within the application and reveal potential signs of intrusion.

Assertions and exception handling are essential in writing robust C++ codes, capable of graceful degradation rather than abrupt failure.

Consider thorough logging in sensitive components, detailing access attempts, error states, and detection of anomalies, while ensuring that logs do not expose sensitive information.

Logging program flows without compromising privacy can be demonstrated as:

```
#include <iostream>

void authenticateUser(const std::string& username, const std::string& password) {
    // Logging an authentication attempt
    std::cout << "Attempting login for user: " << username << std::endl;
    // Authentication logic here without logging credentials
}
```

Secure programming necessitates **compiler security checks**, ensuring the application of security features inherent to modern compilers. Recognizing compilers' warnings and employing features such as stack protection, position-independent code (PIC), and address randomization at the compilation phase crafts an additional security layer.

Continual **vulnerability assessments** and **code reviews** represent proactive steps in identifying and mitigating security weaknesses. Reviews can utilize tools for static code analysis, enhancing the detection of potential vulnerabilities without executing the program. Performing regular security audits cements a proactive security posture.

Ultimately, secure programming is not merely an additive process but a holistic design philosophy embedded throughout the software development lifecycle, fostering resilience to cyber threats and producing secure, robust, and stable applications that protect stakeholders' interests.

Chapter 9

Performance Optimization Techniques

This chapter explores various techniques for optimizing the performance of network applications. It starts by identifying common bottlenecks and offers strategies to enhance the efficient use of CPU, memory, and network resources. Readers will learn methods to optimize data transfer, reduce latency, and leverage concurrency for scalability. The chapter also discusses tools and methods for continuous performance monitoring, equipping developers with the necessary skills to ensure their applications run efficiently and effectively under diverse conditions.

9.1   Identifying Bottlenecks

Identifying performance bottlenecks is a critical step in optimizing network applications. Bottlenecks often act as constraining points in an application, limiting its overall performance. Effective identification and subsequent resolution of these bottlenecks can significantly enhance an application's efficiency and responsiveness. In this section, we delve into various strategies and methodologies for diagnosing and identifying performance bottlenecks in network systems.

A typical network application can have multiple potential sources of bottlenecks, categorized chiefly into CPU, memory, disk I/O, and network constraints. Each of these resources can independently impede performance, necessitating specific techniques for diagnosis.

A crucial first step in bottleneck identification is establishing baseline performance metrics for your application. This involves measuring typical performance indicators under normal operating conditions. Metrics such as throughput, latency, CPU usage, memory usage, and network bandwidth utilization provide a comprehensive performance profile of the application.

```
import psutil

def get_performance_metrics():
    cpu_usage = psutil.cpu_percent(interval=1)
    memory_info = psutil.virtual_memory()
    return {
        "cpu_usage": cpu_usage,
        "memory_used": memory_info.used / (1024 ** 2), # In MB
        "memory_available": memory_info.available / (1024 ** 2) # In MB
    }

metrics = get_performance_metrics()
print(metrics)
```

The above Python code snippet uses the psutil library to collect CPU and memory usage metrics, which serve as an initial step toward understanding potential bottlenecks.

To identify CPU bottlenecks, one should examine CPU utilization patterns. Applications with processes consistently peaking the CPU at above 80% utilization might be CPU-bound. Excessive CPU usage often leads to jackhammer effect process queuing, causing latency spikes and decreased throughput. Profilers such as gprof or more modern tools like Intel's VTune can provide insights into time consumed by different functions or processes within your application. Analyzing CPU cycles wasted on overheads provides actionable insights for optimization.

Memory bottlenecks occur when an application demands more memory than is available in physical RAM, leading to extensive use of swap space and increased page faults. Monitoring paging operations and swap space activities is crucial in identifying memory-related constraints. Tools like vmstat or atop can provide minute insights into memory performance.

Disk I/O bottlenecks are prevalent in applications where storage access is critical, such as databases. High disk read/write times can indicate poor I/O performance. Monitoring disk I/O statistics using tools like iostat provides a clear picture of your storage performance. In situations where disk I/O is a bottleneck, consider employing faster storage solutions like SSDs or distributed storage systems.

Network bottlenecks often manifest in applications with significant network I/O operations. Monitoring network bandwidth utilization is essential for identification. iftop and nload are Unix-based tools that can help visualize real-time usage and traffic patterns. It's pertinent to examine both inbound and outbound traffic behavior, latency through ping tests, and packet drop statistics.

Equally important as real-time indicators are Windows Performance Counters or Linux Performance Counters, which incorporate monitoring hardware performance events. They are integral for identifying fine-grained bottlenecks at the architectural level, offering insights into cache misses, branch mispredictions, and other specific performance events.

Consider a scenario in which a network communication component is suspected to be a bottleneck. For diagnosis, one could deploy logging frameworks that track the duration of network request operations.

```
import logging
import time
import requests

logging.basicConfig(filename='network.log', level=logging.INFO)

def log_network_request(url):
    start_time = time.time()
    response = requests.get(url)
    duration = time.time() - start_time
    logging.info(f"Requested {url} in {duration:.2f} seconds")
    return response

log_network_request('https://example.com')
```

This code snippet introduces a logging mechanism to capture the time taken for HTTP requests. By analyzing the logs over time, one can determine if the network request times are disproportionally large, pointing to a network bottleneck.

For more advanced applications, integrating distributed tracing capabilities can provide end-to-end visibility in multi-tiered applications. Tools like OpenTelemetry allow developers to capture detailed traces across distributed services, revealing latency sources and other bottlenecks that could be obscured in aggregated metrics.

Profiling tools, both language-specific such as Python's cProfile and holistic solutions like New Relic or Dynatrace, offer valuable insights into performance bottlenecks. These tools facilitate the identification of long-running queries, inefficient loops, and excessive object creation, among others.

The application of machine learning techniques can predict bottlenecks before they occur by modeling system performance and foreseeing when thresholds will be exceeded. Predictive analytics can adaptively reallocate resources preemptively to mitigate the impending bottleneck.

In highly dynamic microservices environments, Service Level Indicators (SLIs) and Service Level Objectives (SLOs) define performance expectations and thresholds. Exceeding error rates or latency thresholds indicates potential bottlenecks. Linking these metrics can guide the root cause analysis and prioritization of investigative efforts.

Beyond technical indicators is an examination of architectural design patterns. Monolithic architectures often face bottlenecks due to tight coupling, unlike microservices architectures which enable independent scaling. Understanding the context of bottlenecks frequently leads to re-architecting options beyond simple optimization.

By employing a systemic multi-faceted approach to bottleneck detection, which encompasses runtime metrics, logging, tracing, architectural analysis, and predictive modeling, developers can achieve meaningful identification and remedial steps toward network application optimization.

9.2 Efficient Use of Resources

Efficient use of resources in network applications is paramount for achieving optimal performance and cost-effectiveness. It involves optimizing CPU, memory, and network resources, ensuring that applications run smoothly under varying loads without unnecessary waste. Understanding and managing these resources efficiently requires a deep dive into several techniques and strategies.

The CPU is a fundamental computational resource, and its effective use is critical. CPU efficiency can be enhanced through optimizing algorithms, leveraging parallel processing, and minimizing computational overheads. Algorithmic optimizations often lead to the most significant CPU usage reductions. This involves selecting the right algorithm complexity that fits the task requirements. Consider the task of searching; employing a binary search algorithm with $O(\log n)$ complexity over a linear search algorithm $O(n)$ significantly improves CPU efficiency when handling large datasets.

Utilizing parallel processing capabilities through multi-threading or multiprocessing further boosts CPU utilization. Modern CPUs come with multiple cores and hyper-threading capabilities, allowing concurrent execution of threads. In Python, the concurrent.futures module provides a high-level interface for asynchronously executing functions.

```
import concurrent.futures

def cpu_task(n):
    # Simulate a CPU-bound task
    return sum(i * i for i in range(n))

with concurrent.futures.ThreadPoolExecutor() as executor:
    futures = [executor.submit(cpu_task, 1000000) for _ in range(10)]
    results = [f.result() for f in concurrent.futures.as_completed(futures)]
```

This example demonstrates executing CPU-bound tasks concurrently using a thread pool, enhancing the CPU's workload management.

Memory management is equally vital in ensuring efficient resource use. Inefficient memory usage can lead to high latency and application crashes due to memory exhaustion. Effective memory management strategies include memory pooling, garbage collection tuning, and efficient data storage formats.

Memory pooling reduces the overhead of frequent memory allocation and deallocation by maintaining a pool of pre-allocated objects.
Languages like Java and environments like JVM manage automatic
garbage collection; however, fine-tuning the garbage collector's operation patterns can drastically improve memory performance. For instance, selecting the right garbage collection algorithm or adjusting parameters like MinHeapFreeRatio and MaxHeapFreeRatio can minimize
pause times.

Python, a language integral in network applications, employs automatic garbage collection to manage memory. However, developers can
optimize memory usage by leveraging data structures with efficient in-
memory representation, like deque over list for queue operations, and
using slots to reduce memory overhead in classes.

```
class OptimizedObject:
    ___slots___ = ['attribute1', 'attribute2']

    def ___init___(self, attribute1, attribute2):
        self.attribute1 = attribute1
        self.attribute2 = attribute2

# Memory usage is reduced as ___slots___ prevent the creation of ___dict___ for each
    object
```

This approach utilizes ___slots___, which optimizes attribute storage
by preventing Python from creating a per-instance ___dict___.

Data serialization and deserialization significantly impact memory and
network resource use. Efficient serialization formats like Protocol
Buffers and Avro offer advantages over JSON and XML due to their
compact binary format, reducing both memory footprint and network
transmission time.

Effective use of network resources ensures data transfer completion under optimal conditions, minimizing bandwidth saturation and latency.
Techniques such as data compression, rate limiting, and efficient protocol use can lead to improved resource utilization.

Data compression reduces network load by minimizing the size of data
packets, trading off increased CPU use for reduced bandwidth consumption. In server-client architectures, enabling gzip or Brotli compression can significantly reduce payload sizes, facilitating faster transmission times.

Rate limiting constrains the amount of data sent or received over a network, alleviating congestion and ensuring a fair distribution of bandwidth across multiple users. Implementing algorithms like token bucket or leaky bucket can manage rate limits effectively.

One of the enhancements in network utilization involves choosing the right network protocols tailored to application requirements. For example, employing HTTP/2 over HTTP/1.1 introduces multiplexing capabilities, reducing latency by allowing multiple concurrent streams over a single connection.

```
import hyper

conn = hyper.HTTPConnection('http2.example.com')
conn.request('GET', '/index.html')
response = conn.get_response()
print(response.read())
```

The hyper library facilitates the use of HTTP/2 protocol, allowing developers to exploit its performance improvements over traditional protocols.

Adaptability dynamically alters resource allocation based on real-time demand, optimizing resource utilization. Cloud providers like AWS and Azure offer tools for dynamic scaling. By analyzing resource utilization metrics, applications can automatically extend or reduce computing resources, ensuring efficient operation under varying load conditions.

Containerization technologies such as Docker offer resource isolation and utilization capabilities by using container orchestration tools like Kubernetes. It provides fine-grained control over CPU and memory allocation, allowing applications to scale efficiently without over-provisioning physical hardware resources.

Profiling and monitoring tools play a critical role in resource optimization, enabling real-time and historical performance analysis. Prometheus combined with Grafana provides an excellent open-source stack for monitoring and visualizing metrics, allowing developers to observe resource consumption patterns and pinpoint optimization opportunities.

```
# prometheus.yml configuration snippet
scrape_configs:
  - job_name: 'my_application'
```

```
static_configs:
 - targets: ['localhost:9090']
```

This configuration establishes a Prometheus job for monitoring a local application, paving the way for automated efficiency analysis.

Optimal resource utilization is a continuous process driven by analysis, proactive strategies, and adaptable architecture. It integrates thorough understanding and application of best practices in algorithms, memory management, serialization, protocol choice, containerization, and cloud resource management. Furthermore, continuous monitoring backed by profiling provides insights conducive to sustained performance enhancement. By strategically applying these principles, network applications can effectively manage resources, optimizing both performance and cost-efficiency.

9.3 Optimizing Data Transfer

Optimizing data transfer is crucial for enhancing the performance of network applications, particularly when dealing with large data volumes or requiring real-time data exchange. Effective strategies reduce transmission time, minimize latency, and improve overall application responsiveness. This section explores various techniques for enhancing data transfer efficiency, including compression, data aggregation, choosing the right protocols, and employing content delivery networks (CDNs).

Data compression is a fundamental method for optimizing data transfer. By reducing the size of data, the time taken to transmit it over the network diminishes, leading to quicker response times. Compression can be applied at different layers of the network stack and to various types of data. For textual data, algorithms like gzip and Brotli provide significant size reductions while maintaining data integrity.

```
import brotli

data = "This is a sample response data to be sent over the network."

# Compress data using Brotli
compressed_data = brotli.compress(data.encode('utf-8'))

# Decompressing the data
```

```
decompressed_data = brotli.decompress(compressed_data).decode('utf-8')

print(len(data), len(compressed_data)) # Original vs Compressed lengths
```

This example demonstrates how to utilize Brotli for compressing HTTP response data, illustrating size reduction that enhances data transmission speeds.

For binary data, formats such as Protocol Buffers or Avro provide efficient serialization and compact representation. These formats are particularly advantageous in reducing data payload sizes, resulting in more efficient network utilization compared to plain text formats like JSON or XML.

Data aggregation involves combining multiple data packets into a single transmission unit, thus reducing the overhead associated with individual packet headers and increasing throughput. This technique is especially beneficial in applications with frequent but small-sized data packets, such as IoT devices or telemetry transmission.

To illustrate, suppose a monitoring application collects sensor data at regular intervals. Instead of sending each data point immediately, the application can aggregate several readings and send them as a batch.

```
import json
import time
import requests
import threading

data_buffer = []

def aggregate_and_send():
    while True:
        if data_buffer:
            aggregated_data = json.dumps(data_buffer)
            # Send the aggregated data to the server
            requests.post('https://example.com/api/data', data=aggregated_data)
            data_buffer.clear()
        time.sleep(5) # Aggregate every 5 seconds

threading.Thread(target=aggregate_and_send, daemon=True).start()

# Example of appending data to buffer
data_buffer.append({"temperature": 22.5, "humidity": 45.2})
```

In this code snippet, data aggregation is performed by collecting metrics into a buffer and sending them periodically as a single consolidated packet, enhancing the efficiency of network resource utilization.

Choosing the right data transfer protocols plays a vital role in optimizing data transmissions. Protocols such as HTTP/2 and HTTP/3 (which leverages QUIC) offer significant improvements over traditional HTTP/1.1 through features like multiplexing, header compression, and reduced latency over TLS. Similarly, for real-time applications, using WebSockets allows for full-duplex communication channels over a single connection, significantly optimizing bidirectional data flow.

```
const socket = new WebSocket('wss://example.com/data');

socket.addEventListener('open', (event) => {
    socket.send('Hello Server!');
});

socket.addEventListener('message', (event) => {
    console.log('Message from server ', event.data);
});
```

The example demonstrates establishing a WebSocket connection, achieving efficient real-time data transfer between client and server with significantly lower overhead than traditional HTTP polling methods.

Employing Content Delivery Networks (CDNs) is another powerful strategy. CDNs cache static resources like images, CSS, and JavaScript files across geographically distributed servers, ensuring that requests for these resources are served from a location proximate to the user, reducing latency and offloading traffic from the origin server.

Furthermore, employing caching strategies and leveraging browser cache settings can drastically enhance data transfer efficiency. Setting appropriate cache-control headers for static resources reduces redundant data transfers, minimizing latency for repeated requests.

Network congestion is a common hindrance to effective data transfer. Implementing congestion control algorithms, such as TCP BBR (Bottleneck Bandwidth and Round-trip propagation time), instead of traditional congestion avoidance algorithms like Reno or CUBIC, results in superior throughput and latency reduction under high-volume data transfers.

Monitoring and analytics play an essential role in optimizing data transfers. Real-time performance monitoring provides insights into data transfer rates, round-trip times, retransmission rates, and error rates, enabling proactive bottleneck identification and resolution.

```
import psutil

def network_io_status():
    # Get total bytes sent and received over network
    net_io = psutil.net_io_counters()
    return {
        "bytes_sent": net_io.bytes_sent,
        "bytes_recv": net_io.bytes_recv,
        "packets_sent": net_io.packets_sent,
        "packets_recv": net_io.packets_recv
    }

network_status = network_io_status()
print(network_status)
```

Utilizing the 'psutil' library, this example monitors network I/O, providing essential metrics to evaluate data transfer performance and uncover inefficiencies.

By combining these practices, applications can significantly enhance data transfer efficiency, resulting in lower operational costs, improved user satisfaction due to reduced latency, and the ability to handle increased loads without degrading performance. Applying a systematic approach by continuously evaluating existing data transfer methodologies, implementing compression, aggregation, selecting efficient protocols, leveraging CDNs, and employing effective caching strategies results in robust data transfer optimization.

9.4 Latency Reduction Strategies

Reducing latency is pivotal for enhancing the responsiveness and user experience of network applications. Latency, the delay between a request initiation and its completion, can significantly affect the perceived speed and overall usability of an application. This section examines various strategies to minimize latency in network communication, focusing on architectural optimizations, data handling improvements, and network protocol enhancements.

At the core of latency reduction lies the understanding of its sources. Latency can originate from several core areas: network transmission delays, server processing times, and client-side processing inefficiencies. Each of these contributes cumulatively to the total latency experi-

243

enced by users.

Network latency often results from the time data takes to traverse the physical media and network infrastructure. Reducing network hops and optimizing routing paths can significantly reduce this type of latency. Implementing technologies like Anycast routing can help by allowing data to be delivered from the closest possible point, reducing traversal time and consequently lowering latency.

```
# Ping a server to measure network latency
ping -c 4 example.com
```

Running a 'ping' command provides an estimate of the round-trip time (RTT), helping identify latency bottlenecks in the network path.

Caching is a powerful strategy for reducing latency by eliminating the need to fetch fresh data for every request. Web caching, where frequently accessed resources like HTML pages, images, and stylesheets are stored locally or on a proxy server, can drastically cut down retrieval time. On a more granular level, database query caching reduces latency by storing the results of expensive queries, eliminating the need for repeated execution of the same computation-heavy SQL statements.

Data retrieval optimization also plays a critical role. This involves not only caching but also efficient data structuring and retrieval methods. Utilizing indexes in databases, reducing query complexity, and avoiding data over-fetching (fetching only necessary data) are crucial.

On the client side, optimizing asset delivery through techniques like lazy loading can remarkably reduce initial load times, enhancing perceived latency reduction. Lazy loading ensures that only critical resources are loaded initially, while non-essential elements are retrieved when needed.

```
<img src="lazy-image.jpg" loading="lazy" alt="Lazy Loaded Image">
```

This HTML snippet showcases the 'loading="lazy"' attribute, deferring the image load until it enters the viewport, effectively reducing initial page load latency.

Server-side latency can be minimized by optimizing processing algorithms and leveraging asynchronous operations, particularly when dealing with I/O-bound tasks. Utilizing asynchronous programming models, such as those found in Node.js or Python's 'asyncio', can alleviate bottlenecks by allowing other processes to execute while waiting for I/O operations to complete.

```
import asyncio
import aiohttp

async def fetch_url(url):
    async with aiohttp.ClientSession() as session:
        async with session.get(url) as response:
            return await response.text()

# Running the coroutine
url_data = asyncio.run(fetch_url('https://example.com'))
```

The above example shows the use of Python's 'aiohttp' library for non-blocking HTTP requests, enabling concurrent execution and reducing effective latency for network-bound operations.

Reducing latency through protocol optimization involves shifting from older protocols to newer standards that inherently support latency-reduction features. HTTP/2 and HTTP/3 present substantial improvements over HTTP/1.1 by supporting multiplexing, header compression, and other mechanisms, reducing both latency and overhead.

With HTTP/2, multiple requests are allowed concurrently on the same connection without head-of-line blocking, which reduces the need for multiple parallel connections to improve throughput. Implementing TLS session resumption and optimizing encryption settings could further reduce latency incurred by cryptographic operations.

In addition to network and server optimizations, edge processing and computing capabilities provided through platforms like AWS Lambda@Edge or Cloudflare Workers allow for certain tasks to be processed closer to the user, effectively cutting down on round-trip time for data processing and reducing perceived latency.

Real-time applications such as video conferencing, VoIP, or online gaming can benefit enormously by leveraging UDP over TCP for communication, particularly in environments where packet loss is less of a concern than latency. Systems like WebRTC utilize UDP for efficient real-time media transmission, ensuring lower latency due to the absence of TCP's strict acknowledgment and retransmission policies.

Another vital approach includes employing predictive prefetching strategies, where an application anticipates the user's next activity and preloads the required data. This approach can reduce latency significantly if predictions are accurate, although it requires sophisticated analytics and understanding user behavior patterns.

Testing and monitoring tools like Wireshark provide detailed insights into latency characteristics present within the network path, revealing bottleneck areas for targeted optimization.

Finally, latency testing should be conducted in conditions that closely mimic the user environment, using globally distributed servers to test geographical latency variances. Synthetic transaction monitoring tools or real user monitoring can provide invaluable data regarding how latency affects end-user performance across varying conditions.

By combining these strategies with a rigorous and continuous profiling and feedback loop for performance monitoring, developers can significantly mitigate latency issues within their applications, providing end-users with a seamless and responsive experience. Consequently, latency reduction is not merely a singular technique but a comprehensive approach comprising architectural, protocol, data management, and client-side considerations.

9.5 Concurrency and Scalability

Concurrency and scalability are pivotal in developing robust network applications capable of handling numerous simultaneous requests and managing increasing workloads. Concurrency refers to the ability of an application to perform multiple tasks at the same time, while scalability denotes the capability of a system to handle growth in workload effectively by adding resources.

Effective concurrency design exploits the inherent parallelism in application tasks, maximizing resource utilization and performance. Concurrency models can be broadly categorized into multi-threading, multi-processing, and asynchronous programming.

Multi-threading allows an application to create multiple threads of execution within a single process, sharing the same memory space. This model is especially beneficial in I/O-bound applications where a thread can perform other tasks while waiting for I/O operations to complete. However, multi-threading requires careful synchronization to prevent race conditions and deadlocks, often utilizing constructs like locks, semaphores, and condition variables.

```python
import threading
import time

def thread_task(name):
    time.sleep(2)
    print(f'Task {name} completed')

threads = []
for i in range(5):
    t = threading.Thread(target=thread_task, args=(f'Thread-{i}',))
    threads.append(t)
    t.start()

for t in threads:
    t.join()
```

This example utilizes Python's 'threading' module to demonstrate basic multi-threading, initiating multiple threads to execute tasks concurrently.

Multi-processing, in contrast, involves running separate processes, each with its own memory space. This model is pertinent in CPU-bound applications requiring intensive computation, allowing complete parallel execution without the limitations imposed by the Global Interpreter Lock (GIL) in languages like Python.

```python
from multiprocessing import Process

def process_task(name):
    print(f'Processing task {name}')

processes = []
for i in range(5):
    p = Process(target=process_task, args=(f'Process-{i}',))
    processes.append(p)
    p.start()

for p in processes:
    p.join()
```

The use of Python's 'multiprocessing' module here illustrates how processes are spawned and executed independently, leveraging multiple cores for enhanced performance.

Asynchronous programming models, prevalent in languages like

JavaScript and Python (with 'asyncio'), offer a non-blocking execution workflow suitable for applications with high I/O operations. Asynchronous constructs like 'async' and 'await' allow functions to yield control until awaited operations complete, thus enhancing concurrency.

```
import aiohttp
import asyncio

async def fetch_data(session, url):
    async with session.get(url) as response:
        return await response.text()

async def main():
    async with aiohttp.ClientSession() as session:
        tasks = [fetch_data(session, 'https://example.com') for _ in range(5)]
        return await asyncio.gather(*tasks)

data = asyncio.run(main())
```

This asynchronous programming example makes use of 'aiohttp' to perform non-blocking web requests concurrently, showcasing improved handling of I/O-bound tasks.

Scalability in network applications is generally approached through vertical and horizontal strategies. Vertical scalability involves adding more resources, such as CPU and memory, to existing machines, enhancing their capacity. However, vertical scaling is often limited by cost and hardware limits.

Horizontal scalability, on the other hand, entails adding more machines or nodes to distribute the load. A load balancer directs incoming requests across nodes, ensuring balanced server load. This model supports growth without significant constraints and is the backbone of many scalable architectures, such as microservices.

Microservices architecture further enhances scalability through decoupling application components into smaller, independent services. Each service can be deployed, scaled, and managed independently, enabling fine-grained scaling based on functional load demands.

Containerization technologies such as Docker facilitate scalable deployments by creating isolated environments that replicate across different systems. Using orchestration tools like Kubernetes, developers can automate deployment, scaling, and management of containerized applications, ensuring consistent performance as application demand changes.

Stateful versus stateless designs also affect concurrency and scalability. Stateless systems, which don't retain client session data, are inherently more scalable due to their simplicity and ease of replication. Stateful systems require additional mechanisms such as distributed caches (e.g., Redis) or persistent storage solutions to manage and maintain state, introducing complexity but enabling functionality that necessitates user state persistence.

Distributed systems further push the envelope of scalability by allowing applications to run across a cluster of nodes, each handling a part of the workload. Managing these systems requires handling data consistency and availability trade-offs, often using distributed consensus algorithms like Paxos or Raft.

```
import redis

# Connect to Redis instance
r = redis.StrictRedis(host='localhost', port=6379, decode_responses=True)

# Set a key-value pair in the cache
r.set('key', 'value')

# Fetch the key-value pair from the cache
value = r.get('key')
print(value)
```

This code shows a simple interaction with a Redis cache, demonstrating how external caching solutions can assist in scaling stateful applications.

Designing applications for concurrency and scalability requires a systemic approach to application architecture, leveraging appropriate models, tools, and technologies at every level from code concurrency to full-system deployment. Ensuring optimal design not only addresses immediate performance concerns but also sets the foundation for long-term sustainability as user demands evolve. Scalability and concurrency should therefore be integrated into the core principles of application development, allowing applications to thrive under increasing demand and advancing technologies.

9.6 Performance Monitoring Tools

Performance monitoring is an essential practice for ensuring that network applications run efficiently and effectively under diverse conditions. Monitoring tools collect, visualize, and analyze metrics relating to application performance, resource utilization, and system health, providing developers and IT operations with critical insights into potential bottlenecks and system failures. This section explores various performance monitoring tools and methodologies, examining how they contribute to maintaining optimal application performance.

Effective performance monitoring facilitates several key objectives: identifying performance degradation before it affects users, understanding system behavior under load, and providing data-driven insights for capacity planning and resource optimization. Modern performance monitoring solutions often integrate with application code, infrastructure, and third-party services, offering a comprehensive view of system performance.

1. Application Performance Monitoring (APM)

APM solutions provide insights into application-specific metrics, such as request throughput, response times, error rates, and service dependencies. By instrumenting application code, APM tools trace transactions across distributed components, identifying bottlenecks and providing detailed transaction logs.

Prominent APM tools like New Relic, Datadog, and Dynatrace offer sophisticated features such as distributed tracing, error detection, and real-time alerting. These tools deploy agents within application environments to collect metrics and transmit them to centralized servers for processing and visualization.

```
# Install New Relic agent for Node.js
npm install newrelic --save

# Set the New Relic license key and application name in newrelic.js
# Configure the agent to collect performance metrics
```

This installation example for New Relic shows the straightforward setup for instrumenting a Node.js application, enabling developers to track performance metrics with minimal setup.

2. Infrastructure Monitoring

Infrastructure monitoring tools focus on the underlying hardware and virtual resources supporting network applications. Metrics include CPU usage, memory consumption, disk I/O, and network bandwidth, providing insights into the health and efficiency of physical or cloud infrastructure components.

Prometheus and Grafana form a powerful open-source stack for collecting and visualizing infrastructure metrics. Prometheus gathers and stores metrics from various sources, while Grafana provides dashboards for graphical representation and analysis.

```
scrape_configs:
 - job_name: 'node'
   static_configs:
   - targets: ['localhost:9100']
```

The configuration snippet adds Prometheus' Node Exporter for monitoring system-level metrics, paving the way for a comprehensive infrastructure monitoring solution.

3. Log Management and Analysis

Log management tools aggregate, search, and analyze log data generated by applications and infrastructure systems. Such logs often contain error messages, transaction details, and other operational insights, crucial for diagnosing runtime issues and debugging.

Elastic Stack (ELK), comprising Elasticsearch, Logstash, and Kibana, is widely used for log management and analysis. Logs are parsed and ingested by Logstash, indexed by Elasticsearch, and visualized in Kibana for detailed analysis and searchability.

```
input {
  file {
    path => "/var/log/myapp/*.log"
    start_position => "beginning"
  }
}
```

251

```
output {
  elasticsearch {
    hosts => ["localhost:9200"]
    index => "myapp-logs"
  }
}
```

This Logstash configuration specifies the file input plugin for collecting logs from specified directories and forwarding them to Elasticsearch for indexing.

4. Network Monitoring Tools

Network monitoring tools evaluate the performance and reliability of network components — routers, switches, firewalls, and links — crucial for maintaining uninterrupted, high-performance communication.

Wireshark, an open-source packet analyzer, allows detailed inspection of live or recorded network traffic, making it invaluable for troubleshooting at the packet level. SolarWinds Network Performance Monitor (NPM) and Nagios provide comprehensive network monitoring, including SNMP polling, performance analysis, and automated alerting.

```
# Capture network packets on the eth0 interface
tcpdump -i eth0 -w network_traffic.pcap

# Analyze the captured packets in-depth with Wireshark
```

Here, 'tcpdump' captures network packets on an interface for detailed post-analysis in Wireshark, illustrating packet-level insight into network activity.

5. Real User Monitoring (RUM) and Synthetic Monitoring

Real User Monitoring captures the interactions of real users with web applications, measuring load times, transaction speeds, and error rates under actual usage conditions. Tools like Google Analytics and New Relic Browser offer valuable user-centric performance data, helping optimize the end-user experience.

Synthetic Monitoring involves testing applications using pre-defined scripts mimicking user paths and actions, running from multiple locations globally. Tools like Pingdom and Uptime Robot simulate user interactions to verify performance and availability, crucial for maintaining SLAs.

```
# Check latency and server response with curl
curl -o /dev/null -s -w "%{http_code} %{time_total}\n" http://example.com
```

This simple 'curl' command sends a request to a URL and returns latency and HTTP status code, a rudimentary form of synthetic monitoring.

6. Alerting and Incident Management

Effective monitoring solutions integrate alerting systems and incident management processes, notifying operators of performance anomalies in real-time. Tools like PagerDuty and Opsgenie provide alerting services, integrating with monitoring tools to deliver immediate notifications via email, SMS, or mobile push messages.

Integrating automatic remediation processes, where possible, reduces MTTR (Mean Time to Resolution), enhancing the resilience of managed environments. AI-driven anomaly detection and predictive analytics further refine alerting systems, identifying abnormal patterns before system performance degrades.

Incorporating these diverse but synergistic tools into a cohesive monitoring strategy empowers development and IT operations teams to ensure their network applications meet rigorous performance and operational metrics. Defining clear SLAs, extracting value from comprehensive data analytics, and adopting a proactive stance towards system monitoring are crucial steps for ensuring optimal performance and enhancing user satisfaction. Through vigilant application and infrastructure monitoring, coupled with effective alerting mechanisms, organizations can maintain high performance standards and minimize service disruptions, fortifying applications against the dynamic challenges of modern network environments.

Chapter 10

Practical Network Application Development

This chapter guides readers through the detailed process of developing practical network applications. It outlines the initial stages of project planning and design, including the selection of protocols and tools that best fit specific application needs. The chapter provides a hands-on approach to building client-server applications, emphasizing error handling and debugging techniques. It also covers testing methodologies to ensure applications meet functional and performance benchmarks, and discusses deployment best practices and ongoing maintenance strategies for sustaining robust and efficient network software solutions.

10.1   Project Planning and Design

The initial phase of any network application development project involves meticulous planning and design. This process is critical, as it lays the foundation for subsequent development stages and ensures that the final output aligns with user requirements and technical constraints. The overarching goal in this phase is to carry out a thorough analysis to understand the needs and translate them into a comprehensive architectural blueprint. This section delves into the significant steps involved in effective project planning and design, focusing on requirements gathering and architectural design.

Requirements gathering is the bedrock of project planning, and it involves understanding the problem space, identifying stakeholders, and defining clear, actionable objectives. A systematic approach towards capturing requirements aids in minimizing ambiguities and sets realistic expectations for all parties involved. During this step, it is imperative to conduct stakeholder interviews, questionnaires, and workshops. Moreover, documenting existing workflows through flowcharts can provide insights into current processes and highlight areas for optimization.

The output of the requirements gathering process is typically a requirements specification document, which should detail functional requirements, non-functional requirements, constraints, and user expectations. Non-functional requirements, such as scalability, availability, and latency, are particularly significant in network applications where performance metrics often dictate the success of the application.

Upon gathering requirements, the focus shifts towards architectural design. This phase involves high-level structuring of the application in terms of modules, data flow, and network interactions. A successful design ensures that the application is modular, scalable, and maintainable. Architectural patterns such as client-server, peer-to-peer, or microservices should be evaluated contextually to address the specific use cases and constraints highlighted in the requirements phase.

Central to architectural design is the choice of data flow mechanisms and communication protocols. For instance, in a client-server architecture, one must decide on synchronous versus asynchronous communication based on the expected response time and bandwidth usage. Consideration must also be given to state management and data consistency, particularly in distributed systems. Consistency models, such as eventual consistency or strong consistency, need to be carefully analyzed for their impact on the user experience and system performance.

To illustrate a practical application of these concepts, consider a client-server network application that involves monitoring IoT devices spread across various geographical regions. The primary functional requirement is to collect sensor data in real-time and enable analysis by backend servers.

```
import socket

HOST = '192.168.1.100' # The server's hostname or IP address
PORT = 65432 # The port used by the server

with socket.socket(socket.AF_INET, socket.SOCK_STREAM) as s:
    s.connect((HOST, PORT))
    s.sendall(b'Hello, world')
    data = s.recv(1024)

print(f'Received {data!r}')
```

The above Python code snippet demonstrates a simplistic client-side implementation of a socket connection intended to communicate with a designated server. By utilizing TCP sockets, the application ensures reliable, ordered communication which is crucial for synchronizing data packets in real time.

On the server-side, a basic implementation capable of accepting incoming connections and reading data might look as follows:

```
import socket

HOST = '192.168.1.100'
PORT = 65432

with socket.socket(socket.AF_INET, socket.SOCK_STREAM) as s:
    s.bind((HOST, PORT))
    s.listen()
    conn, addr = s.accept()
    with conn:
        print(f'Connected by {addr}')
        while True:
            data = conn.recv(1024)
            if not data:
                break
            conn.sendall(data)
```

Through these examples, the importance of designing robust and resilient network layers becomes evident. Such designs provide the backbone upon which more advanced functionalities, such as authentication, data encryption, and load balancing, can be seamlessly layered.

When addressing architectural design, it is also vital to consider network latency and bandwidth, as these will influence user experience and application throughput. Techniques such as data compression and caching can mitigate latency and reduce bandwidth consumption. Load balancing and replication strategies must be devised to handle varying loads and ensure high availability.

Consider the following theoretical scenario within the same IoT context: As the network of IoT devices scales up from tens to thousands, architectural strategies need to evolve. Load should be distributed effectively across multiple servers to prevent bottlenecks. Here, introducing a load balancer can be an optimal strategy, where the load balancer forwards incoming requests to a pool of application servers. This architectural adjustment ensures that no single server becomes overwhelmed, enhancing both performance and fault tolerance.

In addition, consideration of data integrity and security is nonnegotiable. Securing data in transit using protocols such as TLS (Transport Layer Security) and implementing authentication measures using OAuth or similar frameworks should be factored into initial architectural designs. These measures prevent unauthorized access and interception of sensitive information.

Design tools such as UML (Unified Modeling Language) diagrams are beneficial during the architectural design to visualize system components, their interactions, and dependencies. These diagrams help in communicating the architecture to developers and stakeholders, ensuring clarity in understanding the system's functionality and its relation to other systems.

The planning and designing of a network application project require a detailed examination of every possible interaction within the system. Tools such as mockups or prototypes can be useful for gaining stakeholder feedback early in the design process, allowing for iterative refinement of the application before full-scale development begins.

Effective planning and design are indispensable in mitigating risks associated with scope creep, unrealistic expectations, and architectural flaws. Extracting precise requirements and defining a strong architecture are cornerstones that directly influence the quality, reliability, and maintainability of the final network application output. This meticulous approach ensures that development efforts translate into a product that meets user needs, performs efficiently under targeted conditions, and adapts seamlessly to future technological landscapes.

10.2 Choosing the Right Protocols and Tools

The selection of appropriate protocols and tools is a critical phase in the development of network applications, as it influences the application's performance, scalability, and overall efficiency. The protocols dictate how data is transmitted across the network, ensuring secure, reliable, and efficient communication between entities. Simultaneously, the tools selected affect the ease of development, deployment, and mainte-nance processes. This section explores key considerations and strate-gies for selecting the right protocols and tools tailored to diverse net-work application needs.

Protocols serve as the operational guidelines for data interchange over a network, facilitating end-to-end communication between sending and receiving devices. The choice of protocol is context-dependent, heavily influenced by the application's functionality, security needs, and operational constraints. Two of the most widely used transport layer protocols are TCP (Transmission Control Protocol) and UDP (User Datagram Protocol), both of which offer distinct characteristics conducive to various application scenarios.

TCP is a connection-oriented protocol, offering reliable data trans-mission through error checking, acknowledgment, and retransmission processes. It is highly suitable for applications where data integrity and order are paramount, such as web servers, file transfer protocols (FTP), and email services. Its built-in flow control mechanism ensures that a sender does not overwhelm a receiver, which is crucial for maintaining application stability under varying network conditions.

```
import socket

# Setup TCP client socket
with socket.socket(socket.AF_INET, socket.SOCK_STREAM) as s:
    s.connect(('example.com', 80))
    s.send(b'GET / HTTP/1.0\r\nHost: example.com\r\n\r\n')
    response = s.recv(4096)
    print(response.decode('utf-8'))
```

In contrast, UDP is a connectionless protocol that provides expedited data transfer with less overhead but without the reliability mechanisms inherent in TCP. Applications such as video streaming, online gaming, and voice over IP (VoIP) leverage UDP to capitalize on its low latency and minimal delay features, accepting the trade-off for potential packet loss.

```
import socket

# Setup UDP client socket
with socket.socket(socket.AF_INET, socket.SOCK_DGRAM) as s:
    message = b'UDP Packet'
    s.sendto(message, ('example.com', 5005))
    data, server = s.recvfrom(4096)
    print(f'Received {data} from {server}')
```

Beyond the network layer, application layer protocols provide specific features that enhance data delivery according to application requirements. HTTP/HTTPS, MQTT, and CoAP are prominent examples, each serving distinct application requirements and environments.

HTTP/HTTPS is foundational for delivering hypermedia via the World Wide Web. Using HTTPS ensures encrypted communications and enhanced security, addressing privacy concerns associated with plain HTTP. For APIs, RESTful web services commonly operate over HTTP/HTTPS, providing a scalable and stateless interface for network resources.

MQTT (Message Queuing Telemetry Transport) is designed for lightweight, publish-subscribe networks ideal for constrained environments such as IoT. It reduces network bandwidth usage and improves response times, making it an excellent choice for sensor networks and other scenarios necessitating real-time operation.

CoAP (Constrained Application Protocol) is another protocol tailored for simple devices with limited power and processing capability, typical in IoT systems. Operating over UDP, CoAP supports multicast, supports cache proxy, and offers efficient RESTful communication features.

Tool selection is equally pivotal and depends on the development team's expertise, the application's complexity, and the operational ecosystem. Integrated Development Environments (IDEs) such as Visual Studio Code, PyCharm, and IntelliJ IDEA enhance productivity by offering extensive features like code completion, debugging tools, and version control integration.

Version control systems (VCS) such as Git remain indispensable in software development. Git's distributed architecture facilitates concurrent collaboration among developers, maintains comprehensive project histories, and provides branches for seamless parallel development. GitHub, GitLab, and Bitbucket are popular platforms offering cloud-based repository hosting and additional features such as issue tracking and continuous integration.

Containerization tools like Docker further bolster the development and deployment process by enabling application isolation, reproducibility, and accelerated deployment cycles. Kubernetes, an orchestration platform, manages containerized applications' deployment, scaling, and operations, ensuring applications remain robust and scalable across varied environments.

The following is an example of a Dockerfile, outlining steps to containerize a simple Python application:

```
# Use an official Python runtime as a parent image
FROM python:3.9-slim

# Set the working directory to /app
WORKDIR /app

# Copy the current directory contents into the container at /app
ADD . /app

# Install any needed packages specified in requirements.txt
RUN pip install --no-cache-dir -r requirements.txt

# Run app.py when the container launches
CMD ["python", "app.py"]
```

The deployment pipeline is significantly enhanced when employing Infrastructure as Code (IaC) tools like Terraform or Ansible. These enable developers to define infrastructure using codification, allowing for rapid provisioning, configuration management, and consistent deployment across different cloud services.

Monitoring and logging tools such as Prometheus, Grafana, and ELK Stack (Elasticsearch, Logstash, Kibana) form an essential part of the DevOps toolkit. They provide insights into application performance and facilitate quick identification and resolution of issues, promoting optimal application uptime and reliability.

The appropriate choice of protocols and tools is essential for meeting application demand, providing scalability, and ensuring sustainability. Each project's unique requirements necessitate careful evaluation of the available protocols' trade-offs and the suitability of various development and deployment tools. By aligning protocol and tool selection with project objectives and operational constraints, practitioners can ensure optimized network application performance, maintainability, and user satisfaction. Through such informed choices, developers can streamline workflows, reduce time to market, and enhance the overall quality of their network applications.

10.3 Developing a Client-Server Application

Developing a client-server application is a fundamental paradigm in network computing, where tasks are divided between providers of a resource or service (servers) and service requesters (clients). This architecture facilitates centralized resource management, enhances data consistency and security, and is scalable across a multitude of applications such as databases, web services, and content delivery networks. This section explores the intricacies of client-server application development, offering comprehensive insights into design considerations, architecture, and practical implementation.

The client-server model inherently comprises distinct server and client components, each serving unique roles and encapsulating specific functionalities. Servers are tasked with managing resources, processing client requests, and performing complex computations. Clients, operating on individual user devices, initiate requests and interact with the server to display, manipulate, or consume data.

In a typical client-server architecture, the server awaits incoming requests, processes valid requests, and returns results back to the client. The communication between the two entities is governed by specific protocols ensuring orderly data exchange. HTTP(S) is a prevalent protocol for web applications, whereas TCP and UDP are employed in other application scenarios requiring reliable communication or low latency.

The development cycle of a robust client-server application involves several stages: defining requirements, designing the architecture, coding the client and server components, ensuring security, and testing overall functionality.

The architecture design phase is crucial as it lays the groundwork for communication flow between clients and servers. At its core, the architecture is influenced by the number of users, expected load, security requirements, and response time goals. Centralized, distributed, or hybrid models might be chosen based on these factors.

Consider a real-world scenario: a library management system where users can search for, reserve, or renew books online. The server, hosting the database containing up-to-date book information, processes user requests, checks for access permissions, and logs transactions.

For a straightforward client-server interaction example, let's design a basic HTTP server in Python using the Flask framework and complement it with a client communicating over HTTP.

```python
# Flask server example
from flask import Flask, jsonify, request

app = Flask(__name__)

# Sample data
books = [
    {'id': 1, 'title': '1984', 'author': 'George Orwell'},
    {'id': 2, 'title': 'To Kill a Mockingbird', 'author': 'Harper Lee'}
]

@app.route('/books', methods=['GET'])
def get_books():
    return jsonify({'books': books})

@app.route('/book/<int:book_id>', methods=['GET'])
def get_book(book_id):
    book = next((b for b in books if b['id'] == book_id), None)
    return jsonify({'book': book} if book else {'error': 'Book not found'})

if __name__ == '__main__':
    app.run(host='0.0.0.0', port=5000)
```

This Flask server implementation includes endpoints to retrieve book listings and specific book data using the book_id. It listens for incoming requests on port 5000, providing a simplified but effective server mechanism for managing book information.

263

On the client side, a Python script utilizing the requests library can interact with this RESTful API to retrieve data.

```
import requests

# Base URL of the server
BASE_URL = 'http://localhost:5000'

# Fetch list of books
response = requests.get(f'{BASE_URL}/books')
if response.status_code == 200:
    print('List of books:', response.json())

# Get details of a specific book
book_id = 1
response = requests.get(f'{BASE_URL}/book/{book_id}')
if response.status_code == 200:
    print(f'Details of book {book_id}:', response.json())
else:
    print('Error fetching book details.')
```

The above client code sends HTTP GET requests to the server's endpoints and processes responses, demonstrating client-server interaction effectively.

Security is a critical concern in client-server architectures. Implementing authentication and authorization ensures that only legitimate users access server resources. Techniques like OAuth, JWT (JSON Web Token), or simple API keys can handle these security requirements efficiently. Moreover, employing HTTPS instead of HTTP encrypts the communication channel, protecting data integrity and confidentiality.

The separation of concerns in client-server applications enhances maintainability. For instance, changes to the server logic do not necessitate changes to client code, provided the API remains consistent. This architectural separation also allows for greater flexibility in scaling components independently to meet demand fluctuations. Horizontal scaling, for instance, can introduce additional server instances under a load balancer to distribute traffic evenly.

Testing client-server applications encompasses unit testing individual components and integration testing to ensure coordinated functionality. Tools like Postman can test server endpoints, simulating various client requests. Automated tests can be integrated into continuous integration pipelines, providing rapid feedback and fault detection.

Designing and implementing a client-server application involves careful consideration of architectural patterns, understanding protocol efficiencies, securing the communication landscape, and thorough testing. These components work in unison to produce an application that not only aligns with user expectations but also scales with increasing demand while safeguarding data integrity and privacy. A solid grasp of these elements enables developers to create scalable, secure, and efficient client-server architectures, tailored to meet a wide variety of practical computing needs.

10.4 Error Handling and Debugging

Error handling and debugging are integral components of software development, paramount in ensuring applications are robust, reliable, and user-friendly. Effective error handling anticipates potential issues and provides mechanisms to gracefully manage them, preventing unexpected crashes and preserving user experience. Debugging, on the other hand, is the systematic process of identifying, tracing, and rectifying defects in the code. In this section, we explore the methodologies, tools, and best practices for efficient error handling and debugging within the context of network applications.

Errors in network applications can be broadly categorized into three types: syntax errors, runtime errors, and logical errors. Syntax errors arise from incorrect code syntax and are typically caught by the compiler or interpreter. Runtime errors occur during execution, often due to unforeseen conditions such as invalid input, network unavailability, or resource exhaustion. Logical errors stem from wrong algorithm implementation or incorrect logic and, despite being the most challenging to detect, lead to incorrect output.

Effective error handling begins with understanding these error types and implementing appropriate strategies for managing each. One fundamental approach is the use of language-specific constructs for error handling. In Python, for example, the try-except block is employed to catch and handle exceptions that might occur during program execution.

```
try:
    # Code that may raise an exception
    data = fetch_data_from_network()
```

```
except NetworkTimeoutError as e:
    # Handle specific exception
    print(f'Network timeout: {e}')
except Exception as e:
    # Handle all other exceptions
    print(f'An error occurred: {e}')
else:
    # Code to execute if no exception occurred
    process_data(data)
finally:
    # Code that will run irrespective of an exception
    print('Execution completed.')
```

In the above example, specific exceptions are caught and handled, allowing the application to recover or degrade gracefully instead of terminating abruptly. The final block ensures that clean-up actions are executed, for instance, closing open network connections or releasing resources, mitigating potential resource leaks.

The concept of exception hierarchies allows developers to create custom exception classes tailored to the unique requirements of their application, thus enhancing clarity and specificity in error handling. For example, network applications can define custom exceptions like NetworkTimeoutError or ConnectionFailedError to better encapsulate network-specific errors.

Logging is an indispensable practice in error handling and debugging, providing a permanent record of application activity that developers can reference when diagnosing problems. Logs should be informative yet concise, capturing information such as timestamps, error messages, stack traces, and relevant contextual data. Python's logging module offers a robust framework for adding logging capabilities to an application.

```
import logging

# Configure logging
logging.basicConfig(filename='app.log', level=logging.INFO,
                    format='%(asctime)s %(levelname)s:%(message)s')

try:
    logging.info('Attempting to fetch data from network.')
    data = fetch_data_from_network()
except NetworkTimeoutError as e:
    logging.error(f'Network timeout: {e}')
else:
    logging.info('Data fetched successfully')
finally:
    logging.info('Network operation completed.')
```

Using different logging levels (INFO, WARNING, ERROR, DEBUG, CRITICAL), developers can fine-tune their logging output, thus distinguishing normal operational messages from critical error alerts. This differentiation assists both in actively monitoring an application in production environments and during post-mortem analysis.

Debugging is the systematic pursuit of anomalies and the endeavor to fix them, and it is often coupled with error handling to ensure comprehensive software quality. The debugging process typically involves reproducing bugs, diagnosing the root cause, applying fixes, and testing the solution.

Interactive debuggers are invaluable tools for developers. They allow for real-time examination of program execution, inspection and modification of the state, and execution control through breakpoints and step execution. Tools like PDB in Python or GDB for C/C++ facilitate line-by-line execution analysis, enabling developers to inspect variable states and dynamically evaluate expressions.

For example, debugging a Python program via PDB might involve the following steps:

1. Start the Python debugger by importing the module and inserting pdb.set_trace() at the location in the script where debugging is required:

```
import pdb

def complex_calculation(data):
    result = data / 0  # Deliberate error for debugging
    return result

pdb.set_trace()

print(complex_calculation(5))
```

2. Run the script, and when it reaches pdb.set_trace(), it enters interactive mode. 3. Use commands like n (next), s (step into), p (print variable), c (continue), etc., to inspect and control execution.

Unit testing frameworks such as PyTest for Python, JUnit for Java, or NUnit for .NET are essential in the debugging cycle, promoting a test-driven development approach. These frameworks enable automated testing, ensuring code changes do not introduce regression bugs and verifying that new code behaves as intended. A well-tested codebase vastly simplifies the debugging process, as failures are rapidly detected and isolated.

Consider the following simple unit test using PyTest for a hypothetical function that processes network data:

```
def process_data(data):
    if not data:
        raise ValueError('No data provided.')
    # Processing logic
    return len(data)

def test_process_data():
    assert process_data([1, 2, 3]) == 3, "Data length should be 3"
    assert process_data([]) == 0, "Processing empty data should raise ValueError"
```

Running this test will immediately reveal a critical issue—the assumption that processing empty data will simply return zero is incorrect; a ValueError should be raised instead. By addressing this through unit tests, developers can catch such errors in early stages of development, reducing the debugging effort required later.

Profiling tools, while traditionally focused on performance, can also aid in debugging by revealing code hotspots and anomalies. Identifying sections of code that execute unexpectedly long helps pinpoint inefficient algorithms or resource-releasing errors, guiding optimization efforts.

In sophisticated applications, contextual error tracing might be implemented using correlation IDs—unique identifiers attached to requests across distributed systems. Correlation IDs assist in piecing together logs from various services, revealing the whole transaction sequence and highlighting precisely where an error occurs in a microservices architecture.

Error handling and debugging practices should remain integral throughout the software development lifecycle, not merely as ad hoc resolutions during crises. Regular code reviews and peer programming can complement automated and manual testing, providing a fresh perspective that often uncovers subtle bugs or potential failure points. These comprehensive approaches ensure that applications are both robust and user-friendly, fostering a positive user experience and safeguarding against operational disruptions.

In summary, embracing systematic error handling and debugging practices lays the foundation for developing resilient applications that gracefully manage unexpected conditions, maintain seamless operations, and consistently deliver intended outcomes.

10.5   Testing Network Applications

Testing is an essential phase in the development lifecycle of network applications, ensuring that they function correctly under varied conditions and meet agreed performance and reliability standards. Unlike desktop applications, network applications must navigate the complexities of data exchange over networks, including latency, bandwidth, reliability, and security challenges. Therefore, comprehensive testing approaches are vital to ensure they operate seamlessly once deployed. This section discusses strategies, methodologies, and tools used for testing network applications effectively.

To start, it's essential to identify the types of testing applicable to network applications, which typically include functional testing, performance testing, load testing, stress testing, security testing, and usability testing. Each type is designed to validate specific aspects of the application, ensuring it meets its prescribed requirements and user expectations.

Functional testing assesses whether the network application functions as expected under normal usage conditions. This type of testing focuses on specific features and functionality outlined in the requirements specification. It involves testing APIs, data integrity, and the proper operation of network protocols. Tools such as Selenium for web application automated testing, JUnit for Java applications, and pytest for Python enable automated functional testing, which is invaluable for regression testing and achieving consistent results.

Consider a RESTful API server that provides book information. The following Python pytest-based test example illustrates how functional testing can validate API responses:

```
import requests

BASE_URL = 'http://localhost:5000'

def test_get_books():
```

```
    response = requests.get(f'{BASE_URL}/books')
    assert response.status_code == 200
    assert isinstance(response.json(), list) # Expect a list of books

def test_get_individual_book():
    book_id = 1
    response = requests.get(f'{BASE_URL}/book/{book_id}')
    assert response.status_code == 200
    assert 'title' in response.json()['book']
```

This functional test checks the API endpoints for expected HTTP status codes and verifies data structure integrity, thus confirming compliance with specified functionality.

Performance testing evaluates the application's responsiveness, throughput, and stability under expected usage. Load testing and stress testing are subcategories that assess how the application performs under heavy traffic conditions and beyond normal operational capacity, respectively. Tools like Apache JMeter and Gatling allow developers to simulate realistic user loads, measure server responses, and detect potential bottlenecks before they affect end-users.

In a simulated environment using JMeter, configure a test plan to generate requests emulating several users accessing a server concurrently, monitoring server metrics such as CPU and memory usage, response time, and error rates. Such tests make it possible to tune server parameters and optimize application performance by identifying and eliminating bottlenecks.

Stress testing examines application behavior under extreme conditions, often pushing it to the breaking point to understand its limits and establish thresholds for acceptable performance. The aim is to identify the failure points and ensure that the application degrades gracefully under high load instead of crashing.

Security testing safeguards network applications against vulnerabilities that could be exploited by malicious agents. Identifying security flaws in authentication processes, data encryption, and access controls prevents unauthorized access and data breaches. Tools like OWASP ZAP (Zed Attack Proxy) and Burp Suite facilitate vulnerability scanning and penetration testing, helping engineers fortify applications against potential threats.

For example, using OWASP ZAP, testers can execute automated and manual testing processes against HTTP endpoints, identifying issues such as SQL injections, XSS (Cross-Site Scripting), and insecure data transmissions. Such vulnerabilities must be addressed to protect sensitive data and maintain application integrity. Implementing security headers, input validation, and secure coding practices are further measures to enhance security test outcomes.

Usability testing, although often overlooked in network applications, ensures that the end product offers an intuitive and positive user experience. Usability testing scenarios include checking user navigation, accessibility, and overall satisfaction. This can be performed through user testing sessions or employing tools to analyze user interactions.

A key element of testing network applications involves setting up an equivalent testing environment that mirrors the production scenario. This facilitates accurate testing conditions, as networking components such as firewalls, load balancers, and DNS can influence application behavior. DevOps practices, including the use of Infrastructure as Code (IaC) tools like Terraform, allow for provisioning consistent, replicable testing environments, reducing the risk of environment-specific issues affecting results.

Integration testing is another critical testing facet for network applications, particularly as they often consist of multiple interconnected components or services. Integration testing verifies that these components function together seamlessly. For instance, ensuring that a server correctly communicates with a database or that API endpoints correctly aggregate microservice responses are vital integration points to verify.

End-to-end (E2E) testing extends integration testing by simulating real user scenarios and testing application workflows from start to finish. E2E tests, while more costly and complex to maintain, are invaluable for validating the entire application stack and pinpointing integration errors in complex workflows. Popular tools for E2E testing include Cypress for web applications and Appium for mobile app testing.

Continuous Testing is a cornerstone of modern software development, fostering a culture of quality and allowing teams to detect and resolve issues rapidly. Continuous Integration (CI) pipelines facilitate continuous testing by automating and executing tests against every code change. Deployment pipelines can incorporate stages like code quality

271

checking, unit testing, integration testing, and deployment to testing environments, providing feedback early and ensuring a high level of software reliability.

Incorporating monitoring and logging into network applications supports testing efforts by offering insights into application performance and user behavior post-deployment. Logs enable developers to trace issues during testing that did not appear during initial bug resolution phases. Likewise, monitoring systems such as Prometheus and Datadog offer metrics that further validate testing assumptions and recognize performance anomalies.

Testing network applications requires meticulous planning and execution, encompassing a host of testing types to ensure functionality, performance, security, and usability. Effective testing strategies incorporate automated testing for scalability and efficiency, supplemented by manual tests for intricate scenarios requiring human judgment. Network applications that undergo rigorous, thorough testing stand a better chance of delivering reliable, high-performance solutions that meet or exceed user expectations while remaining resilient to the ever-evolving network and security landscapes. Through diligent testing practices, developers and testers not only assure the immediate quality of a network application but also lay down a foundation for its sustainable, long-term success.

10.6   Deployment and Maintenance

Deployment and maintenance are critical phases in the lifecycle of network applications, ensuring that software is not only delivered efficiently to end-users but also remains operational and updated over time. Effective deployment strategies ensure a smooth transition from development to production while minimizing downtime and user disruption. Maintenance encompasses the long-term monitoring, updating, and improvement of the application to maintain its relevance and address emerging issues. This section explores the intricacies and best practices for deploying and maintaining network applications.

The deployment process transitions an application from the development environment into a production setting where users can access and interact with it. Given the complexity inherent in network applications, deploying these systems often involves many components including application servers, databases, network configurations, and security protocols.

Continuous Integration and Continuous Deployment (CI/CD) pipelines have revolutionized how applications are deployed. By automating the build, testing, and deployment processes, CI/CD pipelines reduce the time to market, enhance quality control, and minimize human errors. Popular CI/CD tools include Jenkins, GitHub Actions, and GitLab CI, which streamline these workflows.

A typical deployment pipeline may involve the following stages:

- **Build Stage**: Compile application code from the source repository into executable artifacts and perform initial tests. Tools like Maven for Java or Gradle for diversified environments manage dependencies and build logic.

- **Testing Stage**: Execute automated test suites, including unit, integration, and performance tests, to validate the application's readiness for deployment. Utilizing robust testing tools like Selenium or PyTest during this stage ensures that any defects are addressed promptly.

- **Release Stage**: Package and deploy the application artifacts to a staging environment, providing an opportunity for final validation. This environment should mirror production closely to ensure that the release is robust and any potential issues are caught early.

- **Deployment Stage**: Transitioning an application into the production environment often employs strategies like blue-green deployments or canary releases. These techniques facilitate the deployment of new versions with minimized risk. For example, blue-green deployments maintain two identical production environments — one live (blue) and one idle (green). While users access the blue environment, the green can be updated and tested. Upon successful validation, traffic is switched to green, minimizing downtime.

273

The following YAML configuration illustrates a simplified CI/CD pipeline using GitLab CI for a Python application:

```yaml
stages:
  - build
  - test
  - deploy

build:
  stage: build
  script:
    - pip install -r requirements.txt

test:
  stage: test
  script:
    - pytest tests/

deploy:
  stage: deploy
  script:
    - apt-get install python3-flask
    - nohup python3 app.py &
  only:
    - master
```

Leveraging containerization with Docker also simplifies deployment. Containers encapsulate applications in standardized units, containing everything needed to run: code, runtime, system tools, libraries, and settings. This promotes consistency across different environments and simplifies scaling applications across cloud infrastructures like AWS, Google Cloud, and Azure.

Docker-compose facilitates multi-container orchestration, managing the lifecycle of containers as a cohesive unit. Define services, set dependencies, and specify build instructions in a docker-compose.yml file:

```yaml
version: '3'

services:
  web:
    build: .
    ports:
      - "8000:8000"
    depends_on:
      - db

  db:
    image: postgres
    environment:
      POSTGRES_DB: example_db
      POSTGRES_USER: user
      POSTGRES_PASSWORD: password
```

Once deployed, the maintenance phase keeps applications operating optimally. This involves regular monitoring, updating, and optimizing processes. Effective monitoring leverages tools like Prometheus for metrics collection and Grafana for visualization, enabling proactive issue detection and resolution.

Monitoring encompasses both application performance metrics (e.g., response time, error rates, throughput) and infrastructure health metrics (CPU and memory usage, network latency). Implementing alerts for thresholds ensures timely intervention before user experience is impacted.

Security updates and patch management are vital maintenance activities. As new vulnerabilities emerge, maintaining an updated security posture through patches shields applications from exploits. Automation tools like Ansible or Puppet can streamline patch management by orchestrating updates across servers with minimal disruptions.

Regular audits, including code reviews and vulnerability assessments, enhance application security and quality. Code reviews encourage sharing best practices, identifying vulnerabilities, and fostering collaborative development, while vulnerability scanning tools like Nessus or Snyk address weaknesses before they are exploited.

Database maintenance secures data integrity, availability, and performance. Regular backups, optimized queries, and indexed tables improve database performance. Automating backups and employing failover mechanisms guard against data loss and downtime.

Elastic scaling ensures applications adapt to fluctuating loads, employing auto-scaling in cloud environments to dynamically allocate resources based on demand. This elasticity improves cost efficiency, allowing resources to scale up during peak usage and down in low-traffic periods. Tools like Kubernetes further enhance scaling strategies through efficient container orchestration across environments.

Continuous feedback loops involve soliciting user feedback and monitoring user behavior to inform future updates. This feedback fosters an iterative development approach and keeps the application aligned with user needs. Implementing feature flags or toggles permits experimentation with new features in real users' environments, reducing release risks and gathering behavioral data to inform product decisions.

Documentation is a cornerstone of effective maintenance, providing a comprehensive knowledge base for developers and operators. Well-maintained documentation covers APIs, architecture, deployment scripts, and troubleshooting guides, accelerating onboarding and easing modifications.

Effective deployment and maintenance are ongoing processes emphasizing stability and scalability, transforming network applications into continuously evolving, robust systems. By adopting CI/CD, leveraging containerization, and prioritizing monitoring and documentation, applications are poised to thrive in dynamic environments and deliver sustained value to users. Through strategic deployment and diligent maintenance, organizations not only drive operational efficiency but ensure that their network applications remain secure, performant, and able to meet the evolving demands of users and businesses alike.